MW00414815

PEOPLE'S COMMENTARY BIBLE

Jeremiah Lamentations

David M. Gosdeck

CPH
SAINT LOUIS

The interior illustrations were originally executed by James Tissot (1836–1902).

Commentary and pictures are reprinted from JEREMIAH/LAMENTATIONS (The People's Bible Series), copyright © 1994 by Northwestern Publishing House. Used by permission.

3558 S. Jefferson Avenue, St. Louis, MO 63118-3968
Manufactured in the United States of America

1 2 3 4 5 6 7 8 9 10 04 03 02 01 00 99 98 97 96 95

CONTENTS

LAMENTATIONS

ILLUSTRATIONS

PREFACE

The People's Bible Commentary is just what the name implies—a Bible and commentary for the people. It includes the complete text of the Holy Scriptures in the popular New International Version. The commentary following the Scripture sections contains personal applications as well as historical background and explanations of the text.

The authors of *The People's Bible Commentary* are men of scholarship and practical insight, gained from years of experience in the teaching and preaching ministries. They have tried to avoid the technical jargon which limits so many commentary series to professional Bible scholars.

The most important feature of these books is that they are Christ-centered. Speaking of the Old Testament Scriptures, Jesus himself declared, "These are the Scriptures that testify about me" (John 5:39). Each volume of *The People's Bible Commentary* directs our attention to Jesus Christ. He is the center of the entire Bible. He is our only Savior.

We dedicate these volumes to the glory of God and to the good of his people.

The Publishers

JEREMIAH

INTRODUCTION

Jeremiah is meant to be read with the ear. Few people in Jeremiah's time, even the great and powerful, could read. So Jeremiah spoke the Lord's Word to his audience. He did not write down any of his prophecy until he had been at work over twenty years. This helps to explain some of his style and manner of writing.

Jeremiah is hard reading because his was a hard message. This message was delivered over a period of forty-one years. It was not given all at once, so more than one generation had time to grasp it. Because it was delivered over such a long period of time and to many different audiences, there is much repetition. As with rich food, it is best to eat and rest, and then to eat some more and rest again. A slow and thoughtful reading will bring great profit. God had Jeremiah write his prophecy with all generations in mind, ". . . so that through endurance and the encouragement of the Scriptures we might have hope" (Romans 15:4).

The Author

Jeremiah was a young man when the Lord called him to his life's work. From the moment of his call to the end of his life, he was steadfast and unwavering in his devotion to the Lord's work. He was found faithful. But his was not a happy mission. Like Noah, he was called to preach in an age when people would not listen.

Because Jeremiah was close to his people, their unbelief troubled him deeply. He was sensitive both to the pain of his people and to the hatred of his opponents. As a result,

Jeremiah reveals more of his inner turmoil and personal feelings than any of the other prophets. From the height of joy to the depths of despair, Jeremiah was open and honest in his emotions. The special burden he carried was his loneliness. For the Lord had forbidden him to marry or to enjoy the normal social relationships that others could enjoy (Jeremiah 16:1-9).

In his preaching Jeremiah soared, for the Lord had given him a poet's eye and ear. He used that gift to the fullest. At his hand simple truths became powerful proclamations. "Even the stork in the sky knows her appointed seasons, and the dove, the swift and the thrush observe the time of their migration. But my people do not know the requirements of the LORD" (Jeremiah 8:7). Jeremiah's preaching brought few to repentance, but he was true to the call God had given him. And God asks no more.

Content and Purpose

Except, perhaps, for chapter fifty-two, the entire book is the work of the prophet Jeremiah. He himself did not actually write the material, but he dictated it to his secretary or scribe, Baruch, who then wrote it on a scroll. More than half of the book is dated, that is, we know the exact year in which the Lord gave this or that message to Jeremiah. We have more history in Jeremiah than in any other of the prophets. The book contains large sections of both poetry and narrative.

The purpose of the book is given in the first chapter and in the following prophecy. We may summarize it as follows:

1. To preach repentance to an ungodly nation in the hope that all who heard the message would repent.
2. To proclaim certain judgment if they did not repent.

3. To leave them without excuse so that in the future the survivors might repent.
4. To give the believers among them an understanding of what God was doing.
5. To comfort the believers with the sure promises of the Lord.

The General Political Situation in Jeremiah's Time

For hundreds of years the dominant nation in the Middle East had been Assyria. About the time Jeremiah began his ministry (627 B.C.), Assyria began the sharp decline that would lead to her total destruction. A few years before, the Egyptians, under the father of Pharaoh Necho, regained their independence. From that point the chief interest of the Egyptians was to protect Egypt by controlling Judah and Syria, the lands to the immediate north of Egypt. These lands provided the only invasion route over which any conqueror had to pass in order to attack Egypt.

In the year 626 B.C. the Babylonians under Nabopolassar and his son, Nebuchadnezzar, successfully gained their independence from Assyria. Father and son together led campaigns that won for them most of the Assyrian empire, which stretched north and east of Israel. In 612 B.C. the Babylonians with their allies, the Medes, captured and destroyed Nineveh, the capital of Assyria. At Haran in 610 B.C. they administered the final defeat to the remnants of Assyria.

In 605 B.C. Nabopolassar died, leaving Nebuchadnezzar sole ruler of the new Babylonian empire. Nabopolassar's death occurred while Nebuchadnezzar was engaged with Pharaoh Necho and his allies at Carchemish in a decisive battle for control of the Middle East. The Pharaoh was completely defeated. As a result, Judah and Syria became dependencies of Babylon. Pharaoh Necho and his successor,

Pharaoh Hophra, continued to try, though unsuccessfully, to regain control of both Judah and Syria. Their attempts led the kings of Judah, several times, to plot against Nebuchadnezzar. The final result was the total destruction of Jerusalem in the year 587/586 B.C.

Throughout this period Judah, as always, was caught in the middle. As a kingdom she was weak and small, unable to do much about the events around her. In 609 B.C. King Josiah tried to stop Pharaoh Necho in a battle at Megiddo. This foolhardy attempt cost him his life and cost Judah whatever independence it might have had. Though weak and small, Judah was important because she was the land bridge between Babylon to the north and east, and Egypt to the south and west. For this reason, each tried to control her.

Easily the most important political figure of the age in which Jeremiah lived and worked was Nebuchadnezzar. He ruled Babylon from 605 B.C. to 562 B.C. Under his vigorous leadership the new Babylonian empire spread until it covered an area from Iran in the east to Egypt in the west. His great renown, however, was not in war, but in building. He transformed Babylon into the most magnificent city of its time. After his death, his empire rapidly declined and became part of the Persian empire founded by Cyrus the Great.

The Kings of Judah at Jeremiah's Time

Jeremiah began his prophetic activity under Josiah, the last good and pious king of Judah. He had ascended the throne in 640 B.C. at the age of eight after the violent death of his father. His reign followed a long period of godlessness. The worship of the Lord had been almost wiped out by the idolatrous practices of his grandfather and father, Manasseh and Amon. The heart of the whole nation had been perverted. Josiah tried valiantly to restore the true worship of the Lord.

He was spurred on by the discovery of the book of the Law in the year 622 B.C., the year he began the great temple reform (2 Kings 22—23:3).

For all of his zeal Josiah was only able to achieve a limited measure of reform. He met his untimely death in a battle with Pharaoh Necho at Megiddo. His character is best described by the writer of 2 Kings 23:25, "Neither before nor after Josiah was there a king like him who turned to the LORD as he did—with all his heart and with all his soul and with all his strength, in accordance with all the Law of Moses." He was so much loved and admired that special songs were composed and regularly sung in his memory (2 Chronicles 35:25). The Bible records his life in 2 Kings 21:24—23:30 and in 2 Chronicles 34 and 35.

The people of Judah, perhaps wanting to maintain some independence from Egypt and perhaps fearing the character of the older brother Jehoiakim, put Jehoahaz (Shallum) on the throne after the death of his father in 609 B.C. Jehoahaz was allowed to rule only a short time. Preferring Jehoahaz's brother, Pharaoh Necho deposed Jehoahaz and took him to Egypt, where he died in exile. The Bible records his life in 2 Kings 23:31-33 and in 2 Chronicles 36:1-4.

A puppet of the Pharaoh, Jehoiakim (also called Eliakim) began his rule in 609/608 B.C. Cruel and greedy, he was primarily concerned about personal pleasure and entertainment. He was hostile to the worship of the Lord. He murdered at least one of the Lord's prophets, a man by the name of Uriah. He tried to murder Jeremiah but was restrained by the Lord and by powerful princes, who had imbibed some of the spirit of Josiah. He was faithless to Nebuchadnezzar. Finally after several warnings, Nebuchadnezzar attacked Jerusalem and took Jehoiakim captive. But before the king of Babylon was actually able to carry him away to Babylon, Jehoiakim died in chains. The Bible records his life in 2 Kings 23:34—24:7 and in 2 Chronicles 36:5-8.

Like father like son. Jehoiachin succeeded his father in 597 B.C. He proved to be an equally unreliable ally for Nebuchadnezzar. Three months after Jehoiachin became king, Nebuchadnezzar deported him to Babylon. The Bible records his life in 2 Kings 24:8-16 and in 2 Chronicles 36:9,10.

The last king of Judah from the line of David was Zedekiah (also called Mattaniah). He was the son of Josiah, the brother of Jehoiakim and the uncle of Jehoiachin. He was weak and indecisive. He too was an unreliable ally of the Babylonians. Worse yet, he never could commit himself to the Lord. He kept on wavering until the destruction of Jerusalem in 587/586 B.C. After he was captured by the enemy, he was forced to witness the death of his sons and was then blinded and carried away in chains to exile. His unhappy life is recorded in 2 Kings 24:17—25:7 and in 2 Chronicles 36:11-14.

Short Chronicle of Judah's Dealings with Babylon

During the twenty years from the time Jehoiakim ascended the throne until the destruction of Jerusalem, the Babylonians punished the Jews many times for their resistance to Babylonian rule. The following chronology will assist the reader in understanding these encounters and their significance for the work of the prophet.

605 B.C.—Judah under Jehoiakim becomes a vassal of Nebuchadnezzar. A few hostages, perhaps Daniel and his friends among them, are taken to Babylon.

602 B.C.—Jehoiakim rebels against Nebuchadnezzar, who punishes Judah by sending bands of raiders to devastate the land.

598/597 B.C.—The Babylonians capture Jerusalem for the first time. Jehoiakim dies. Nebuchadnezzar deports 3,023 Jews to Babylon.

597 B.C.—After only three months and ten days on the throne Jehoiachin, the son of Jehoiakim, is also deported to Babylon, along with 10,000 nobles, fighting men, and skilled workers. It was during this period that the prophet Ezekiel was taken away to Babylon. Zedekiah, Jehoiakin's uncle, was placed on the throne.

587/6 B.C.—Judah's last rebellion is crushed. Babylonian forces completely destroy Jerusalem. Zedekiah, the last king, is also deported to Babylon.

582 B.C.—745 more Jews are carried off to Babylon.

An Outline of Jeremiah

THEME: ONE LAST TIME THE LORD PLEADS WITH JUDAH TO REPENT

I. The Lord delivers that message through Jeremiah (Jeremiah 1)

II. The Lord points Judah to some lessons from the past (2—6)

A. The lesson of their forefathers (2:1—3:5)
B. The lesson of the ten northern tribes (3:6—4:31)
C. The lesson of Sodom and Gomorrah (5,6)

III. The Lord warns Judah that false religion cannot save her (7—11)

A. They had made the temple into a center of idolatry (7:1—8:3)

B. They had encouraged and listened to false teachers (8:4—9:6)
C. They acted as if the Lord were no different from any idol (9:17—10:25)
D. Their only hope for deliverance lies in returning to the covenant the Lord had made with them (11:1-23)

IV. The Lord's action troubles the prophet (12—14)

A. Jeremiah questions the Lord's ways (12)
B. The Lord teaches Jeremiah with the object lesson of the linen belt (13)
C. Jeremiah wrestles with the Lord in prayer (14)

V. Judah's impenitence seals the Lord's judgment against her (15—20)

A. No one can turn it aside (15)
B. Jeremiah's manner of life is witness to it (16)
C. The condition of their hearts demonstrates that it is just (17)
D. The Lord brings it home to them in the object lessons of the clay jars (18—20:6)
E. Jeremiah staggers under its burden (20:7-18)

VI. Judah's behavior exposes her impenitence (21—29)

A. The people deceive themselves to the very end (21)
B. They ignore the tragic end of their most immediate kings (22)
C. They keep on clinging to the delusions of their false prophets (23)
D. They see themselves in a different light than the Lord—the vision of the figs (24)
E. They hope they can escape the cup of wrath (25)

F. They try to silence the voice of God's prophet (26)
G. They deny all reality (27—29)

VII. The Lord remains faithful (30—33)

A. He promises a return from exile (30)
B. He promises a new covenant (31)
C. He confirms the promise through the object lesson of Jeremiah's purchase of a field (32:1—33:13)
D. He makes the promise even more glorious (33:14-26)

VIII. Judah's continuing impenitence finally brings down the Lord's judgment (34—39)

A. They respond half-heartedly to any attempts to keep faith with the Lord (34)
B. The Recabites show them up (35)
C. They betray their real attitude by despising God's Word and his prophet (36—38)
D. The Lord brings down the final curtain on Jerusalem (39)

IX. The few survivors learn nothing from the disaster (40—44)

A. They destroy their one slim hope (40:1—41:10)
B. They ignore the Lord's warning by fleeing to Egypt (41:11—43:7)
C. They will find no escape from the consequences of their impenitence in Egypt (43:8—44:30)

X. The Lord sends a message to Baruch (45)

XI. The Lord will judge the nations (46—51)

XII. The Lord sends a ray of hope in the midst of exile (52)

THE LORD DELIVERS HIS MESSAGE THROUGH JEREMIAH
JEREMIAH 1

**1 The words of Jeremiah son of Hilkiah, one of the priests at
Anathoth in the territory of Benjamin. [2]The word of the
LORD came to him in the thirteenth year of the reign of Josiah
son of Amon king of Judah, [3]and through the reign of Jehoiakim son of Josiah king of Judah, down to the fifth month
of the eleventh year of Zedekiah son of Josiah king of Judah,
when the people of Jerusalem went into exile.**

The Call of Jeremiah

[4]The word of the LORD came to me, saying,

**[5]"Before I formed you in the womb I knew you,
before you were born I set you apart;
I appointed you as a prophet to the nations."**

**[6]"Ah, Sovereign LORD," I said, "I do not know how to speak;
I am only a child."**

**[7]But the LORD said to me, "Do not say, 'I am only a child.'
You must go to everyone I send you to and say whatever I command you. [8]Do not be afraid of them, for I am with you and
will rescue you," declares the LORD.**

**[9]Then the LORD reached out his hand and touched my
mouth and said to me, "Now, I have put my words in your
mouth. [10]See, today I appoint you over nations and kingdoms
to uproot and tear down, to destroy and overthrow, to build
and to plant."**

At the very beginning of his prophecy, Jeremiah tells us a little bit about himself. He was the son of a priest, living in the home town of Abiathar, who had served as high priest under David. That town was the village of Anathoth, located two and one-half miles northeast of Jerusalem. Next he tells us how long his prophetic ministry lasted. He began his work in the year 627 B.C. under the pious and good king Josiah. His ministry came to an end about the year 586 B.C. after the destruction of Jerusalem. His ministry lasted for over forty years. Few other prophets served as long as Jeremiah.

The Lord had determined Jeremiah's future long before his mother conceived or gave birth to him. From eternity the Lord had chosen him to be a prophet. The Lord's choice was wholly rooted in his grace. In effect, the Lord said to Jeremiah, "Because of my goodness and for my own purpose I have loved you and called you my very own."

This word from the Lord (verse 5) would be the anchor of Jeremiah's life, holding him securely in all the fierce tests he would face. In the face of doubt, uncertainty, and rejection Jeremiah knew without question that he belonged to the Lord and was about the Lord's business. How often he would gain comfort by returning to these words!

The Lord, too, has chosen each of us to be his own, even before our conception or birth. At our baptism, he made that choice known to us. As we look to our baptism, we will find the same kind of promise, assurance, and anchor in the Lord as Jeremiah did by looking back to the promise given to him at his call.

Jeremiah protested the Lord's call. He felt he was far too young and inexperienced in public speaking. But the Lord had shaped him for this very purpose. The Lord himself had made him and equipped him. To spur him on to the task ahead, the Lord in a vision reached out his hand and touched Jeremiah's mouth. In this fashion the Lord empowered him for his work. The prophet would not go alone or in his own name. He was the Lord's spokesman.

The means by which Jeremiah would accomplish the Lord's mission was the Word. With the Word he would uproot and tear down, destroy and overthrow. With the same Word he would build and plant. This Word was all he had. This Word was all he needed, for it was living and powerful, accomplishing all of God's purposes. The Lord would never abandon him or fail him. His heart put at rest by the might of the Lord's promise, the prophet accepted his calling. He was ready.

**11The word of the LORD came to me: "What do you see,
Jeremiah?"**

"I see the branch of an almond tree," I replied.

**12The LORD said to me, "You have seen correctly, for I am
watching to see that my word is fulfilled."**

**13The word of the LORD came to me again: "What do you
see?"**

**"I see a boiling pot, tilting away from the north," I an-
swered.**

**14The LORD said to me, "From the north disaster will be
poured out on all who live in the land. 15I am about to summon
all the peoples of the northern kingdoms," declares the LORD.**

"Their kings will come and set up their thrones
in the entrance of the gates of Jerusalem;
they will come against all her surrounding walls
and against all the towns of Judah.
16I will pronounce my judgments on my people
because of their wickedness in forsaking me,
in burning incense to other gods
and in worshiping what their hands have made.

**17"Get yourself ready! Stand up and say to them whatever I
command you. Do not be terrified by them, or I will terrify
you before them. 18Today I have made you a fortified city, an
iron pillar and a bronze wall to stand against the whole
land—against the kings of Judah, its officials, its priests and**

the people of the land. [19]They will fight against you but will not overcome you, for I am with you and will rescue you," declares the LORD.

Jeremiah knew something of the message he was to deliver. Though he would do some building and planting, though he would preach the good news of the gospel, the main theme of his preaching would be the law. By the law he was to bring Judah to a knowledge of her sins. In these verses God outlined the prophet's message in greater detail.

In the first vision Jeremiah saw an almond branch. The almond bush was the first to come to life in the spring. The blossoming of the pink flowers (the flowers came before the leaves) of the almond tree was a sure sign that spring was coming. So the almond branch was a symbol of the coming fulfillment of the Lord's Word. The Lord was watching over his Word to carry it out. Jeremiah plays on words. The Hebrew word for "watch" in this text has a root that sounds like the word for "almond branch." The Lord will carry out his Word without delay. The period of waiting, the period of warning, was almost over; the time of judgment on Judah and Jerusalem had come. The Lord would delay no longer; now he would surely act.

The second vision, the vision of the boiling pot tilting from the north, tells us what the judgment is and by what means the Lord would carry it out. The most important thing to learn from this vision is that the Lord is the ONE who is doing the judging. The invasion of the Babylonians and their allies from the north was no accident of history. The Lord planned and directed the entire operation. The vision proclaims the complete defeat of Judah and Jerusalem.

At the end of the vision the Lord announced the reason for this terrible judgment. Judah did not lack religion or the worship that goes with it, but Judah was practicing false religion. The people had created their own religion. Because of their idolatry, the Lord would judge them. They had rejected his promises and the Giver of those promises. They were faithless and impenitent. In heart and action they had rejected the Lord who had embraced them and loved them. These then are the repeated themes of Jeremiah: the judgment will soon come; the Lord will accomplish his judgment through the Babylonians; the judgment will come because of unbelief. The time to repent is now.

The prophet blanched at the message he was to deliver. He knew all too well the stubbornness of the heart of Judah. How could he carry on with such work? How could he keep it up? The Lord spoke to the fears of the prophet. He reminded Jeremiah that he was a man under orders. He promised to give him unbreakable strength. The Lord would hold him up.

Here is the secret to the strength Jeremiah displayed throughout his long ministry, a strength he had in common with all believers. The secret is that the Lord strengthens his saints with gracious promises. Through Word and sacrament he sends his Spirit to renew the inner man. His Spirit is a living water springing up to give life and faith for whatever the Lord sets before his people to do. We can do all things through him who strengthens us.

THE LORD POINTS JUDAH TO SOME LESSONS FROM THE PAST

JEREMIAH 2—6

The Lesson of their Forefathers

2 The word of the LORD came to me: [2]"Go and proclaim in the hearing of Jerusalem:

" 'I remember the devotion of your youth,
how as a bride you loved me
and followed me through the desert,
through a land not sown.
[3] Israel was holy to the LORD,
the firstfruits of his harvest;
all who devoured her were held guilty,
and disaster overtook them,' "
declares the LORD.

The Lord knows no time. The days of Israel's deliverance from Egypt were fresh in his mind. What grace he had lavished on Israel! What protection he had given her! At Sinai the people had willingly pledged themselves to the covenant he had made with them. Under Moses and Joshua they had experienced the blessings that come to those who know the Lord's love and treasure it.

[4]Hear the word of the LORD, O house of Jacob,
all you clans of the house of Israel.
[5]This is what the LORD says:
"What fault did your fathers find in me,
that they strayed so far from me?
They followed worthless idols
and became worthless themselves.

6They did not ask, 'Where is the LORD,
who brought us up out of Egypt
and led us through the barren wilderness,
through a land of deserts and rifts,
a land of drought and darkness,
a land where no one travels and no one lives?'
7I brought you into a fertile land
to eat its fruit and rich produce.
But you came and defiled my land
and made my inheritance detestable.
8The priests did not ask,
'Where is the LORD?'
Those who deal with the law did not know me;
the leaders rebelled against me.
The prophets prophesied by Baal,
following worthless idols.
9"Therefore I bring charges against you again,"
declares the LORD.
"And I will bring charges against your children's children.
10Cross over to the coasts of Kittim and look,
send to Kedar and observe closely;
see if there has ever been anything like this:
11Has a nation ever changed its gods?
(Yet they are not gods at all.)
But my people have exchanged their Glory
for worthless idols.
12Be appalled at this, O heavens,
and shudder with great horror,"
declares the LORD.
13"My people have committed two sins:
They have forsaken me,
the spring of living water,
and have dug their own cisterns,
broken cisterns that cannot hold water.

When sudden and unexpected disaster strikes us, it leaves us numb, asking the question, "What happened?" Here the Lord feels numbed. He asked Judah, "What happened?" Using the image of the courtroom, the Lord plays the role of the plaintiff. He asks, "Why?" He had kept his part of the covenant. He had been faithful to his promises. Yet the whole nation, especially the spiritual leaders, had forgotten his grace and turned from him.

The Lord called the whole world to witness. From west to east there had never been anything like this. No nation changes its gods; but that is precisely what Israel had done. It had abandoned the true God for worthless idols.

The Lord illustrated the folly of the nation with a powerful picture. In the semi-arid and desert regions of the holy land nothing is more precious than water. The most valuable of all sources of water was a free-flowing spring. All year long it would gush forth sweet and fresh life-giving water. Such a spring guaranteed life for the people and herds who drank from it. The Lord was such a life-giving fountain to Israel. He had never failed to supply all their wants and needs. In the desert no one would be so foolish as to give up such a spring of water. Yet this was the very thing Israel had done; it had surrendered the Lord of life.

A second source of water in the desert was rainwater that had previously been caught or channeled into cisterns. These cisterns were dug under the ground, carefully plastered and then filled with water during the rainy season. The owners then placed a sealed cover over the cistern to preserve the water for future use. Such cisterns were vital water supplies for travelers and herdsmen. To have the cistern leak and run dry would mean sure death. This was Israel's second sin. It had placed its confidence in itself and its false gods. When it needed help and deliverance none was to be had. As we say, "When they went to the well, they came up empty or dry." Coming up empty is a tough experience; but it is the only result for anyone who gives up Christ and turns elsewhere for help.

14 Is Israel a servant, a slave by birth?
Why then has he become plunder?
15 Lions have roared;
they have growled at him.
They have laid waste his land;
his towns are burned and deserted.
16 Also, the men of Memphis and Tahpanhes
have shaved the crown of your head.
17 Have you not brought this on yourselves
by forsaking the LORD your God
when he led you in the way?
18 Now why go to Egypt
to drink water from the Shihor?
And why go to Assyria
to drink water from the River?
19 Your wickedness will punish you;
your backsliding will rebuke you.
Consider then and realize
how evil and bitter it is for you
when you forsake the LORD your God
and have no awe of me,"
declares the Lord, the LORD Almighty.

20 "Long ago you broke off your yoke
and tore off your bonds;
you said, 'I will not serve you!'
Indeed, on every high hill
and under every spreading tree
you lay down as a prostitute.
21 I had planted you like a choice vine
of sound and reliable stock.

How then did you turn against me
into a corrupt, wild vine?
22 **Although you wash yourself with soda**
and use an abundance of soap,
the stain of your guilt is still before me,"
declares the Sovereign LORD.
23 **"How can you say, 'I am not defiled;**
I have not run after the Baals'?
See how you behaved in the valley;
consider what you have done.
You are a swift she-camel
running here and there,
24 **a wild donkey accustomed to the desert,**
sniffing the wind in her craving—
in her heat who can restrain her?
Any males that pursue her need not tire themselves;
at mating time they will find her.
25 **Do not run until your feet are bare**
and your throat is dry.
But you said, 'It's no use!
I love foreign gods,
and I must go after them.'

Once the nation had turned from her covenant God, its suffering began. Egypt and Assyria, the super powers of the area, successfully plundered the land, carrying off large amounts of booty. The chief reference in our text may be to the invasion of Pharaoh Shishak who carried off to Egypt large amounts of treasure from both the temple and the palace (1 Kings 14:25-28).

To try to find security in the region, the Jewish nation sought out alliances with the great powers, now allying with Egypt, then allying with Assyria. It did not find protection in any of these alliances. It searched for strength in arms, diplomacy, and great leaders. Its search was constant. It adopted a multitude of foreign gods. It looked in every place but the right one. It never looked to the Lord.

The people of Judah and Israel failed to find a solution to their problems because they stubbornly refused to identify the root of those problems. They blamed the prophets; they blamed the kings; they blamed the priests; they blamed the weather; they blamed the Lord. But the fault was their own. Their sin had found them out. The Lord had lavished every blessing upon them. He had "planted them a choice vine," capable of producing good fruit. They were without excuse. The only answer lay in repentance, in turning away from their sin and turning to the Lord and receiving his forgiveness.

Unfortunately their sin was not mere weakness. God's gracious Word had become an unbearable burden. They wanted to be free to do whatever they pleased. In the words of St. Paul, having become free from the righteousness of God, they became slaves to sin. They exulted in their sin. "It's no use," they said. "It's the natural thing to do." "We can't help ourselves." "We like doing what we are doing, and we will not stop." With this lie they excused and deceived themselves, revealing their sinfulness in all its ugliness. Wild and untamed, they ran from one god to the next. Where would it all end?

26 "As a thief is disgraced when he is caught,
so the house of Israel is disgraced—
they, their kings and their officials,
their priests and their prophets.
27 They say to wood, 'You are my father,'
and to stone, 'You gave me birth.'
They have turned their backs to me
and not their faces;
yet when they are in trouble, they say,
'Come and save us!'

28 Where then are the gods you made for yourselves?
Let them come if they can save you
when you are in trouble!
For you have as many gods
as you have towns, O Judah.
29 "Why do you bring charges against me?
You have all rebelled against me,"
declares the LORD.

30 "In vain I punished your people;
they did not respond to correction.
Your sword has devoured your prophets
like a ravening lion.

31 "You of this generation, consider the word of the LORD:

"Have I been a desert to Israel
or a land of great darkness?
Why do my people say, 'We are free to roam;
we will come to you no more'?
32 Does a maiden forget her jewelry,
a bride her wedding ornaments?
Yet my people have forgotten me,
days without number.
33 How skilled you are at pursuing love!
Even the worst of women can learn from your ways.
34 On your clothes men find
the lifeblood of the innocent poor,
though you did not catch them breaking in.
Yet in spite of all this
35 you say, 'I am innocent;
he is not angry with me.'
But I will pass judgment on you
because you say, 'I have not sinned.'
36 Why do you go about so much,
changing your ways?
You will be disappointed by Egypt
as you were by Assyria.

37 You will also leave that place
with your hands on your head,
for the LORD has rejected those you trust;
you will not be helped by them.

From father to son, from mother to daughter, the people of Judah had lived in a spirit of unbelief. By a constant turning from the Lord they had hardened their hearts against him. This, however, was a new generation, able to make decisions for itself. The Lord did not punish these children for the sins of their parents. They still had an opportunity to repent.

The Lord continued to invite Judah to consider his unfailing goodness to his people. How could they possibly forget his grace? No bride forgets her wedding day. According to the custom of the times, even the poorest bride would be bedecked with jewelry and finery fit for a queen. For that one day of her life all her relatives and friends lent her their jewelry. Never again would she be dressed in such splendor. In addition to that borrowed finery and jewelry, she was also dressed with the dowry saved for her by her father and given to her as her share of the family estate. Often she would wear her dowry in the form of gold and silver bracelets and anklets. She would not give up her dowry easily. If any of it were lost, she would search feverishly for it as did the woman in Jesus' parable who lost one of the ten silver coins from her dowry (Luke 15:8-10). How could Israel possibly forget the "dowry" God had given her at Mount Sinai? There he had made them a special people, treasured above all the peoples of the earth. He had given them his word of grace for all time in the words of Moses and the other holy writers. He had kept all of his promises.

Despite all this, the people of Israel had forgotten their God. Their real sin was not weakness, or sin in general. They had committed the greatest of all errors. It lay rooted deeply in their hearts. It found expression in the attitude shown in the words: "I have not sinned." They rejected the very idea that they were sinners who deserved God's punishment. They, therefore, refused to repent. But there could be no help for them in any way until they repented. The Lord asked for nothing from them. He was and is always ready to forgive the one who sorrows for sin.

3 "If a man divorces his wife
and she leaves him and marries another man,
should he return to her again?
Would not the land be completely defiled?
But you have lived as a prostitute with many lovers—
would you now return to me?"
declares the LORD.
2 "Look up to the barren heights and see.
Is there any place where you have not been ravished?
By the roadside you sat waiting for lovers,
sat like a nomad in the desert.
You have defiled the land
with your prostitution and wickedness.
3 Therefore the showers have been withheld,
and no spring rains have fallen.
Yet you have the brazen look of a prostitute;
you refuse to blush with shame.
4 Have you not just called to me:
'My Father, my friend from my youth,
5 will you always be angry?
Will your wrath continue forever?'
This is how you talk,
but you do all the evil you can."

In this section God uses a picture that he uses elsewhere throughout the Old Testament. He pictures himself as Israel's husband. His chosen nation is therefore his wife. In this case God is a husband whose wife has left him. Not only has she left him, but she has given her favors to many men. Judah has committed idolatry everywhere. The shrines to false gods were usually built on suitable, open high places, "the barren heights." Because of their idolatry, Judah had corrupted the land. The Lord had punished the nation by withholding the rains. The early rains came in October and lasted through December. These rains softened the soil for plowing and planting, and gave the crops a good start. The late (latter) rains or spring rains came in late February and March and filled the crops out. Both rainy seasons were essential for a good crop. The people of Judah had experienced drought and famine; but still they did not know the reason.

They went on as if nothing had happened. Outwardly, they worshiped the Lord as before. They continued to claim a special relationship to him. They reminded him of his promise to Abraham, whose descendants they were. But they did not change the way they lived. They continued to do all the evil they could. Under such conditions could the Lord forgive them?

The Lesson of the Ten Northern Tribes

6During the reign of King Josiah, the LORD said to me,
"Have you seen what faithless Israel has done? She has gone
up on every high hill and under every spreading tree and has
committed adultery there. 7I thought that after she had done
all this she would return to me but she did not, and her un-
faithful sister Judah saw it. 8I gave faithless Israel her certifi-
cate of divorce and sent her away because of all her adulteries.
Yet I saw that her unfaithful sister Judah had no fear; she also
went out and committed adultery. 9Because Israel's immorality
mattered so little to her, she defiled the land and committed

adultery with stone and wood. [10]In spite of all this, her unfaithful sister Judah did not return to me with all her heart, but only in pretense," declares the LORD.

If the example of their forefathers were not enough, the Lord provides the people of Judah with a second more vivid lesson about the results of unbelief. The prophet delivered these words at the time of King Josiah (640–609 B.C.). The renewed devotion to the true worship of the Lord fostered by King Josiah did not take root in the hearts of his people. They said the right things and offered the right sacrifices, but their hearts remained distant from the Lord.

So the Lord directs their attention to the disaster that befell the ten tribes of the north, known after the breakup of the kingdom (931 B.C.) as Israel. In 722 B.C., after the Lord's repeated warnings, the Assyrians brought an end to the kingdom of Israel by capturing its capital, Samaria, and deporting its people to a distant place in the vast Assyrian empire. This exile happened because the Israelites did not listen to the prophets sent to them.

To use the picture of the husband and wife, the Lord made the divorce final. He gave Israel what it had asked for, a final release from him. This chilling lesson had no impact on the people of Judah. Without fear and with even greater determination, Judah kept on committing the same sins as her sister to the north. She kept plunging along the same path to destruction.

[11]The LORD said to me, "Faithless Israel is more righteous than unfaithful Judah. [12]Go, proclaim this message toward the north:

" 'Return, faithless Israel,' declares the LORD,
'I will frown on you no longer,

for I am merciful,' declares the LORD,
'I will not be angry forever.
13 Only acknowledge your guilt—
you have rebelled against the LORD your God,
you have scattered your favors to foreign gods
under every spreading tree,
and have not obeyed me,' "
declares the LORD.

14 "Return, faithless people," declares the LORD, "for I am
your husband. I will choose you—one from a town and two
from a clan—and bring you to Zion. 15 Then I will give you
shepherds after my own heart, who will lead you with knowl-
edge and understanding. 16 In those days, when your numbers
have increased greatly in the land," declares the LORD, "men
will no longer say, 'The ark of the covenant of the LORD.' It
will never enter their minds or be remembered; it will not be
missed, nor will another one be made. 17 At that time they will
call Jerusalem The Throne of the LORD, and all nations will
gather in Jerusalem to honor the name of the LORD. No longer
will they follow the stubbornness of their evil hearts. 18 In those
days the house of Judah will join the house of Israel, and to-
gether they will come from a northern land to the land I gave
your forefathers as an inheritance.

19 "I myself said,

" 'How gladly would I treat you like sons
and give you a desirable land,
the most beautiful inheritance of any nation.'
I thought you would call me 'Father'
and not turn away from following me.
20 But like a woman unfaithful to her husband,
so you have been unfaithful to me, O house of Israel,"
declares the LORD.

The Lord calls Israel more righteous than Judah because Judah had the benefit of her sister's warning example but ignored it. By comparison, Judah's sin made Israel's sin look small. In that sense Israel was more righteous than Judah. By making this comparison, the Lord shows his true character. With great affection and tenderness he begs the sinner, here portrayed by Israel, to return to him. He invites the sinner to confess his sins from the heart.

In grace the Lord proposes to do the unthinkable. He would receive back the wife who had given herself over to shameless prostitution. He would once again embrace her who had sinned so greatly. In describing his grace the Lord leads the reader beyond the Old Testament era to the time of the Messiah, the long awaited Savior. To replace the faithless, false spiritual leaders who had deceived his people, the Lord would send leaders after his own mind. They would guide his people with a knowledge born of intimate acquaintance with God's Word.

Those days would be the time when the shadows of the Old Testament would have found their fulfillment in Jesus Christ, God's very own Son. God would be present with his people, no longer in a place, but in a person. In the person of Christ he would accomplish the great salvation from sin that he had promised. It would be so great a salvation from sin that the temple and the ark of the covenant would no longer be remembered or needed. It would be a time when the nations and the Jews turned to the Lord and believed in Jesus Christ.

We are living in that time. For the gospel has been preached over the whole earth. Men and women and children of every nation have heard its message and believed it to their own eternal salvation. The Lord was concerned not only with future grace and promise. The Lord is the God of eternal grace. He had hoped his revelation of future grace would convince the people of Jeremiah's day that he still loved them, and he hoped that they would repent. But such repentance was not to be. The Lord could only reflect on what might have been had Judah changed her ways.

21 A cry is heard on the barren heights,
the weeping and pleading of the people of Israel,
because they have perverted their ways
and have forgotten the LORD their God.

22 "Return, faithless people;
I will cure you of backsliding."

"Yes, we will come to you,
for you are the LORD our God.
23 Surely the idolatrous commotion on the hills
and mountains is a deception;
surely in the LORD our God
is the salvation of Israel.
24 From our youth shameful gods have consumed
the fruits of our fathers' labor—
their flocks and herds,
their sons and daughters.
25 Let us lie down in our shame,
and let our disgrace cover us.
We have sinned against the LORD our God,
both we and our fathers;
from our youth till this day
we have not obeyed the LORD our God."

4 "If you will return, O Israel,
return to me,"
declares the LORD.
"If you put your detestable idols out of my sight
and no longer go astray,
2 and if in a truthful, just and righteous way
you swear, 'As surely as the LORD lives,'
then the nations will be blessed by him
and in him they will glory."

These verses picture for us the Lord's fervent hope. He hoped to sing the duet we hear sung in these verses. The Lord invites his penitent people to return to him. By his Spirit and with his Word he would heal them. He would apply to them the healing balm of the gospel. He would forgive them. Their true sorrow would be a sign that their healing had already begun. He hoped that they would respond to his invitation with the words expressing true repentance.

If the people of Judah had responded to the Lord's invitation in repentance and faith, they would have confessed that all their false worship had done them no good. They would have admitted that they could find real help in no one but the Lord, that they had wasted their time and money for nothing. Holding nothing back, they would not have tried to excuse their sins but would have made a complete confession of sin. Taking their cue from the Lord's invitation, they would have thrown themselves wholly on his mercy. Believers give God no greater honor than believing his promise and looking to him as their savior. This is the kind of honor he had hoped Judah would give him.

Such repentance would have brought the greatest blessings, not only for Judah, but for all the nations. Seeing the Lord's mercy toward Judah they would have been drawn to the Lord. The Lord had promised Abraham that in him all the nations of the earth would be blessed (Genesis 12:3). This promise included all nations and would be realized as the nations came to know the Lord through his acts of love and faithfulness, first toward his chosen people and then toward all, in the person of his own Son, Jesus Christ.

3This is what the LORD says to the men of Judah and to Jerusalem:

"Break up your unplowed ground
and do not sow among thorns.

4Circumcise yourselves to the LORD,
circumcise your hearts,
you men of Judah and people of Jerusalem,
or my wrath will break out and burn like fire
because of the evil you have done—
burn with no one to quench it.
5"Announce in Judah and proclaim in Jerusalem and say:
'Sound the trumpet throughout the land!'
Cry aloud and say:
'Gather together!
Let us flee to the fortified cities!'
6Raise the signal to go to Zion!
Flee for safety without delay!
For I am bringing disaster from the north,
even terrible destruction."

7A lion has come out of his lair;
a destroyer of nations has set out.
He has left his place
to lay waste your land.
Your towns will lie in ruins
without inhabitant.
8So put on sackcloth,
lament and wail,
for the fierce anger of the LORD
has not turned away from us.

The Lord requires a genuine, heartfelt response to his invitation. The Lord looks for a change in the inner self. For that reason he calls upon Judah to circumcise its heart. A mere mark on the body did not then and does not now make one right with God. True righteousness begins in the heart. For if the heart is pure, then the whole person is pure. Cleanse the heart with forgiveness and faith, then all the rest is good. If the inner self is not cleansed and renewed, then everything else still remains polluted and impure.

Without such genuine repentance, the people of Judah could experience only the wrath of God. That wrath burns like an unquenchable fire, for the only means of putting it out is the gospel. The gospel alone purifies and cleanses the heart with forgiveness and faith. Reject that forgiveness, say no to that gospel, and there is nothing left to turn away the wrath of God.

Since the people of Judah did not repent from the heart, the Lord had no choice but to bring fiery judgment down upon them. They would have to leave the unprotected countryside for the fortified cities. The Lord would turn loose a lion from the north. The lion, of course, is a symbol of a powerful conqueror and a great king. Because the Lord was with this attacker, there would be no stopping him.

9"In that day," declares the LORD,
"the king and the officials will lose heart,
the priests will be horrified,
and the prophets will be appalled."

10Then I said, "Ah, Sovereign LORD, how completely you have deceived this people and Jerusalem by saying, 'You will have peace,' when the sword is at our throats."

11At that time this people and Jerusalem will be told, "A scorching wind from the barren heights in the desert blows toward my people, but not to winnow or cleanse; 12a wind too strong for that comes from me. Now I pronounce my judgments against them."

13Look! He advances like the clouds,
his chariots come like a whirlwind,
his horses are swifter than eagles.
Woe to us! We are ruined!
14O Jerusalem, wash the evil from your heart and be saved.
How long will you harbor wicked thoughts?
15A voice is announcing from Dan,
proclaiming disaster from the hills of Ephraim.

16"Tell this to the nations,
proclaim it to Jerusalem:
'A besieging army is coming from a distant land,
raising a war cry against the cities of Judah.
17They surround her like men guarding a field,
because she has rebelled against me,'"
declares the LORD.

Because the nation chose to ignore all the warnings it had received, the Lord's judgment would catch the whole nation by surprise. Many prophets, Jeremiah chief among them, had predicted the coming judgment. Despite the warnings, the leaders and people of Judah had chosen to believe the wispy peace the false prophets had promised. This, too, was part of the Lord's judgment; he let his stubborn people believe the lie.

The prophets of the Lord had sounded the warning trumpet for so long and so many times that when the final judgment came upon Jerusalem nobody could believe it was really happening. For years the Lord had sent them chastisements, forms of discipline. He had designed these chastisements to correct them and to lead them to repentance. But because they had failed to learn from them, the Lord ended his attempts at correction. Instead, he promised to send a scorching desert wind which would sweep them from the threshing floor and consume them.

The Lord himself would lead the advance against them. They were opposing not some other human being but the Lord himself. There is no hope for people like that. From Dan in the very north of the country, one frightened messenger after another passed the message: "A besieging army is coming. . . ."

18"Your own conduct and actions
have brought this upon you.

This is your punishment.
How bitter it is!
How it pierces to the heart!"
19 Oh, my anguish, my anguish!
I writhe in pain.
Oh, the agony of my heart!
My heart pounds within me,
I cannot keep silent.
For I have heard the sound of the trumpet;
I have heard the battle cry.
20 Disaster follows disaster;
the whole land lies in ruins.
In an instant my tents are destroyed,
my shelter in a moment.
21 How long must I see the battle standard
and hear the sound of the trumpet?

Jeremiah here expresses his personal feelings and what he felt as a representative of the nation as a whole. We all make mistakes, some worse than others. The most painful mistakes are those that hurt ourselves or others, mistakes we could have avoided. Such was the pain Jeremiah expressed here. The nation could have turned away the judgment of the Lord. It chose not to. That choice made its punishment all the more bitter. The fault was its own.

Jeremiah felt the pain of his people. He knew the word he proclaimed was the truth. The burden of this preaching tore him up. He wished he could preach another message; but as long as the nation refused to repent he had to preach God's message of law and judgment. Judah's continued impenitence was all the more reason to preach. The people of Judah had to be made to listen. Jeremiah could not keep silent.

22 "My people are fools;
they do not know me.

They are senseless children;
they have no understanding.
They are skilled in doing evil;
they know not how to do good."

23 I looked at the earth,
and it was formless and empty;
and at the heavens,
and their light was gone.
24 I looked at the mountains,
and they were quaking;
all the hills were swaying.
25 I looked, and there were no people;
every bird in the sky had flown away.
26 I looked, and the fruitful land was a desert;
all its towns lay in ruins
before the LORD, before his fierce anger.

27 This is what the LORD says:

"The whole land will be ruined,
though I will not destroy it completely.
28 Therefore the earth will mourn
and the heavens above grow dark,
because I have spoken and will not relent,
I have decided and will not turn back."

29 At the sound of horsemen and archers
every town takes to flight.
Some go into the thickets;
some climb up among the rocks.
All the towns are deserted;
no one lives in them.

30 What are you doing, O devastated one?
Why dress yourself in scarlet
and put on jewels of gold?
Why shade your eyes with paint?
You adorn yourself in vain.

Your lovers despise you;
they seek your life.

31 **I hear a cry as of a woman in labor,**
a groan as of one bearing her first child—
the cry of the Daughter of Zion gasping for breath,
stretching out her hands and saying,
"Alas! I am fainting;
my life is given over to murderers."

The people of Judah had shut the Lord out. Because they no longer believed him, they could not make any sense out of what he said. Because of their folly, they would receive the reward of fools. In his mind Jeremiah painted a picture of the devastation of the land. There are grays and browns. No green, no signs of life. The heavens were black and silent, the towns empty.

Perhaps no person was more responsible for the ruin of Israel, the northern kingdom, than Jezebel. For it was through Jezebel that Baal worship became a part of the fabric of the religious life of the people of the north. Her name was synonymous with unbelief. The people of Israel never recovered from her deception. The Lord cursed her with the promise of a violent death. As his instrument, God raised up the new king Jehu. Jezebel, dressed in her finest, tried to the very last to prevent her own execution (2 Kings 9:30ff). That's how Judah behaved, down to her very end. Caught in the consequences of her unbelief, she did not repent, but turned all the more to idol worship. It would do no good. Having the example of Israel and ignoring it, Judah would receive the same punishment as Israel did. In Judah's case, though, because of the promises made to David, the Lord would spare a small remnant.

The Lesson of Sodom and Gomorrah

5 **"Go up and down the streets of Jerusalem,**
look around and consider,
search through her squares.

If you can find but one person
who deals honestly and seeks the truth,
I will forgive this city.
2 Although they say, 'As surely as the LORD lives,'
still they are swearing falsely."

3 O LORD, do not your eyes look for truth?
You struck them, but they felt no pain;
you crushed them, but they refused correction.
They made their faces harder than stone
and refused to repent.
4 I thought, "These are only the poor;
they are foolish,
for they do not know the way of the LORD,
the requirements of their God.
5 So I will go to the leaders
and speak to them;
surely they know the way of the LORD,
the requirements of their God."
But with one accord they too had broken off the yoke
and torn off the bonds.
6 Therefore a lion from the forest will attack them,
a wolf from the desert will ravage them,
a leopard will lie in wait near their towns
to tear to pieces any who venture out,
for their rebellion is great
and their backslidings many.

7 "Why should I forgive you?
Your children have forsaken me
and sworn by gods that are not gods.
I supplied all their needs,
yet they committed adultery
and thronged to the houses of prostitutes.
8 They are well-fed, lusty stallions,
each neighing for another man's wife.

9 Should I not punish them for this?"
declares the LORD.
"Should I not avenge myself
on such a nation as this?

10 "Go through her vineyards and ravage them,
but do not destroy them completely.
Strip off her branches,
for these people do not belong to the LORD.
11 The house of Israel and the house of Judah
have been utterly unfaithful to me,"
declares the LORD.

The Lord had first compared Judah with Israel. That comparison was not flattering. Now the Lord made an even more odious comparison. The Lord compared Judah with the cities of Sodom and Gomorrah. In Old Testament literature no place on earth was more wicked than Sodom and Gomorrah. Yet the Lord had promised Abraham that if he found ten righteous people in those cities he would spare them from his judgment. That same, all-searching God now issued a challenge to Jeremiah: "Find one righteous person in the city of Jerusalem and I will spare it from the doom I have spoken over it."

The Lord would have spared Sodom and Gomorrah for the sake of ten believers. The Lord promised to spare Jerusalem if he found only one believer—if one can be found! With this challenge the Lord wanted to show the extent of the evil of Jerusalem. He wanted the citizenry to realize the danger of their present course.

In spirit Jeremiah conducted his search. He scoured the city from the least to the greatest but could not find one believer. No argument, no reason could be advanced to spare the city. We know from Jeremiah's prophecy that some (and certainly more than one) in the city of Jerusalem believed what Jeremiah had said. But he drew this picture to drive home to the city's inhabitants the critical danger into which their impenitence had placed them.

12 They have lied about the LORD;
they said, "He will do nothing!
No harm will come to us;
we will never see sword or famine.
13 The prophets are but wind
and the word is not in them;
so let what they say be done to them."

14 Therefore this is what the LORD God Almighty says:

"Because the people have spoken these words,
I will make my words in your mouth a fire
and these people the wood it consumes.
15 O house of Israel," declares the LORD,
"I am bringing a distant nation against you—
an ancient and enduring nation,
a people whose language you do not know,
whose speech you do not understand.
16 Their quivers are like an open grave;
all of them are mighty warriors.
17 They will devour your harvests and food,
devour your sons and daughters;
they will devour your flocks and herds,
devour your vines and fig trees.
With the sword they will destroy
the fortified cities in which you trust.

Words, words, words—nothing but words. That was how the people received the message of the prophet. They insisted on believing that the Lord would not do anything. They were absolutely sure that they had a lock on God. They were his people, no matter how bad they were. He could not turn away from them. They rejected his warning message also because they no longer believed that God was around. They did not deny the existence of God, but they did deny that he had much to do with their day-to-day living. For them God was far away in the distant heavens. He was a spirit who has little to do with our world. The people of Judah dreamed that, and people are still dreaming that today. By their dreaming they thought they could get rid of God and their responsibility to him.

Such an attitude calls down God's curse. Here God confirmed the authority of the prophet. The Word they had refused to believe would be the Word that would judge them and consume them. The Lord described further the fierce nature of the attacker from the north. He would be a stranger without sympathy for the people of Judah. He would take everything for himself. He would level their most secure fortresses, because the Lord would be with him.

18 "Yet even in those days," declares the LORD, "I will not de-
stroy you completely. 19 And when the people ask, 'Why has the
LORD our God done all this to us?' you will tell them, 'As you
have forsaken me and served foreign gods in your own land, so
now you will serve foreigners in a land not your own.'

20 "Announce this to the house of Jacob
and proclaim it in Judah:
21 Hear this, you foolish and senseless people,
who have eyes but do not see,
who have ears but do not hear:
22 Should you not fear me?" declares the LORD.
"Should you not tremble in my presence?
I made the sand a boundary for the sea,
an everlasting barrier it cannot cross.
The waves may roll, but they cannot prevail;
they may roar, but they cannot cross it.
23 But these people have stubborn and rebellious hearts;
they have turned aside and gone away.
24 They do not say to themselves,
'Let us fear the LORD our God,

who gives autumn and spring rains in season,
who assures us of the regular weeks of harvest.'
25 **Your wrongdoings have kept these away;**
your sins have deprived you of good.

26 **"Among my people are wicked men**
who lie in wait like men who snare birds
and like those who set traps to catch men.
27 **Like cages full of birds,**
their houses are full of deceit;
they have become rich and powerful
28 **and have grown fat and sleek.**
Their evil deeds have no limit;
they do not plead the case of the fatherless to win it,
they do not defend the rights of the poor.
29 **Should I not punish them for this?"**
declares the LORD.
"Should I not avenge myself
on such a nation as this?

30 **"A horrible and shocking thing**
has happened in the land:
31 **The prophets prophesy lies,**
the priests rule by their own authority,
and my people love it this way.
But what will you do in the end?

The Lord again promised that he would leave a small group of survivors to confirm that he had indeed spoken the truth. How stupid this people had become. Just as God had threatened, they felt the drought and its effects. But they imagined it was no more than bad luck. There had to be some logical explanation for it. Perhaps the prevailing wind currents were wrong, the ocean currents cold. In this way they attempted to sidestep the God who had created all the universe and established the laws by which it is governed.

The people of Judah were willing to believe any reason for their trouble except the real one—their own sinfulness. Their evil leaped all bounds. They showed little concern for the rights and needs of others. Everywhere their conduct betrayed the motives of their hearts.

Judah's "prophets" told the people what they wanted to hear. In every age liars will appear to tell whatever lies the religious market calls for. The priests twisted God's Word to suit their own purposes. No one objected. This is the way the people wanted it. And let us not think that these were the worst of all people. For they were no worse than any other unbelievers. All unbelievers are just as wicked in God's holy eyes.

Jerusalem Under Siege

6 "Flee for safety, people of Benjamin!
Flee from Jerusalem!
Sound the trumpet in Tekoa!
Raise the signal over Beth Hakkerem!
For disaster looms out of the north,
even terrible destruction.
2 I will destroy the Daughter of Zion,
so beautiful and delicate.
3 Shepherds with their flocks will come against her;
they will pitch their tents around her,
each tending his own portion."
4 "Prepare for battle against her!
Arise, let us attack at noon!
But, alas, the daylight is fading,
and the shadows of evening grow long.
5 So arise, let us attack at night
and destroy her fortresses!"

6 This is what the LORD Almighty says:

"Cut down the trees
and build siege ramps against Jerusalem.

This city must be punished;
it is filled with oppression.
7 As a well pours out its water,
so she pours out her wickedness.
Violence and destruction resound in her;
her sickness and wounds are ever before me.
8 Take warning, O Jerusalem,
or I will turn away from you
and make your land desolate
so no one can live in it."

9 This is what the LORD Almighty says:

"Let them glean the remnant of Israel
as thoroughly as a vine;
pass your hand over the branches again,
like one gathering grapes."

The people of the nation snoozed in their lies. Their true condition was far from the false peace they had imagined for themselves. Once again, therefore, the prophet Jeremiah sounded the warning. News of the invading army rumbled down from the north. It would be a powerful army. Many allies would form it. Neither the heat of the day nor the dark of the night would stop their attack.

Wickedness cannot and would not go unpunished. The people of Judah had heaped up unrepented sin till it overflowed. There was no restraint. All they could do was sin. Such is the nature of the sinful flesh. In this way sin grows until it controls the whole person. This sin, this impenitence must be punished. The enemy would leave not a single thing. Like a grape-picker, it would not be satisfied until it had picked the very last grape.

10 To whom can I speak and give warning?
Who will listen to me?

Their ears are closed
so they cannot hear.
The word of the LORD is offensive to them;
they find no pleasure in it.
11 But I am full of the wrath of the LORD,
and I cannot hold it in.
"Pour it out on the children in the street
and on the young men gathered together;
both husband and wife will be caught in it,
and the old, those weighed down with years.
12 Their houses will be turned over to others,
together with their fields and their wives,
when I stretch out my hand
against those who live in the land,"
declares the LORD.
13 "From the least to the greatest,
all are greedy for gain;
prophets and priests alike,
all practice deceit.
14 They dress the wound of my people
as though it were not serious.
'Peace, peace,' they say,
when there is no peace.
15 Are they ashamed of their loathsome conduct?
No, they have no shame at all;
they do not even know how to blush.
So they will fall among the fallen;
they will be brought down when I punish them,"
says the LORD.

16 This is what the LORD says:

"Stand at the crossroads and look;
ask for the ancient paths,
ask where the good way is, and walk in it,
and you will find rest for your souls.
But you said, 'We will not walk in it.'

17 I appointed watchmen over you and said,
'Listen to the sound of the trumpet!'
But you said, 'We will not listen.'

The people of Judah had much more time and opportunity to repent than the people of Sodom and Gomorrah had. For centuries they had heard the preaching of the Word by the prophets. Through time, however, they had hardened themselves. They no longer listened. More tragically, they no longer could listen, for the Lord had hardened the hearts of many of them. Such hardening begins with neglect. It continues with more neglect. It ends with total neglect of the preaching of the Word. The devil is the happiest when people will no longer listen to the preaching of the Word.

Jeremiah had a message to deliver, but there was no one to listen. The people, the entire nation, had surrendered themselves to greed or covetousness. They had bowed down to the greatest idol of all. This idol has more worshipers than any other religion. Love for this world, the passion for the things that this life has to offer, has rooted itself solidly in every human heart. Judah's spiritual leaders had pandered to these unwholesome desires. They knew what great profit and popularity they could gain from such a stance. Their preachers ignored the disease, suppressed the symptoms, and continued to preach the "gospel of success, prosperity, and fulfillment."

In important matters, a time comes for decision. Time for weighing the choices runs out. The decision must be one way or the other. The Lord invited his people to make that choice. They were standing at the crossroads of their national existence. The good, ancient path stretched out before them. The Lord invited his people to follow the example of Joshua, Samuel, and David by following the Lord. He invited them to repent, to listen, to find true peace, true healing, and fulfillment by believing the gospel message. But they chose to go a different way. They had made their choice, and now they had to live with it.

18 Therefore hear, O nations;
observe, O witnesses,
what will happen to them.
19 Hear, O earth:
I am bringing disaster on this people,
the fruit of their schemes,
because they have not listened to my words
and have rejected my law.
20 What do I care about incense from Sheba
or sweet calamus from a distant land?
Your burnt offerings are not acceptable;
your sacrifices do not please me."

21 Therefore this is what the LORD says:

"I will put obstacles before this people.
Fathers and sons alike will stumble over them;
neighbors and friends will perish."

22 This is what the LORD says:

"Look, an army is coming
from the land of the north;
a great nation is being stirred up
from the ends of the earth.
23 They are armed with bow and spear;
they are cruel and show no mercy.
They sound like the roaring sea
as they ride on their horses;
they come like men in battle formation
to attack you, O Daughter of Zion."

24 We have heard reports about them,
and our hands hang limp.

Anguish has gripped us,
pain like that of a woman in labor.
25 Do not go out to the fields
or walk on the roads,
for the enemy has a sword,
and there is terror on every side.
26 O my people, put on sackcloth
and roll in ashes;
mourn with bitter wailing
as for an only son,
for suddenly the destroyer
will come upon us.

The people of Judah had made their choice. They confirmed it in their manner of worship. To be sure, they heaped sacrifices on the temple altar. The temple was a busy place. The pilgrims and worshipers crowded in. To all appearances religion was on the upswing. But the Lord found no pleasure in what they were doing, for their hearts were not clean. Their hearts were full of unbelief. They lived in the delusion that the mere performance of temple rituals would save them. In truth, theirs was a religion of works. They believed that they would gain favor with God by what they did. This great lie fights with covetousness for first place in the human heart. Both had won in the hearts of the people of Judah.

Having abandoned the sure safety of the Lord's promises, the people of Judah would find no rest. Despair would feed upon them. Fear would surround them. Death would call to them on every side. They would weep the tears they would not shed in repentance. Their grief would be the kind of grief one grieves for an only child. There would be nothing that could soften it. Pain killers couldn't kill the pain. The hand of the Lord would weigh heavily upon them until it crushed them into the dust.

27 "I have made you a tester of metals
and my people the ore,
that you may observe
and test their ways.
28 They are all hardened rebels,
going about to slander.
They are bronze and iron;
they all act corruptly.
29 The bellows blow fiercely
to burn away the lead with fire,
but the refining goes on in vain;
the wicked are not purged out.
30 They are called rejected silver,
because the LORD has rejected them."

Jeremiah's function was to bring out the truth. By his fierce preaching of the law, he was to burn away all the impurities of the people. He was to expose the motive of the heart. He had been busy. The hearts of the people stood exposed. Since they had chosen to stand on their own before the Lord, he found nothing in them of value. His righteous judgment was to throw them aside on the slag heap.

THE LORD WARNS JUDAH THAT FALSE RELIGION CANNOT SAVE HER

JEREMIAH 7—11

False Religion Worthless

**7 This is the word that came to Jeremiah from the LORD:
2“Stand at the gate of the LORD’s house and there proclaim
this message:**

**“ ‘Hear the word of the LORD, all you people of Judah who
come through these gates to worship the LORD. 3This is what
the LORD Almighty, the God of Israel, says: Reform your ways
and your actions, and I will let you live in this place. 4Do not
trust in deceptive words and say, “This is the temple of the
LORD, the temple of the LORD, the temple of the LORD!” 5If you
really change your ways and your actions and deal with each
other justly, 6if you do not oppress the alien, the fatherless or
the widow and do not shed innocent blood in this place, and if
you do not follow other gods to your own harm, 7then I will let
you live in this place, in the land I gave your forefathers for
ever and ever. 8But look, you are trusting in deceptive words
that are worthless.**

**9“ ‘Will you steal and murder, commit adultery and perjury,
burn incense to Baal and follow other gods you have not
known, 10and then come and stand before me in this house,
which bears my Name, and say, “We are safe”—safe to do all
these detestable things? 11Has this house, which bears my
Name, become a den of robbers to you? But I have been watching! declares the LORD.**

These words are all the more striking because Jeremiah may have preached them during the reign of pious King Josiah. Josiah had attempted to restore to its fullness the ancient religion of Israel. Josiah himself was a devout believer. In 622 B.C. he had begun his great reform of the Jewish religion. Through this reform he attempted to bring back the true worship of God. As part of the reform, Josiah cleansed and redecorated the temple.

For most of the people the reform never went beyond decoration. Josiah's reform never took root in the hearts of the people. In fact, the renewal of the temple and its ritual life gave people a false sense of security. Many of them believed that the temple was like a charm. Its mere presence would protect them, they thought. As long as they kept the temple in good repair and went through the motions of worship, the temple and the capital city would never be destroyed. In the shadow of the temple they could live safely, regardless of how they lived. With this misunderstanding they twisted the purpose of the temple and lost sight of the reasons for which God had established it.

From the time of Moses the Lord had promised that he would choose a place for his Name to dwell (Deuteronomy 12). In other words, he would select a location in which he would reveal his saving name to his chosen people through his Word and the rituals of worship and sacrifice. His name would unveil his true character and show that he is a God of free grace and mercy. For God's name is all that he has revealed to us about himself. To the people of Israel he made that revelation when he delivered them from Egypt. There and then he proved himself a savior. This was the purpose of temple worship—to give the people an opportunity to meet with their God, to learn to know him, and to receive abundantly of his grace.

Unfortunately, God's people forgot for what purpose the Lord had given them the temple. They had begun to view the temple as an amulet or a charm offering them sure protection.

They had put the building above the Builder, the creature before the Creator. They had come to believe that no matter how they lived or acted, God would not destroy his temple. Even worse, they felt they were doing God a favor by maintaining the temple and offering sacrifices.

In this manner they had entirely reversed the purpose for which God had established the temple. Instead of coming to the temple as penitents to receive pardon and grace from the Lord, they came unrepentant, demanding what they felt God owed them. They misused the temple and used the priest as judge in legal disputes in order to steal from the helpless. They were confident that no one could touch them. Their confidence was misplaced. The Lord would not allow his name to be used in vain.

12 "'Go now to the place in Shiloh where I first made a
dwelling for my Name, and see what I did to it because of the
wickedness of my people Israel. 13 While you were doing all
these things, declares the LORD, I spoke to you again and
again, but you did not listen; I called you, but you did not an-
swer. 14 Therefore, what I did to Shiloh I will now do to the
house that bears my Name, the temple you trust in, the place I
gave to you and your fathers. 15 I will thrust you from my pres-
ence, just as I did all your brothers, the people of Ephraim.'

16 "So do not pray for this people nor offer any plea or peti-
tion for them; do not plead with me, for I will not listen to you.
17 Do you not see what they are doing in the towns of Judah and
in the streets of Jerusalem? 18 The children gather wood, the fa-
thers light the fire, and the women knead the dough and make
cakes of bread for the Queen of Heaven. They pour out drink
offerings to other gods to provoke me to anger. 19 But am I the
one they are provoking? declares the LORD. Are they not
rather harming themselves, to their own shame?

20 "'Therefore this is what the Sovereign LORD says: My
anger and my wrath will be poured out on this place, on man

and beast, on the trees of the field and on the fruit of the ground, and it will burn and not be quenched.

The people of Jerusalem thought the Lord would never destroy the temple. But the Lord told them to remember another lesson from the past. For years the tabernacle had been located at Shiloh, twenty miles north of Jerusalem. Under the high priesthood of Eli and his sons, the people began to treat the tabernacle like a magic charm (1 Samuel 3,4). Even though Eli's sons abused their priestly privileges, their father did not restrain them. The people lost much respect for the priesthood and for the Lord. They turned to superstition. Faced with an attack by their ancient enemy, the Philistines, the people asked that the ark of the covenant be brought to the battlefield. With the ark among them, they could not suffer defeat. That day they lost thousands of men; the ark was captured; Eli died from shock. Shiloh was never again a worship center.

The lesson is clear: trusting in things, however sacred they might be, cannot save anyone. The only way to salvation is faith in the Lord. Because the people of Eli's day did not believe, they lost the ark. Because the people of Jeremiah's time did not believe, they would lose the temple.

The prospect of losing the temple, the heart of Israel's worship, was shocking. Jeremiah recoiled at that prospect. He begged the Lord for mercy. The Lord knew what was on the heart of Jeremiah and ordered him not to pray for this people. Idolatry had penetrated to the deepest recesses of their hearts. They had made it a family affair. They all involved themselves in the worship of false gods. The "Queen of Heaven" was a fertility goddess to whom the worshiper offered little ritual cakes. The Lord could not help but judge such sin. Their sins did not harm the Lord. The Lord did not suffer from the sins of the people of Judah. No, their sins hurt only themselves.

**21 "'This is what the LORD Almighty, the God of Israel, says:
Go ahead, add your burnt offerings to your other sacrifices
and eat the meat yourselves! 22 For when I brought your forefathers out of Egypt and spoke to them, I did not just give them
commands about burnt offerings and sacrifices, 23 but I gave
them this command: Obey me, and I will be your God and you
will be my people. Walk in all the ways I command you, that it
may go well with you. 24 But they did not listen or pay attention;
instead, they followed the stubborn inclinations of their evil
hearts. They went backward and not forward. 25 From the time
your forefathers left Egypt until now, day after day, again and
again I sent you my servants the prophets. 26 But they did not
listen to me or pay attention. They were stiff-necked and did
more evil than their forefathers.'**

**27 "When you tell them all this, they will not listen to you;
when you call to them, they will not answer. 28 Therefore say to
them, 'This is the nation that has not obeyed the LORD its God
or responded to correction. Truth has perished; it has vanished
from their lips. 29 Cut off your hair and throw it away; take up
a lament on the barren heights, for the LORD has rejected and
abandoned this generation that is under his wrath.**

What the people of Judah were doing in the temple they were doing for themselves and not for the Lord. So the Lord told them to eat the meat of the sacrifice themselves, since it was to themselves and for themselves that they were offering it. They had sorely missed the point of the whole law of Moses. The sacrifices and other rituals and laws were not ends in themselves. The whole purpose of the law of Moses was to bring the people to a knowledge of their sins every day, and every day to lead them to a deeper understanding of the great mercy of God by which they were forgiven and by which they lived. If the people of Israel had embraced that purpose, then they would be God's people, rejoicing to do his will.

Despite the Lord's constant effort through the prophets, the people rejected his Word. Through time they lost the truth. They became unresponsive. They would not listen. Therefore they fell under his fierce wrath.

The Valley of Slaughter

**30"'The people of Judah have done evil in my eyes, declares
the LORD. They have set up their detestable idols in the house
that bears my Name and have defiled it. 31They have built the
high places of Topheth in the Valley of Ben Hinnom to burn
their sons and daughters in the fire—something I did not command, nor did it enter my mind. 32So beware, the days are coming, declares the LORD, when people will no longer call it
Topheth or the Valley of Ben Hinnom, but the Valley of
Slaughter, for they will bury the dead in Topheth until there is
no more room. 33Then the carcasses of this people will become
food for the birds of the air and the beasts of the earth, and
there will be no one to frighten them away. 34I will bring an end
to the sounds of joy and gladness and to the voices of bride and
bridegroom in the towns of Judah and the streets of Jerusalem,
for the land will become desolate.**

**8 "'At that time, declares the LORD, the bones of the kings
and officials of Judah, the bones of the priests and prophets, and the bones of the people of Jerusalem will be removed
from their graves. 2They will be exposed to the sun and the
moon and all the stars of the heavens, which they have loved
and served and which they have followed and consulted and
worshiped. They will not be gathered up or buried, but will be
like refuse lying on the ground. 3Wherever I banish them, all
the survivors of this evil nation will prefer death to life, declares the LORD Almighty.'**

Once the people of Judah had lost the truth, they served the lie with a vengeance. They filled the temple with false gods of every kind. They committed the ultimate horror. Following the worship of the god Molech, they sacrificed their own children in a fiery blaze of inhumanity and idolatry. They performed these human sacrifices in a place called Topheth, which was in the Valley of Ben Hinnom south of Jerusalem. Once having become the servants of sin, they could only fall deeper into the pit of shame.

The Lord's judgment would match their sin. Most of them would die violent deaths. The number of the dead would be so large that there would be no room in the graves. Their death would be so swift that there would be no time and no one to bury them. This lack of burial was frightening to them, for many believed that the soul would not rest without a decent burial. God warned them and their leaders that there would be no rest or escape for them even in the grave. Such is the punishment for unrepented sin. It follows the sinner to the grave and even beyond.

Sin and Punishment

4"Say to them, 'This is what the LORD says:

" 'When men fall down, do they not get up?
When a man turns away, does he not return?
5 Why then have these people turned away?
Why does Jerusalem always turn away?
They cling to deceit;
they refuse to return.
6 I have listened attentively,
but they do not say what is right.
No one repents of his wickedness,
saying, "What have I done?"
Each pursues his own course
like a horse charging into battle.

7 Even the stork in the sky
knows her appointed seasons,
and the dove, the swift and the thrush
observe the time of their migration.
But my people do not know
the requirements of the LORD.

8 " 'How can you say, "We are wise,
for we have the law of the LORD,"
when actually the lying pen of the scribes
has handled it falsely?
9 The wise will be put to shame;
they will be dismayed and trapped.
Since they have rejected the word of the LORD,
what kind of wisdom do they have?
10 Therefore I will give their wives to other men
and their fields to new owners.
From the least to the greatest,
all are greedy for gain;
prophets and priests alike,
all practice deceit.
11 They dress the wound of my people
as though it were not serious.
"Peace, peace," they say,
when there is no peace.
12 Are they ashamed of their loathsome conduct?
No, they have no shame at all;
they do not even know how to blush.
So they will fall among the fallen;
they will be brought down when they are punished,
says the LORD.

The unbelief of the people of Judah was a strange phenomenon, contrary to nature. Nature moves according to the laws laid down by God at creation. In a way unknown to us or them, the birds carry out their annual migrations with amazing precision. Yet the people of Judah, with the Lord's Word to guide them on the way, were lost. Lost because they did not let the Word be their guide! Lost because they would not entertain any thought of guilt! Lost because their teachers had misled them!

Although the nation of Israel had accumulated great wealth of learning, there was abysmal ignorance. The scribes were professional interpreters of the law of Moses. They had studied and expounded the law of Moses at great length. They had memorized great portions of the Old Testament. But they did not know anything, because they had thrown away the key to understanding. Sin and grace, repentance and faith—the heart of God's message in the Bible—was a mystery to them. Since they had rejected the kernel of scriptural truth, they were left with only the shell. Thinking themselves wise, they became fools. Being fools, they entangled their people in their folly.

What a lesson for us! Mere knowledge of Scripture, however great it might be, is not wisdom. Wisdom begins when the sinner trembles before the righteous God. Wisdom flowers when the forgiven sinner lives by the grace of the Lord. Without this wisdom, no matter how much a person knows of the Bible, he remains in darkness. In darkness there is no hope.

13 " 'I will take away their harvest,
declares the LORD.
There will be no grapes on the vine.
There will be no figs on the tree,
and their leaves will wither.
What I have given them
will be taken from them.' "

14 "Why are we sitting here?
Gather together!

Let us flee to the fortified cities
and perish there!
For the LORD our God has doomed us to perish
and given us poisoned water to drink,
because we have sinned against him.
15 We hoped for peace
but no good has come,
for a time of healing
but there was only terror.
16 The snorting of the enemy's horses
is heard from Dan;
at the neighing of their stallions
the whole land trembles.
They have come to devour
the land and everything in it,
the city and all who live there."
17 "See, I will send venomous snakes among you,
vipers that cannot be charmed,
and they will bite you,"
declares the LORD.

What the Lord had given the nation, he would now take away from them, for he is the owner of it all. The people of Judah had hopes, but their hopes were now dashed, for their hopes were morning mists. They did not rest on God's Word. Nor had the people who held those hopes changed their hearts or ways. Not even in the face of the destruction of their national existence did they understand their God or the way back to him. How sad!

18 O my Comforter in sorrow,
my heart is faint within me.
19 Listen to the cry of my people
from a land far away:
"Is the LORD not in Zion?
Is her King no longer there?"

"Why have they provoked me to anger with their images,
with their worthless foreign idols?"

20 "The harvest is past,
the summer has ended,
and we are not saved."
21 Since my people are crushed, I am crushed;
I mourn, and horror grips me.
22 Is there no balm in Gilead?
Is there no physician there?
Why then is there no healing
for the wound of my people?
9 Oh, that my head were a spring of water
and my eyes a fountain of tears!
I would weep day and night
for the slain of my people.
2 Oh, that I had in the desert
a lodging place for travelers,
so that I might leave my people
and go away from them;
for they are all adulterers,
a crowd of unfaithful people.

3 "They make ready their tongue
like a bow, to shoot lies;
it is not by truth
that they triumph in the land.
They go from one sin to another;
they do not acknowledge me,"
declares the LORD.

4 "Beware of your friends;
do not trust your brothers.
For every brother is a deceiver,
and every friend a slanderer.
5 Friend deceives friend,
and no one speaks the truth.

They have taught their tongues to lie;
they weary themselves with sinning.
6 You live in the midst of deception;
in their deceit they refuse to acknowledge me,"
declares the LORD.

The tender-hearted prophet grieved bitterly for his people. He sorrowed that they refused to listen to his message, for he knew that the chance to repent would soon pass. We remember how Jesus wept as he approached the city of Jerusalem for the last time. He wept because he knew the people of that city would not receive him. We think of Paul who wrote, "I have great sorrow and unceasing anguish in my heart. For I could wish that I myself were cursed and cut off from Christ for the sake of my brothers, those of my own race" (Romans 9:2,3). How many pastors have grieved in the same way for impenitents in congregations! How many believers have grieved for those among them who have drifted away from the Lord and have refused to return! Jeremiah found relief only in the Lord who comforts in time of sorrow.

Far away in Babylon, the Jews who already had been carried away into exile, could not believe it. With their own hopes for a quick return shattered, they wondered what would happen. Has the Lord abandoned Jerusalem for good?

Jeremiah could not stop crying. It was as if a spring of tears flowed from within him. The healers could not heal themselves. The balm of Gilead, a region across the Jordan to the northwest, was famous in the ancient Middle East for its curative powers. This balm could not help the people of Judah in their hour of crisis. They had thrown away the one balm capable of healing them. They refused to apply the only remedy of the gospel to the wound of their sin and guilt.

The prophet's grief was greater because of the role he now had to play. He would just as soon have run from the responsibilities of his office and from those who would not listen. On top of that, the Lord warned him that he had not yet seen the worst. In fact, the worst was yet to come. He would have to be on guard against his own relatives and friends. They might listen when he preached and greet him in the square, but their hearts were full of murder. It was not long before these very friends would attempt to kill him. The prophet could expect little else from a people who tried to deceive God himself. In the end they had deceived only themselves.

7 Therefore this is what the LORD Almighty says:

"See, I will refine and test them,
for what else can I do
because of the sin of my people?
8 Their tongue is a deadly arrow;
it speaks with deceit.
With his mouth each speaks cordially to his neighbor,
but in his heart he sets a trap for him.
9 Should I not punish them for this?"
declares the LORD.
"Should I not avenge myself
on such a nation as this?"

10 I will weep and wail for the mountains
and take up a lament concerning the desert pastures.
They are desolate and untraveled,
and the lowing of cattle is not heard.
The birds of the air have fled
and the animals are gone.

11 "I will make Jerusalem a heap of ruins,
a haunt of jackals;
and I will lay waste the towns of Judah
so no one can live there."

12What man is wise enough to understand this? Who has
been instructed by the Lord and can explain it? Why has the
land been ruined and laid waste like a desert that no one can
cross?

13The LORD said, "It is because they have forsaken my law,
which I set before them; they have not obeyed me or followed
my law. 14Instead, they have followed the stubbornness of their
hearts; they have followed the Baals, as their fathers taught
them." 15Therefore, this is what the LORD Almighty, the God of
Israel, says: "See, I will make this people eat bitter food and
drink poisoned water. 16I will scatter them among nations that
neither they nor their fathers have known, and I will pursue
them with the sword until I have destroyed them."

17This is what the LORD Almighty says:

"Consider now! Call the wailing women to come;
send for the most skillful of them.
18 Let them come quickly
and wail over us
till our eyes overflow with tears
and water streams from our eyelids.
19 The sound of wailing is heard from Zion:
'How ruined we are!
How great is our shame!
We must leave our land
because our houses are in ruins.' "

20 Now, O women, hear the word of the LORD;
open your ears to the words of his mouth.
Teach your daughters how to wail;
teach one another a lament.
21 Death has climbed in through our windows
and has entered our fortresses;
it has cut off the children from the streets
and the young men from the public squares.

22 Say, "This is what the LORD declares:

" 'The dead bodies of men will lie
like refuse on the open field,
like cut grain behind the reaper,
with no one to gather them.' "

The people of Judah left the Lord no choice. He would rather have forgiven them and received them back as his own, but they would not return. So he would leave their land as empty as the hearts of those who lived in it.

Who can explain this judgment? Wise men scratch their heads. Some speculate that it was a series of bad decisions, that the people of Judah simply picked the wrong side in the power struggle of the time. Others might say nothing could be done; it was simply bad luck. None of these explanations touched the heart of the matter. The Lord supplies the reason: the people would not listen to my Word. The reason for my judgment is their unbelief. Having rejected the Lord, the people of Judah could have only one expectation, ". . . a fearful expectation of judgment and of raging fire that will consume the enemies of God" (Hebrews 10:27).

The Lord orders the wake to begin. He bids the people of Judah to summon the wailing women. According to the funeral customs of that time, when a family member died, the family hired professional mourners. These professional mourners (always women) would shriek and wail to show grief for the deceased. They would beat themselves and tear at their hair. Now, not only a few, but all the women of the land were to mourn, for death was everywhere. Neither great nor small could escape. Like the cold damp of winter, death penetrated every corner of the land and house. It left behind a gruesome trail. Apart from the life which God's mercy provides, there is only death, "For the wages of sin is death . . ." (Romans 6:23).

23 This is what the LORD says:

"Let not the wise man boast of his wisdom
or the strong man boast of his strength
or the rich man boast of his riches,
24 but let him who boasts boast about this:
that he understands and knows me,
that I am the LORD, who exercises kindness,
justice and righteousness on earth,
for in these I delight,"

declares the LORD.

25 "The days are coming," declares the LORD, "when I will
punish all who are circumcised only in the flesh—26 Egypt, Ju-
dah, Edom, Ammon, Moab and all who live in the desert in
distant places. For all these nations are really uncircumcised,
and even the whole house of Israel is uncircumcised in heart."

It is the nature of the creature, and especially of the human creature, to exult in himself. In his first epistle St. John calls it "the boasting of what he has and does" (1 John 2:16). Such boasting shoots up from the pride of our sinful nature. We tend to forget God and claim credit for everything. The Lord warns us here against such boasting. No wise person ought to boast of his wisdom, for by our own wisdom we will not find a right relationship with God. The strong man ought not boast of his strength, for without God he has none. The rich man ought not boast of his riches, for they are God's gift. In using our gifts for ourselves we forget the Giver. There dare not be any trust or boasting in the creature, for "the paths of glory lead but to the grave" (Thomas Gray).

There is only one boast anyone dare make. There is only one boast God invites us to make. God invites us to boast in him. Once Moses begged to see God in all of his unveiled glory. God's answer was to show Moses his goodness and to proclaim to Moses his name. For through his name he has made himself known. To know his name is to know the fullness of the Lord's mercy and grace.

To know his name is to know Christ and to trust in him as the Savior. This is true wisdom, strength, and riches. So Paul confessed, "May I never boast except in the cross of our Lord Jesus Christ . . ." (Galatians 6:14). Such boasting is a confession that we live by the grace of God and that whatever we are or have is by his grace alone. If only Judah had learned such boasting, she would have lived.

The Lord makes no distinctions. Be it Judah or her pagan neighbors, because of their unbelief they all stand under equal condemnation. Therefore all must be punished. The same is true for any person. Whoever stands outside of the grace of God suffers the judgment God's holy law pronounces upon all sinners. For apart from the cover of his grace, there is no salvation.

God and Idols

10 Hear what the LORD says to you, O house of Israel.
2 This is what the LORD says:

"Do not learn the ways of the nations
or be terrified by signs in the sky,
though the nations are terrified by them.
3 For the customs of the peoples are worthless;
they cut a tree out of the forest,
and a craftsman shapes it with his chisel.
4 They adorn it with silver and gold;
they fasten it with hammer and nails
so it will not totter.
5 Like a scarecrow in a melon patch,
their idols cannot speak;
they must be carried
because they cannot walk.

Do not fear them;
they can do no harm
nor can they do any good."

6 No one is like you, O LORD;
you are great,
and your name is mighty in power.
7 Who should not revere you,
O King of the nations?
This is your due.
Among all the wise men of the nations
and in all their kingdoms,
there is no one like you.
8 They are all senseless and foolish;
they are taught by worthless wooden idols.
9 Hammered silver is brought from Tarshish
and gold from Uphaz.
What the craftsman and goldsmith have made
is then dressed in blue and purple—
all made by skilled workers.
10 But the LORD is the true God;
he is the living God, the eternal King.
When he is angry, the earth trembles;
the nations cannot endure his wrath.

11 "Tell them this: 'These gods, who did not make the heavens and the earth, will perish from the earth and from under the heavens.' "

12 But God made the earth by his power;
he founded the world by his wisdom
and stretched out the heavens
by his understanding.
13 When he thunders, the waters in the heavens roar;
he makes clouds rise from the ends of the earth.
He sends lightning with the rain
and brings out the wind from his storehouses.

14Everyone is senseless and without knowledge;
every goldsmith is shamed by his idols.
His images are a fraud;
they have no breath in them.
15They are worthless, the objects of mockery;
when their judgment comes, they will perish.
16He who is the Portion of Jacob is not like these,
for he is the Maker of all things,
including Israel, the tribe of his inheritance—
the LORD Almighty is his name.

The hope of Judah and Jerusalem was in the Lord, but they had abandoned the Lord for idols. They had left the living God for nothing. For that is what idols are. Following the example of Isaiah (chapters 40:19,20; 41:7,9; 44:9-20; 46:5-7), Jeremiah teaches the people once again that idols are what one falsely trusts with one's whole heart. Indeed, they are no more than products of human ingenuity. The craftsman fashions the idol from wood and precious stones and metal.

Times and conditions change, but every age has its idols. We, too, fashion idols. We may no longer manufacture statues. But remember that an idol is whatever one falsely trusts and relies upon with his whole heart. Consequently our idols may be our riches, our technology, our impressive buildings and modern transportation systems, our enviable system of government, our vacation cottages—in short, whatever we put ahead of the Lord. These products are as good and powerful as their makers.

How foolish to worship the products of our own hands! Yet, such worship is the most evident consequence of sin. Paul told the Romans, "since what may be known about God is plain to them, because God has made it plain to them . . . so that men are without excuse. For although they knew God, they neither glorified him as God nor gave thanks to him, . . . their foolish hearts were darkened . . . and [they] exchanged the glory of the immortal God for images . . ." (1:19-21,23). How powerless are these idols! They cannot talk. They cannot walk. They are like a scarecrow in a melon patch, flapping in the breeze, frightening only a few dumb birds. For someone to worship them proves the hold that sin has upon him. To give up God for idols is not only wrong, it's stupid.

This was the disaster the nation of Judah had brought upon itself. But Judah could still avoid this disaster by turning to the Lord. There is no one like him. He is the creator; by his wisdom and power he fashioned all that we see and know. He is the eternal and living king and God, in control of all that he made, providing for us a sure and safe foundation upon which to rest and trust. He has shown and revealed himself to us in Christ, so that we need not grope or search for signs of his presence or person. He has not left us outside the door to peer into his house through a frosted window, finding him as best we can. Through the perfect life and the innocent death of Christ, he has made us his own, drawn us to himself, forgiven us for Christ's sake. For in Christ he has drawn near to us and become our Helper. It's no wonder that St. John urges his readers, "Dear children, keep yourselves from idols" (1 John 5:21).

Coming Destruction

17Gather up your belongings to leave the land,
you who live under siege.
18For this is what the LORD says:
"At this time I will hurl out
those who live in this land;
I will bring distress on them
so that they may be captured."

19Woe to me because of my injury!
My wound is incurable!
Yet I said to myself,
"This is my sickness, and I must endure it."
20My tent is destroyed;
all its ropes are snapped.
My sons are gone from me and are no more;
no one is left now to pitch my tent
or to set up my shelter.
21The shepherds are senseless
and do not inquire of the LORD;
so they do not prosper
and all their flock is scattered.
22Listen! The report is coming—
a great commotion from the land of the north!
It will make the towns of Judah desolate,
a haunt of jackals.

Without the Lord's help nothing is left for Judah. She has no power. When the siege is laid against her, those in the cities may choose only flight, for God will sling them out. The only saving grace will be to accept the punishment that their sins have deserved. By themselves and through their leaders, the shepherds, they have lost everything. They can only throw themselves upon the mercy of the God whom they have forsaken. Their punishment is inescapable.

Jeremiah's Prayer

23I know, O LORD, that a man's life is not his own;
it is not for man to direct his steps.
24Correct me, LORD, but only with justice—
not in your anger,
lest you reduce me to nothing.
25Pour out your wrath on the nations
that do not acknowledge you,
on the peoples who do not call on your name.

For they have devoured Jacob;
they have devoured him completely
and destroyed his homeland.

Jeremiah interjects a personal prayer and confession. Though Judah had followed idols, those idols meant nothing. Jeremiah acknowledged that the direction for life comes from the Lord. As the proverb goes: Man proposes, but God disposes.

In these verses Jeremiah prepares us for what is to come in his prophecy. He was going to walk in a path that he himself had not chosen; the Lord had chosen it for him. In the following chapters we will see many instances in which the prophet questions and challenges the way of the Lord. To him God's way at times seemed unjust and wrong. For him personally that way will prove to be almost unbearable. Jeremiah wants us to realize that from the beginning of his prophetic service he had submitted himself to God's way, however hard such submission was for him.

Jeremiah asked God to correct him. He knew his sinful nature would resist the way of the Lord all his life and that he needed the Lord's help to keep him on the way the Lord had chosen. He therefore asked for such correction to come with justice and not in anger. If God were to act in anger, in his righteous wrath, no sinner, no human being, could stand. By justice Jeremiah means that righteousness which God has extended to us in Christ Jesus—in short, the mercy and forgiveness with which our God has embraced and covered us. That righteousness or justice controls all of God's actions toward us. By contrast, those who have not known or believed in the Lord can expect nothing but wrath.

The Covenant Is Broken

11 This is the word that came to Jeremiah from the LORD:
2"Listen to the terms of this covenant and tell them to

the people of Judah and to those who live in Jerusalem. [3]Tell them that this is what the LORD, the God of Israel, says: 'Cursed is the man who does not obey the terms of this covenant—[4]the terms I commanded your forefathers when I brought them out of Egypt, out of the iron-smelting furnace.' I said, 'Obey me and do everything I command you, and you will be my people, and I will be your God. [5]Then I will fulfill the oath I swore to your forefathers, to give them a land flowing with milk and honey'—the land you possess today."

I answered, "Amen, LORD."

[6]The LORD said to me, "Proclaim all these words in the towns of Judah and in the streets of Jerusalem: 'Listen to the terms of this covenant and follow them. [7]From the time I brought your forefathers up from Egypt until today, I warned them again and again, saying, "Obey me." [8]But they did not listen or pay attention; instead, they followed the stubbornness of their evil hearts. So I brought on them all the curses of the covenant I had commanded them to follow but that they did not keep.' "

Jeremiah returns to the main theme of this section. He had pointed out the worthlessness of idols and of the religion and worship associated with them. Now he shows the people of Judah that their only hope lay in the covenant that the Lord had made with them and in the terms of the covenant which the Lord himself had laid down. The prophet, therefore, urges them twice, "Listen to the terms of this covenant."

The terms of that covenant were spelled out in the law of Moses announced at Mt. Sinai. We find them in Exodus 19:3-6 and especially in Deuteronomy chapters 28 and 29. In Deuteronomy 28:1-14 the Lord promised the people of Israel many material and spiritual blessings if they obeyed the terms of his covenant. At the same time, he announced he would curse them for their disobedience.

The Sinaitic covenant came from the Lord. Because of his love, purely by grace, and because of an earlier covenant made with Abraham to bring the Savior into the world through Abraham's descendants, the Lord made this second covenant with Israel at Sinai. The Sinai covenant was a disciplinary mechanism; it was never intended to be God's last word to the human race. Its purpose was to mold and shape an immature and rebellious people into God's kind of people until the Savior would come.

This Sinaitic covenant was rooted in the faithfulness of God, his determination to keep his word. The Lord would not break the covenant on his part. But the Sinai covenant was not one-sided like the unconditional promise of the Savior given to Abraham. The terms of the covenant of Sinai also called for sincere obedience on the part of the people. The Israelites could not expect the Lord to shower them with blessings if they did not observe their part, that is, if they did not obey the terms of the covenant. For this reason Jeremiah had preached, "Listen to the terms of the covenant." In their hardness of heart, the Israelites had deceived themselves into believing and expecting that the Lord would bless them no matter what they did. They could not have been more wrong.

The covenant itself consisted of a whole series of regulations covering the entire life of the chosen nation and of every person belonging to that nation. These regulations and laws are given in the books of Exodus, Leviticus, Numbers, and Deuteronomy. To these laws God commanded perfect obedience.

The Lord knew full well the weakness brought about by sin and that the Israelites would fail to keep the terms of the covenant. So throughout the laws and ceremonies and sacrifices of the Sinai covenant the Lord provided many means for ancient Israel to return to a right covenant relationship with their Lord. Their continual breaking of the covenant, their failure to keep God's law, along with God's explicit threats to punish them for their disobedience, was meant to remind the Israelites continually of their need for God's unconditional promise of the Savior which God had given to Abraham. In that unconditional promise of salvation, believing Israelites found the strength to serve the Lord under the terms of the Sinai covenant. Unbelieving Israelites, on the other hand, who lived in defiant rebellion of the Lord's covenant, were left with only the curses which the Lord had pronounced in the Sinai covenant.

9 Then the LORD said to me, "There is a conspiracy among
the people of Judah and those who live in Jerusalem. 10 They
have returned to the sins of their forefathers, who refused to
listen to my words. They have followed other gods to serve
them. Both the house of Israel and the house of Judah have
broken the covenant I made with their forefathers. 11 Therefore
this is what the LORD says: 'I will bring on them a disaster they
cannot escape. Although they cry out to me, I will not listen to
them. 12 The towns of Judah and the people of Jerusalem will go
and cry out to the gods to whom they burn incense, but they
will not help them at all when disaster strikes. 13 You have as
many gods as you have towns, O Judah; and the altars you
have set up to burn incense to that shameful god Baal are as
many as the streets of Jerusalem.'

14 "Do not pray for this people nor offer any plea or petition
for them, because I will not listen when they call to me in the
time of their distress.

15 "What is my beloved doing in my temple
as she works out her evil schemes with many?
Can consecrated meat avert your punishment?
When you engage in your wickedness,
then you rejoice."

16The Lord called you a thriving olive tree
with fruit beautiful in form.
But with the roar of a mighty storm
he will set it on fire,
and its branches will be broken.

17The Lord Almighty, who planted you, has decreed disaster for you, because the house of Israel and the house of Judah have done evil and provoked me to anger by burning incense to Baal.

The Lord knew what his people were doing and thinking. He realized that they had not from the heart obeyed the terms of his covenant with them. They had carefully followed some of the external rituals of the covenant. Because of that they had deceived themselves into thinking that going through the motions of worship was enough. Hardly!

The great reformation effected by the pious King Josiah had removed some of the paraphernalia of their idol worship, but that reformation had not penetrated to their hearts. Because they had repeatedly broken the first and greatest commandment, "You shall have no other gods," whatever else they did would be of no value. They had filled the temple and the towns of Judah and the streets of Jerusalem with the worship of the obscene Baal, the great fertility god of the Canaanites.

Having abandoned their Health, as sick men desperate for cures, they multiplied their gods. As people addicted to idolatry, they ran from one false god to another, making their condition even more hopeless. Through it all one factor remained constant: they refused to turn to the Lord. In this respect the Israelites mirror for us our own times. Today many have abandoned God's truth or refuse to acknowledge it. Addicted to the novel and exciting, too many follow every new sect, cult, and movement that comes along. But, like Judah, they find no peace or answers.

The fault certainly was not the Lord's. Jeremiah says: "You were a thriving olive tree when the Lord called you." The olive tree begins to bear fruit at about seven years and reaches its maturity at fifteen or twenty. Then it can live and produce fruit for a very long time—in some cases for nearly a thousand years. In ancient Israel the olive tree was a symbol of prosperity. So the Lord had blessed his people from the very beginning with every grace and good gift, enabling them to be fruitful for him. But because they had turned against him, he would now destroy them. He had already destroyed Israel (the ten tribes of the north). Judah, whose heart was in full rebellion, would not fare any better.

The Lord confirmed the seriousness of his intention by commanding the prophet not to pray for this people. For the second time Jeremiah records this solemn command. If Judah persisted in its disobedience, nothing could stop the fiery judgment of God. No prophetic nor priestly intercession would do any good. Surely this command would show the people how desperate their position was.

Plot Against Jeremiah

18Because the LORD revealed their plot to me, I knew it, for
at that time he showed me what they were doing. 19I had been
like a gentle lamb led to the slaughter; I did not realize that
they had plotted against me, saying,

"Let us destroy the tree and its fruit;
let us cut him off from the land of the living,
that his name be remembered no more."
20But, O LORD Almighty, you who judge righteously
and test the heart and mind,
let me see your vengeance upon them,
for to you I have committed my cause.

21"Therefore this is what the LORD says about the men of
Anathoth who are seeking your life and saying, 'Do not proph-

esy in the name of the LORD or you will die by our hands'— [22]therefore this is what the LORD Almighty says: 'I will punish them. Their young men will die by the sword, their sons and daughters by famine. [23]Not even a remnant will be left to them, because I will bring disaster on the men of Anathoth in the year of their punishment.' "

Jeremiah's preaching had hit home—too close to home. His own fellow-villagers turned against him. Anathoth is located in the territory of Benjamin and was assigned to the priests. Although Jeremiah was related to the priestly clan, his kinsmen found his message incredible. They had witnessed the great renewal under Josiah. That renewal was certainly a move in the right direction. What more did Jeremiah want? Why did he keep preaching his harsh message? Why not give credit for the progress already made? Didn't his preaching threaten to undermine everything? Surely God's people, and especially his priests, did not need someone telling them what to do or how to think. Jeremiah began to experience firsthand the truth of the proverb once used by Jesus, "A prophet has no honor in his own country" (John 4:44).

Jeremiah had no idea how angry his own townspeople were. Perhaps he simply was unable to face or understand that anger. Perhaps he still hoped against hope for much better from Judah. He still wanted to believe that, in fact, the people of Judah would listen to the Lord's message through his prophet and change their ways. Because he was a man wholly dedicated to the Lord's work and because he trusted the Lord with all his heart, Jeremiah was convinced that the people, too, shared his faith. But this incident was to shatter his illusions. It demonstrated to him how little the reformation of Josiah had reached their hearts. The people had not changed, and they did not want to change their ways. Thus

Jeremiah gained further insight into the immense difficulty of his ministry as God's prophet.

Jeremiah's kinsmen had threatened to kill him, and they would have succeeded but for the Lord. Though they took their anger out on Jeremiah, their real enemy was not Jeremiah but the Lord himself. Jesus said, "He who listens to you listens to me; he who rejects you rejects me; but he who rejects me rejects him who sent me" (Luke 10:16). Because they opposed the Lord and made him their enemy, Jeremiah called for vengeance and punishment upon them. This call was not for personal satisfaction, but to announce that those who stand against the Lord's Word cannot prosper or escape his judgment. Such vengeance would also serve as a warning to any others who might want to resist or threaten the prophet.

By revealing this plot and protecting Jeremiah from death, the Lord kept the promises he had made to him at the very beginning of his prophetic ministry (Jeremiah 1:18,19). The Lord had indeed been a bronze wall against his enemies; their plot had failed. By protecting Jeremiah, the Lord strengthened him for the greater challenges to come. God taught Jeremiah that he could count on the Lord no matter what the situation.

Paul the apostle once wrote, "everyone who wants to live a godly life in Christ Jesus will be persecuted" (2 Timothy 3:12). Times have not changed. If we want to live a godly life in Christ and hold to the truth of God's Word and confess it and witness to it, we too will find opposition. Our age does not want to hear the law of God any more than Jeremiah's did. Resistance to the law proves even more the need for the Word and its proclamation and its teaching. The Word is the only spiritual remedy for a sick and dying world.

THE LORD'S ACTION TROUBLES THE PROPHET

JEREMIAH 12—14

Jeremiah's Complaint

12 **You are always righteous, O LORD,**
when I bring a case before you.
Yet I would speak with you about your justice:
Why does the way of the wicked prosper?
Why do all the faithless live at ease?
2 You have planted them, and they have taken root;
they grow and bear fruit.
You are always on their lips
but far from their hearts.
3 Yet you know me, O LORD;
you see me and test my thoughts about you.
Drag them off like sheep to be butchered!
Set them apart for the day of slaughter!
4 How long will the land lie parched
and the grass in every field be withered?
Because those who live in it are wicked,
the animals and birds have perished.
Moreover, the people are saying,
"He will not see what happens to us."

Jeremiah approached the Lord with all confidence and boldness, unafraid to ask the Lord the tough questions, the questions that really bothered him. He was sure that the Lord would answer him. He confessed that the Lord was righteous and just in all that he was doing. He did not doubt the justice of the Lord, but he also did not understand the full meaning of God's justice. He had problems with the way the Lord works out his just ways.

Jeremiah asked a question often on the minds and hearts of believers: "Why do the wicked prosper?" The psalmist Asaph asked that same question (Psalm 73). The book of Job revolves around that question and its related question, "Why do the righteous suffer?" The wicked, the hypocrites, the unbelievers give the Lord only lip service, yet often seem to flourish. At the very least, one might conclude that the Lord allows them such success and is in part responsible for it. Nonetheless, Jeremiah could not believe that the Lord was actually blessing them.

The prosperity of the wicked seems especially out of place in view of the faithfulness of the prophet. Jeremiah invited the Lord to test the motives of his heart. His heart was in the right place, yet he was suffering. What bothered the prophet even more was that the success of the wicked was undermining his message. The wicked questioned whether the judgment of the Lord would fall upon them: "He [God] will not see what happens to us." Even the land itself had suffered periodic droughts because of the wicked.

Wickedness still has the same effect today. At any given time we may not be able to point to this disaster or that instance of what Jeremiah is talking about, yet despite all appearances wickedness and unbelief have had their effects in our time and on our land, too.

Jeremiah asked the Lord to take immediate action. "Drag them off to be butchered." He wanted God to send ruin and destruction right then. Like James and John, the sons of thunder, Jeremiah wanted God to bring fire and destruction upon the wicked (Luke 9:51-56). Perhaps he dreamed about great deeds of might such as those performed by Elijah and Elisha the prophets. Even though such destruction would not bring Jeremiah prosperity, at least it would give him personal satisfaction. Jeremiah waited for the Lord's answer, and the answer was not long in coming.

God's Answer

5 "If you have raced with men on foot
and they have worn you out,
how can you compete with horses?
If you stumble in safe country,
how will you manage in the thickets by the Jordan?
6 Your brothers, your own family—
even they have betrayed you;
they have raised a loud cry against you.
Do not trust them,
though they speak well of you.

7 "I will forsake my house,
abandon my inheritance;
I will give the one I love
into the hands of her enemies.
8 My inheritance has become to me
like a lion in the forest.
She roars at me;
therefore I hate her.
9 Has not my inheritance become to me
like a speckled bird of prey
that other birds of prey surround and attack?
Go and gather all the wild beasts;
bring them to devour.
10 Many shepherds will ruin my vineyard
and trample down my field;
they will turn my pleasant field
into a desolate wasteland.
11 It will be made a wasteland,
parched and desolate before me;
the whole land will be laid waste
because there is no one who cares.
12 Over all the barren heights in the desert
destroyers will swarm,

for the sword of the LORD will devour
from one end of the land to the other;
no one will be safe.
13 They will sow wheat but reap thorns;
they will wear themselves out but gain nothing.
So bear the shame of your harvest
because of the LORD's fierce anger."

14 This is what the LORD says: "As for all my wicked neigh-
bors who seize the inheritance I gave my people Israel, I will
uproot them from their lands and I will uproot the house of Ju-
dah from among them. 15 But after I uproot them, I will again
have compassion and will bring each of them back to his own
inheritance and his own country. 16 And if they learn well the
ways of my people and swear by my name, saying, 'As surely
as the LORD lives'—even as they once taught my people to
swear by Baal—then they will be established among my peo-
ple. 17 But if any nation does not listen, I will completely uproot
and destroy it," declares the LORD.

The Lord has invited us to come to him boldly as dear children with all that is on our hearts. If we do that, he promises us an answer. His answer, however, may differ completely from the one we had wanted or expected.

The Lord told Jeremiah: "Things are going to get worse before they get better. You have just begun to see the extent of the opposition you will face. Your family and friends have opposed you, even to the point of threatening your life, but many more will join them as the years pass. What will you do when you face these greater threats and wickedness? If you cannot race with someone who is on foot, how will you manage with someone who is mounted? If you are having problems where the going is easy, how will you make out in the thickets, the almost impassable thorn bushes and brambles near the Jordan River?

"Use this opportunity to toughen up. Rely on me and my wisdom and strength. My child, you are trying to understand matters that are way beyond you. Put judgment into my hands. Realize the riches and blessings I have already showered upon you. Keep hold of the promises I have made to you. These are your true riches.

"You may be sure that my judgment will strike all who oppose me. You must not confuse my patience with delay. My goal is that no one should perish, but that all should come to a knowledge of the truth. The greatness of my patience is the measure of my love for Judah.

"Be sure, the sin of the people Judah has angered me. The false prophets upon whom they have relied will come to nothing. Soon, at my command, their enemies will come in droves. Ask then what prosperity will be to the wicked. No one will be safe. All their labor will be for nothing. That which they have heaped up, thinking they have secured the future for themselves, will be lost."

The anger of the Lord is especially evident in the words of verse eleven, "There is no one who cares" (literally, "no one puts the matter upon his heart"). The wicked did not care. They did not take the Word of the Lord seriously. They believed that the Lord was nothing, that his warnings were empty threats. For that reason the Lord would bring judgment and destruction upon them.

The Lord also promised to punish those nations who would take advantage of Judah's condition to avenge themselves upon her and seize what was hers for their own. The Lord was here referring to Judah's immediate neighbors. What they would get by plundering Judah would do them no good. They, too, would be scattered by invading armies.

Some good, however, would come from this disaster. The Jews who were scattered as a result of the destruction of the nation would have opportunity to confess and teach others the way of the Lord. This opportunity would continue until the time the Lord restored his people to their homeland and even beyond that time. Their return would prove the faithfulness of God. That demonstration of his faithfulness would invite those nations to hear the promises of the Lord and believe them. Then they would share in the blessings of Judah and be counted as part of the people of God. If these nations did not believe, they would be destroyed.

So the Lord taught Jeremiah that the wicked prosper only for a time, but what counts is the end result. He also taught the prophet that out of even the greatest "evils" the Lord can bring good. To convince Jeremiah that he would bring certain judgment, the Lord instructed Jeremiah to deliver two object lessons to Judah.

A Linen Belt

**13 This is what the LORD said to me: "Go and buy a linen
belt and put it around your waist, but do not let it touch
water." 2So I bought a belt, as the LORD directed, and put it
around my waist.**

**3Then the word of the LORD came to me a second time:
4"Take the belt you bought and are wearing around your waist,
and go now to Perath and hide it there in a crevice in the
rocks." 5So I went and hid it at Perath, as the LORD told me.**

**6Many days later the LORD said to me, "Go now to Perath
and get the belt I told you to hide there." 7So I went to Perath
and dug up the belt and took it from the place where I had hidden it, but now it was ruined and completely useless.**

**8Then the word of the LORD came to me: 9"This is what the
LORD says: 'In the same way I will ruin the pride of Judah and
the great pride of Jerusalem. 10These wicked people, who
refuse to listen to my words, who follow the stubbornness of
their hearts and go after other gods to serve and worship them,**

will be like this belt—completely useless! "For as a belt is bound around a man's waist, so I bound the whole house of Israel and the whole house of Judah to me,' declares the LORD, 'to be my people for my renown and praise and honor. But they have not listened.'

At this point in the Jews's history, because of the hardness of their hearts, the Lord often resorted to object lessons and dramatic measures to try to bring his message home to his people. These extreme methods are further evidence of just how thick and unfeeling and unreceptive their hearts had become. The prophet readily obeyed the Lord's command. He probably bought the linen loincloth in public for all to see so that later his message and application would be all the more effective.

The command was to buy a linen belt or loin cloth. This piece of clothing was worn closest to the skin, and was the most personal part of the dress of the day. Linen was preferred because it was cooler. The prophet was to wear the cloth close to himself and above all to keep it dry. Later he received the command to take the cloth to Perath and hide it in a hole in the rocks. No one knows for sure what place is meant by Perath. Perath may be the Euphrates river; that would have been a journey of about 500 miles for Jeremiah. Some scholars believe Perath may be the wadi and spring of Parah several miles northeast of Anathoth, Jeremiah's home town (Joshua 18:23). The place is not as important as the message.

After a long period of time the Lord sent the prophet to dig up the linen belt. Quite obviously the long exposure to water and dirt had completely ruined it. The Lord now applied this lesson to Judah. The Lord had loved them and taken them as no other people to be close to him. He had caused his name to dwell among them and given them the grace of continuing fellowship through his covenant and the worship he instituted at the tabernacle and later at the temple. He had identified himself with them as he had done with no other people. The Lord had been merciful to them to show all nations what kind of God he is. Yet his chosen people rejected him and followed false gods. They had frustrated his purpose for them. In their stubbornness they had turned from him. Now he would turn from them and they would be ruined and worthless, for their value and worth came not from themselves but from him.

Wineskins

12"Say to them: 'This is what the LORD, the God of Israel, says: Every wineskin should be filled with wine.' And if they say to you, 'Don't we know that every wineskin should be filled with wine?' 13then tell them, 'This is what the LORD says: I am going to fill with drunkenness all who live in this land, including the kings who sit on David's throne, the priests, the prophets and all those living in Jerusalem. 14I will smash them one against the other, fathers and sons alike, declares the LORD. I will allow no pity or mercy or compassion to keep me from destroying them.' "

The Lord now used a second powerful picture to call the leaders of the people to repentance. The word translated "wineskin" can mean an animal skin used to hold wine (1 Samuel 1:24; 10:3; 25:18), or it can mean a clay storage jar (Isaiah 30:14). In this context the picture might be more vivid if we think of large storage jars.

The Lord uses a proverb popular among the people. "Every wineskin should be filled with wine." Perhaps this proverb expressed their idea of the good life. If your wine jars are full, you've got it made. Jeremiah's listeners fully agreed. Our world, too, is filled with such images: freshly caught trout cooking over an open fire, a cooler full of beer, and the sun setting over a quiet lake. Unfortunately, that was the only yardstick many in Judah had for measuring the full, good life. But where does God fit in that picture? Their definition had excluded the greatest good.

Because they had made this created world the measure of all things and had looked for satisfaction only in the here and now, the Lord would give them plenty to drink—not the wine of the grape, but rather the wine of his judgment. He would fill them with drunkenness so that they would act as if they were drunk, out of control and helpless, not knowing what they were doing. This drunkenness would be their grief, their astonishment at the severity of his judgment when it came.

The Lord's judgment is pictured in the fiercest terms. As a person might smash clay jars one against another and break them, so God would smash person against person, shattering the dearest of relationships. Nothing would prevent his judgment. The Lord uses three words for compassion or pity to show that he would not have the slightest feeling in any way. No mercy, only the grim work of punishing judgment. We need not be surprised. Apart from the righteousness he gives us in Christ and the love he extends to us in Christ, he is a consuming fire, a whirlwind of doom.

Threat of Captivity

15 Hear and pay attention,
do not be arrogant,
for the LORD has spoken.
16 Give glory to the LORD your God
before he brings the darkness,
before your feet stumble
on the darkening hills.

You hope for light,
but he will turn it to thick darkness
and change it to deep gloom.
17 But if you do not listen,
I will weep in secret
because of your pride;
my eyes will weep bitterly,
overflowing with tears,
because the LORD's flock will be taken captive.

18 Say to the king and to the queen mother,
"Come down from your thrones,
for your glorious crowns
will fall from your heads."
19 The cities in the Negev will be shut up,
and there will be no one to open them.
All Judah will be carried into exile,
carried completely away.

20 Lift up your eyes and see
those who are coming from the north.
Where is the flock that was entrusted to you,
the sheep of which you boasted?
21 What will you say when the LORD sets over you
those you cultivated as your special allies?
Will not pain grip you
like that of a woman in labor?
22 And if you ask yourself,
"Why has this happened to me?"—
it is because of your many sins
that your skirts have been torn off
and your body mistreated.

In the face of the grim judgment to come, once again the Lord called for repentance. Time was running out for the chosen nation. Today is the day, now is the hour, before the darkness comes, the deep darkness in which one may stumble and fall.

Remember that in the days of the prophets there were no street lights or other artificial lights to brighten the night. The nights without clouds and moonlight were really dark. The Lord gives ample time for repentance, but that time comes to an end and then there is only darkness. The prophet urged his hearers to give glory to the Lord. And they could give no greater glory to God than to turn to him for forgiveness and to trust him as Savior.

Jeremiah took no pleasure in announcing the coming judgment. He felt for his people and their pain. He kept his feelings to himself because he was the public servant of the Lord, commanded now to preach unbending condemnation.

The prophet addressed the king and queen mother. The reference is probably to King Jehoiachin and his mother, Nehushta. Jehoiachin succeeded his father Jehoiakim at age eighteen. He was no better than his father. He ruled for only three months and ten days and was carried away by Nebuchadnezzar to Babylon in 597 B.C. These words were probably first spoken about that time and that event.

Because the people of Judah and their rulers had not listened to the Lord, they were going to taste his judgment. The prophet warned the king and his mother to come down. God had removed them from their place and taken their subjects from them. They did not deserve the rulership. There would be no escape. They might try, but the usual escape routes would be closed. There would be no way to get to the cities of refuge in the southern desert region of Judah; the Negev would be shut to them.

The loss of their throne would be painful, for two reasons. For a long time, in spite of the warnings of many prophets, the rulers of Judah had tried to secure their nation by means of political alliances with neighboring nations. One whose favor they had curried was the Babylonians (Isaiah 39). Since their allies now turned against them, that strategy had failed. They had been warned and were without excuse. Their only hope was in the Lord, not in shifting alliances.

The Lord cites a second reason why the loss of their throne would be so painful: "It is because of your many sins." The hardest troubles in life are those for which we are personally, solely responsible. We like to shift the blame and give excuses. How hard it is when there are none! Such was the situation of Judah.

23 Can the Ethiopian change his skin
or the leopard its spots?
Neither can you do good
who are accustomed to doing evil.

24 "I will scatter you like chaff
driven by the desert wind.
25 This is your lot,
the portion I have decreed for you,"
declares the LORD,

"because you have forgotten me
and trusted in false gods.
26 I will pull up your skirts over your face
that your shame may be seen—
27 your adulteries and lustful neighings,
your shameless prostitution!
I have seen your detestable acts
on the hills and in the fields.
Woe to you, O Jerusalem!
How long will you be unclean?"

The Lord had little hope that the king, queen mother, priests, and other leaders in Jerusalem would repent. Their persistent refusal to listen had hardened their hearts against the message and against the Spirit who brings the message. The Lord expressed this truth with the illustrations of the Ethiopian and the leopard. He does not mean to say that he has made it impossible for any to repent and come to him, but that some have made it hard, if not impossible, for themselves. They had become so practiced in their sinning, so used to it, that they found change difficult. They had closed themselves to the Spirit of God. Such is the power of sinful habit; its grip can chain us to our eternal loss.

The chief and abiding sin of Judah was idolatry, the sin against the first commandment. This sin was the source of all their other sins. Idolatry, then, is the sin for which the Lord condemned them. He used extreme, almost offensive language. He wanted them to understand the revolting and repulsive nature of their sin. He compared them to an adulteress or a prostitute who offers her favors to anyone and everyone. She knows no shame nor how to stop. In the same way, Judah had an insatiable lust for other gods. For a time she had been able to conceal this lust underneath a cover of lip service to the Lord. Soon, however, the Lord would tear the cover away, (or, to use the graphic language of the prophet, he will lift her skirts) so that all may see her sin for what it is.

Drought, Famine, Sword

14 This is the word of the LORD to Jeremiah concerning the drought:

2 "Judah mourns,
her cities languish;
they wail for the land,
and a cry goes up from Jerusalem.
3 The nobles send their servants for water;
they go to the cisterns
but find no water.

They return with their jars unfilled;
dismayed and despairing,
they cover their heads.
4 The ground is cracked
because there is no rain in the land;
the farmers are dismayed
and cover their heads.
5 Even the doe in the field
deserts her newborn fawn
because there is no grass.
6 Wild donkeys stand on the barren heights
and pant like jackals;
their eyesight fails
for lack of pasture."

Jeremiah had apparently questioned the Lord about the most recent drought he had sent upon the land. More than once in the past the Lord had sent droughts to call his people to repentance. The most famous of these was the three-and-a-half-year drought at the time of wicked King Ahab (1 Kings 17,18).

The effects of this latest drought were devastating. It had driven the citizens, even the country's leaders, to desperation. They could find no water, even in their secret cisterns. All water reserves had been exhausted. If even the powerful were helpless, we can only imagine its effect upon the small and weak. It shattered the most tender of relationships: even the doe in the field deserted her newborn fawn. The desperate search for water during the drought had turned one person against the other. The toughest were growing faint. The untamable wild donkeys were staggering. But had the people of Judah gotten the message?

7 Although our sins testify against us,
O LORD, do something for the sake of your name.

For our backsliding is great;
we have sinned against you.
7 O Hope of Israel,
its Savior in times of distress,
why are you like a stranger in the land,
like a traveler who stays only a night?
9 Why are you like a man taken by surprise,
like a warrior powerless to save?
You are among us, O LORD,
and we bear your name;
do not forsake us!

10 This is what the LORD says about this people:

"They greatly love to wander;
they do not restrain their feet.
So the LORD does not accept them;
he will now remember their wickedness
and punish them for their sins."

11 Then the LORD said to me, "Do not pray for the well-being
of this people. 12 Although they fast, I will not listen to their cry;
though they offer burnt offerings and grain offerings, I will not accept them. Instead, I will destroy them with the sword, famine and plague."

13 But I said, "Ah, Sovereign LORD, the prophets keep telling them, 'You will not see the sword or suffer famine. Indeed, I will give you lasting peace in this place.' "

Under these difficult conditions Jeremiah again displayed his deep love for his people. As a lonely intercessor, grasping the promise of the Lord, he prayed once more. He offered no excuses to God. For the people he confessed, "We have sinned." Some had insulted the Lord by claiming that he had no long-term interest in the land or its people, that he had abandoned them, that he was like a traveler passing through, like a foreigner living among them temporarily. Some had pictured the Lord as weak and helpless, a warrior grown too old and weak to fight. Jeremiah begged for an answer. He appealed to the Lord's name. The Lord had saved them in the past and was still among his people. Solely for divine love's sake Jeremiah begged God to save Judah.

For the third time the Lord commanded Jeremiah not to pray for the well-being of the nation. What a test this was for the prophet—to face the stony silence of God! We are reminded of the Syrophoenician woman who shouted to Jesus, but he did not reply (Mark 7). We remember the woman in the parable of the unjust judge (Luke 18). What a hard message for the people to hear! Total destruction was on the way: sword, famine, plague. If one did not kill you, another would. They dared not take their sin lightly.

Unfortunately, they still had not gotten God's message. They showed no change in attitude. Oh, they fasted beyond the command of the law and offered more offerings, but they had forgotten what the Lord truly wants: "The sacrifices of God are a broken spirit; a broken and contrite heart, O God, you will not despise" (Psalm 51:17).

The prophet tried to explain his people's behavior by pleading extenuating circumstances. The false prophets had misled the people. They had opposed the truth. When the Lord said that destruction would come, they quickly replied that there would be no sword or famine in this place. The message of the false prophets was always the same. It was constantly a message of peace and prosperity. Their technique was as old as the world itself. At the very beginning Satan had used the same technique, "Did God really say that you will die? You will not surely die!" (Genesis 3) They told the people what the people wanted to hear, and the people listened (1 Kings 22).

**[14]Then the LORD said to me, "The prophets are prophesying
lies in my name. I have not sent them or appointed them or
spoken to them. They are prophesying to you false visions, div-
inations, idolatries and the delusions of their own minds.
[15]Therefore, this is what the LORD says about the prophets who
are prophesying in my name: I did not send them, yet they are
saying, 'No sword or famine will touch this land.' Those same
prophets will perish by sword and famine. [16]And the people
they are prophesying to will be thrown out into the streets of
Jerusalem because of the famine and sword. There will be no
one to bury them or their wives, their sons or their daughters.
I will pour out on them the calamity they deserve.**

[17]"Speak this word to them:

" 'Let my eyes overflow with tears
night and day without ceasing;
for my virgin daughter—my people—
has suffered a grievous wound,
a crushing blow.
[18]If I go into the country,
I see those slain by the sword;
if I go into the city,
I see the ravages of famine.
Both prophet and priest
have gone to a land they know not.' "

The Lord rejected Jeremiah's attempt to shift the blame solely to the false prophets. False prophets were no excuse for the unbelief of his people. People are deceived because they want to be deceived. The source of the false prophets' deception was self-evident—the delusions of their own minds. They may speak, but no one should listen to them or follow their words.

One should apply the test the Lord himself has provided. In Deuteronomy 13, the Lord had given future generations the means to identify false prophets. They needed only to use these means. The Lord had reaffirmed this test through the prophet Isaiah (8:20) when he had urged the people, "To the law and to the testimony! If they do not speak according to this word, they have no light of dawn." Every age and every believer therefore ought to judge false prophets, yes, all new teaching, by the yardstick the Lord himself has supplied. His Word itself is the standard by which he expects every person to judge whatever any religious teacher says.

To remove all doubt from the minds of his people, the Lord told them flat out: "I have not sent these prophets." They had come on their own. Here is another identifying mark of false prophets. Besides throwing aside the clear testimony of Scripture, they speak on their own authority. They are not sent, called, or appointed. They come by their own authority and in their own name and with no more power than that. Their end, God says here, is sealed. The false prophets will be destroyed in a complete disaster. All who listen to them will share the same reward.

To emphasize how certain the coming destruction was, the Lord through his prophet sang a funeral dirge, even before the funeral itself even occurred. He showed his people his deep grief; he takes no pleasure in the death of the wicked. Wherever he looked he saw death. Those who tried to escape to the countryside lay dead by the sword of their pursuers. Those who stayed behind the safety of fortified walls died from starvation. The false prophets were no more, they were either dead or were carried off into exile. The priests who failed in their duty to test and judge false doctrine shared the fate of the false prophets. The outcome can never be any different when a nation or individual surrenders the Word for lies.

19Have you rejected Judah completely?
Do you despise Zion?

Why have you afflicted us
so that we cannot be healed?
We hoped for peace
but no good has come,
for a time of healing
but there is only terror.
20 O LORD, we acknowledge our wickedness
and the guilt of our fathers;
we have indeed sinned against you.
21 For the sake of your name do not despise us;
do not dishonor your glorious throne.
Remember your covenant with us
and do not break it.
22 Do any of the worthless idols of the nations bring rain?
Do the skies themselves send down showers?
No, it is you, O LORD our God.
Therefore our hope is in you,
for you are the one who does all this.

Jeremiah prayed once more. He knew that the Lord had not rejected Judah completely. He clung to this slender thread of promise. He could appeal to none other than the Lord whom his fellow Jews had offended. Again he confessed the guilt of his people, offering no apologies. His prayer is very similar to that of Daniel (Daniel 9). Nothing in this people deserved anything good from the Lord.

The prophet appealed once more to the very character of the Lord. Jeremiah prayed to him because of the kind of God he is, a saving God ("for your name's sake"). Jeremiah prayed to him because of his dwelling place in Jerusalem, the temple, and the mercy he had promised to send out from there. Because of the covenant the Lord had made with this nation and the unfailing faithfulness which lay behind that covenant, the prophet appealed to the Lord to save. The Lord had the power to save. He was not some fiction, some figment of men's minds. No, he is the almighty Creator and Preserver of heaven and earth. "Therefore our hope is in you."

No one could have prayed more fervently and powerfully than the prophet who pleaded with all his heart for his people. Jeremiah shows us how to pray: fervently and persistently, confidently appealing to all that our God has shown himself to be toward us in Christ—loving, faithful, all-powerful.

JUDAH'S IMPENITENCE SEALS THE LORD'S JUDGMENT AGAINST HER

JEREMIAH 15—20

No One Can Turn Aside God's Judgment

**15 Then the LORD said to me: "Even if Moses and Samuel
were to stand before me, my heart would not go out to
this people. Send them away from my presence! Let them go!
2And if they ask you, 'Where shall we go?' tell them, 'This is
what the LORD says:**

> **" 'Those destined for death, to death;**
> **those for the sword, to the sword;**
> **those for starvation, to starvation;**
> **those for captivity, to captivity.'**

**3"I will send four kinds of destroyers against them," declares
the LORD, "the sword to kill and the dogs to drag away and the
birds of the air and the beasts of the earth to devour and destroy. 4I will make them abhorrent to all the kingdoms of the
earth because of what Manasseh son of Hezekiah king of Judah did in Jerusalem.**

Jeremiah might have been troubled about the ineffectiveness of his prayers. Though he had interceded with the Lord, his intercessions seemed to have had no effect. He had no reason to be discouraged by their failure to turn aside the wrath of God. The Lord told him that no one, not even Moses and Samuel, would have done any better.

Moses had saved the people on two occasions: after the sin of the golden calf (Exodus 32) and after the rebellion at the report of the spies (Numbers 14). Both times the Lord had threatened to wipe out the nation. Both times Moses prayed with great passion and power, pleading with the Lord to save them. Moses had even offered his own life in their place. The prophet Samuel, too, had saved the people twice, once at Mizpeh from the Philistines (1 Samuel 7) and again after the people had rejected him and the Lord and asked for a king (1 Samuel 12).

But now the Lord was prepared to listen no more. No one could postpone the outpouring of his fierce anger. God used the examples of Moses and Samuel to remove all doubt from the minds of the people that he meant business. His patience was at an end. The Lord's patience is great and well beyond our expectations, but it does have its limits.

So the Lord told his prophet, "Send them away." Send them away to destruction. To insure that no one would escape, the Lord promised to send a fourfold destroyer. The number four is often used in the Bible in connection with creation. The Lord would bring the full force of creation against those who insisted on living independently of him. He who had made them for his purpose would now also destroy them. He was right and justified in doing this because of the sins of Manasseh. Manasseh had succeeded his father Hezekiah, but he turned against all that his father had stood for. He filled the land with idols and persecuted the faithful, even shedding their blood (2 Kings 21:11,16). His evil spirit had filled all of Judah so that after him most of the people remained far from the Lord. His sin became theirs; they had made it their own.

5 "Who will have pity on you, O Jerusalem?
Who will mourn for you?
Who will stop to ask how you are?
6 You have rejected me," declares the LORD.
"You keep on backsliding.
So I will lay hands on you and destroy you;
I can no longer show compassion.

7 I will winnow them with a winnowing fork
at the city gates of the land.
I will bring bereavement and destruction
on my people,
for they have not changed their ways.
8 I will make their widows more numerous
than the sand of the sea.
At midday I will bring a destroyer
against the mothers of their young men;
suddenly I will bring down on them
anguish and terror.
9 The mother of seven will grow faint
and breathe her last.
Her sun will set while it is still day;
she will be disgraced and humiliated.
I will put the survivors to the sword
before their enemies,"
declares the LORD.

The prophet describes the severity of the coming judgment in vivid terms. No one will mourn for Judah and Jerusalem. We can imagine nothing sadder or lonelier than to have no mourners present at a person's funeral. How little such a life must have counted for! How little the ruin of Judah counted among the nations! The super arrogance of the Jews, their utter contempt for the other nations who were not God's chosen people or descendants of Abraham, would reap its bitter harvest. No one would pity them.

Jeremiah uses another familiar picture of judgment—the winnowing fork. After the farmers had threshed the grain and separated the kernel of grain from the husk, they would winnow it. On a level piece of ground at a time of day when the breeze was blowing the hardest, the farmer with his winnowing fork in hand would toss the mixture of chaff and grain into the air. The wind would carry the chaff away, allowing the heavier grain to drop. John the Baptist later would use this same picture to describe the Lord Jesus as judge of his people (Luke 3:17). So the Lord would use the enemies of Judah as a heavy winnowing fork to throw the Jews as chaff before the merciless wind.

How powerless they would be before this judgment! It would come suddenly and without warning. There would be no deception; it would come in the light of day. Even though they could see it coming, they would not be able to escape. No one would escape. The strength of all would fail. Even those who had gone through the hard time of childbirth, the young mothers in their vigor, and the mother of seven, would be swept away before it. No one would be spared.

10 Alas, my mother, that you gave me birth,
a man with whom the whole land
strives and contends!
I have neither lent nor borrowed,
yet everyone curses me.

11 The LORD said,

"Surely I will deliver you for a good purpose;
surely I will make your enemies plead with you
in times of disaster and times of distress.

12 "Can a man break iron—
iron from the north—or bronze?
13 Your wealth and your treasures
I will give as plunder, without charge,
because of all your sins
throughout your country.
14 I will enslave you to your enemies
in a land you do not know,
for my anger will kindle a fire
that will burn against you."

15 You understand, O LORD;
remember me and care for me.
Avenge me on my persecutors.
You are long-suffering—do not take me away;
think of how I suffer reproach for your sake.
16 When your words came, I ate them;
they were my joy and my heart's delight,
for I bear your name,
O LORD God Almighty.
17 I never sat in the company of revelers,
never made merry with them;
I sat alone because your hand was on me
and you had filled me with indignation.
18 Why is my pain unending
and my wound grievous and incurable?
Will you be to me like a deceptive brook,
like a spring that fails?

19 Therefore this is what the LORD says:

"If you repent, I will restore you
that you may serve me;
if you utter worthy, not worthless, words,
you will be my spokesman.
Let this people turn to you,
but you must not turn to them.
20 I will make you a wall to this people,
a fortified wall of bronze;
they will fight against you
but will not overcome you,
for I am with you
to rescue and save you,"
declares the LORD.
21 "I will save you from the hands of the wicked
and redeem you from the grasp of the cruel."

The monstrous impenitence of Judah and the unbending justice of God caught Jeremiah between them. He staggered under the burden. Struggle as he may (and we see him struggling here), he could not extricate himself from the cold despair, which slowly numbed his faith.

The people of Judah refused to listen, and instead saw the prophet as the enemy. As Ahab once pointed an accusing finger at Elijah, saying, "You are the one who troubles Israel," so Jeremiah's contemporaries lashed out at him. Except for him and his incessant preaching of judgment, the land would be at peace. The Lord told him at the very beginning of his ministry that all would oppose him. Now the reality of that prophecy was bearing down on Jeremiah with all its force. Yet the Lord consoled his prophet with the assurance that everything would turn out according to his good purpose.

The Lord presents us with the picture of iron, the strongest metal known in Jeremiah's day. The reference to iron may be used for the upbuilding of the prophet. So great would be the strength the Lord would supply, so unyielding would the Lord make the prophet, that the prophet would remain unbroken in the face of all the opposition. He would exult with Paul, "For when I am weak, then I am strong" (2 Corinthians 12:10) and "I can do everything through him who gives me strength" (Philippians 4:13). On the other hand, the reference to iron may underscore the words of judgment that follow. As impossible as it is to break iron, so it will be impossible for Judah to escape the disaster the Lord is bringing from the north.

In his effort to fight off the damp darkness creeping into his soul, the prophet turned to the Word, to his certain knowledge of the Lord's character. He confessed that the Lord knew the anguish of his heart and felt with him and for him. The Lord would not let him be taken away. The prophet had been faithful to his calling. How many insults had stung him! How often he had been called the fool for his message! How many times the people of Judah had thrown the question in his face, "Where is the fulfillment of the Lord's Word?"

According to the Lord's own command to him, Jeremiah had stood apart from the normal social activities. By doing so he had given testimony to the terror of the coming judgment. He had always found his strength in the Lord's Word.

God's Word was his support, the food of his life. What pleasure, what force of life came to him as he devoured it! How it lifted his soul and refreshed his spirit! How gladly he bore the name of the Lord! He looked to that Word now to ward off the doubt so swiftly coming upon him. It had not failed him in the past.

This time, however, Jeremiah let the comfort of the Word slip from him. He fell back on his own strength, and soon the pain overwhelmed him. The blackness of despair drawing everything into itself, engulfed the prophet's faith, hope, and very spirit. He could not hold back his doubts any longer. They rushed upon him. They made the Lord's Word seem only a distant whisper. They called God's promise and person into question. Has God become a deceptive brook or a spring that fails? In the heat of trouble does God give out on him? His aching bones and his weary soul cried out; they shouted in the face of God, "Why is my pain unending and my wound grievous and incurable?" His inner pain blotted out hope, all the love he had known from the Lord, and every promise by which he had lived.

The Lord loved Jeremiah, so he shocked him to his senses. In the midst of such unbelief and despair, such smallness and narrowness of vision, God slapped the prophet in the face with the word, "Repent." Turn to me, listen to my voice, serve me, grab hold of my promise, and forget about yourself. The Lord repeated the promise he had made at the very beginning of Jeremiah's work. At that point the Lord had promised to make Jeremiah a bronze wall against all the people (Jeremiah 1:18). Now he urged him to become again the worthy spokesman he had been.

Jeremiah had lost his sense. He had become like those to whom he was preaching; he had begun to turn to them; he had begun to yield the truth of God. The Lord called him back. The Lord told him, "Do not be afraid; trust what I have said, and what you do will not be in vain." We do not hear the prophet's response. We can see by his action, however, that he took to heart what the Lord had told him here and that he continued on with a renewed faithfulness to his calling.

Even great men of faith fall prey to doubt and despair. They are examples for us. If they fear, if they doubt, if they need encouragement, if they need admonition, if they need help, if they need the preaching of the law and the repeated assurance of the promises of God, how much more do we! We may all expect to drink some of the same bitter cup as did the prophet here. We all will need to be shocked out of our stupor by God's call to repentance. But with the Lord's help we will find our way back to him, as did Jeremiah. From these experiences, both Jeremiah's and ours, we are made more ready to be shining lights to others who also drift into the fog of doubt and despair. We have been there and returned. We may be able to help them return, too.

A Living Object Lesson of God's Judgment

16 Then the word of the LORD came to me: [2]"You must not marry and have sons or daughters in this place." [3]For this is what the LORD says about the sons and daughters born in this land and about the women who are their mothers and the men who are their fathers: [4]"They will die of deadly diseases. They will not be mourned or buried but will be like refuse lying on the ground. They will perish by sword and

**famine, and their dead bodies will become food for the birds of
the air and the beasts of the earth."**

**[5]For this is what the LORD says: "Do not enter a house where
there is a funeral meal; do not go to mourn or show sympathy,
because I have withdrawn my blessing, my love and my pity
from this people," declares the LORD. [6]"Both high and low will
die in this land. They will not be buried or mourned, and no
one will cut himself or shave his head for them. [7]No one will offer food to comfort those who mourn for the dead—not even
for a father or a mother—nor will anyone give them a drink to
console them.**

**[8]"And do not enter a house where there is feasting and sit
down to eat and drink. [9]For this is what the LORD Almighty,
the God of Israel, says: Before your eyes and in your days I
will bring an end to the sounds of joy and gladness and to the
voices of bride and bridegroom in this place.**

No customs are more central and important to social relationships and family than those surrounding death and marriage. Few times bring families together more, and few times reveal the fractures and stresses in the family more. Once again the Lord made Jeremiah a living object lesson to the people of Judah. In him they were to see how great and dreadful the judgment of the Lord would be upon a disobedient and apostate nation.

God commanded Jeremiah not to marry or to have any children. This command went against the most powerful forces in Jewish society. All men were expected to marry. Family and its continuation were vital. But because of the present time and its crisis, Jeremiah was to be different. Of all the servants of the Lord in the whole history of the Bible, Jeremiah alone was forbidden to marry.

Jeremiah was also forbidden to attend funerals and weddings. These celebrations, of course, were the chief family get-togethers and important times to renew acquaintances and strengthen family ties. Jeremiah could go to none of them, even for his dearest and closest friends. One can only imagine the stares, the gossip, the tensions his actions produced. No wonder he confessed in 15:17, "I never sat in the company of revelers . . . I sat alone because your hand was on me. . . ." One can only imagine the personal pain and torment the prophet experienced. But God had a purpose in all of this.

In Jeremiah's present circumstances the nation was to see its own future. "In your days," the Lord says, death and destruction will be everywhere. All normal social functions will be interrupted. People will die in droves. No one will be left to mourn or bury them. Such a prospect was utterly abhorrent to the Jew. To allow a body to be unburied or molested by animals or birds was unthinkable. We are reminded of Rizpah the daughter of Aiah who protected the dead bodies of her loved ones from predators for weeks (2 Samuel 21:1-14). Things would be so bad that people would not even bury their fathers or mothers. They would not even be able to offer the usual "cup" which marked the end of the immediate family's fasting and the beginning of the funeral feast.

Jeremiah could not attend any wedding celebrations either. Soon there would be none. The Lord had withdrawn his blessing, his assurance of well-being, the blessing conveyed through the words of the priests (Numbers 6:22-27). He would show no love (the word for love as expressed in and through the terms of the covenant). Because the Israelites had broken their part of God's covenant, the Lord was no longer bound to the promises he had made with them. Any hopes they had in the covenant were gone. He would show no pity. No longer would his deep feeling for their pain and suffering move him to act on their behalf. This harsh message was delivered both through the words and the life of the prophet. What effect would it have?

**[10]"When you tell these people all this and they ask you,
'Why has the LORD decreed such a great disaster against us?
What wrong have we done? What sin have we committed
against the LORD our God?' [11]then say to them, 'It is because
your fathers forsook me,' declares the LORD, 'and followed
other gods and served and worshiped them. They forsook me
and did not keep my law. [12]But you have behaved more wickedly than your fathers. See how each of you is following the stubbornness of his evil heart instead of obeying me. [13]So I will
throw you out of this land into a land neither you nor your fathers have known, and there you will serve other gods day and
night, for I will show you no favor.'**

How little Judah understood! How deeply sin had taken hold of their understanding. They had lost their knowledge of right and wrong. They were so comfortable in their sin, so used to it, that they could imagine no reason for the Lord's anger against them. Nothing conveys the hold of sin upon a people or upon an individual more than the loss or lack of understanding of right and wrong.

The Lord told them that their final payment for the sin of their fathers was coming due. Their fathers had broken the first commandment. We note again that to break the first commandment is the great sin, the fount and beginning of all other sins. They had not kept the law. They did not acknowledge their sin as sin, nor did they look to the Lord for the forgiveness and mercy he had offered them in the promise of the Savior. It was, however, not just the fathers who had sinned. Their children, the people of Jeremiah's time, had outdone their fathers in stubbornness of heart. Despite much more warning and admonishing, they had walked a path more perverse than their fathers. As a result, they would be thrown out of the land. What they had desired they would receive. Day and night in a land unknown to them they would serve false gods.

[14]"However, the days are coming," declares the LORD, "when men will no longer say, 'As surely as the LORD lives, who brought the Israelites up out of Egypt,' [15]but they will say, 'As surely as the LORD lives, who brought the Israelites up out of the land of the north and out of all the countries where he had banished them.' For I will restore them to the land I gave their forefathers.

[16]"But now I will send for many fishermen," declares the LORD, "and they will catch them. After that I will send for many hunters, and they will hunt them down on every mountain and hill and from the crevices of the rocks. [17]My eyes are on all their ways; they are not hidden from me, nor is their sin concealed from my eyes. [18]I will repay them double for their wickedness and their sin, because they have defiled my land with the lifeless forms of their vile images and have filled my inheritance with their detestable idols."

Though the Lord kept his word and judged them, he did not leave the survivors without hope. He promised that the time would come when he would bring his people back from the land of the north just as he had brought his people out of Egypt. That act would be just as much an act of his love and power as the time he had saved them from Egypt.

However, those now listening to the message found little comfort in this promise. Before that promised restoration would come judgment. The Lord used a vivid example to describe his judgment. He would send hunters and fishermen—relentlessly, systematically, ruthlessly—to find their game. They would leave no stone unturned in their pursuit.

The first application of these words of judgment is, of course, to the conquering armies who would chase the hapless fugitives and catch them wherever they tried to hide. Another clear application is to the searching and finding out of sin. No sinner can escape the Lord's justice. Relentlessly, just as the inspector in Victor Hugo's novel *Les Miserables* hunted down his victim, so the law written in the heart, the conscience, and the consequences of sin hunt down the sinner. No one can hide anything from the Lord. No one can escape the punishment due because of sin.

However, the people of Judah could take comfort in the Lord's zeal against sin. For as his anger burns against sin and pursues it, even more his love reaches out and covers the penitent. The justice of God has found satisfaction in Christ's suffering and death. That same justice the Lord gives freely to those who believe in Christ.

19 O LORD, my strength and my fortress,
my refuge in time of distress,
to you the nations will come
from the ends of the earth and say,
"Our fathers possessed nothing but false gods,
worthless idols that did them no good.
20 Do men make their own gods?
Yes, but they are not gods!"

21 "Therefore I will teach them—
this time I will teach them
my power and might.
Then they will know
that my name is the LORD.

Jeremiah prayed again, this time renewed to the task the Lord had given him. He knew what the Lord had in mind. He would disperse his chosen people throughout many nations because of their sin. In this way he would give other nations in great numbers the chance to come to know him. Just as one needs to clear a garden or field of rubble and stones before planting, so the Lord cleared Judah of the rubble of its sins and prepared to use Judah to plant the seed for an even greater harvest.

Through the confession of Judah's exiles and the demonstration of the Lord's saving power, many nations would see the emptiness of their worship, the worthlessness of their gods. "Do men make their own gods? Yes. . . ." How true! Men still make their own gods. Our world is full of them. "But they are not gods"—no more than the false gods of the nations of Judah's time.

The Lord now speaks and offers Jeremiah a glorious vision. The Lord himself would teach them by his power and might that he alone is the Lord, the Savior of all. That lesson he taught in the life and person of his own Son, Jesus Christ. That lesson he teaches through the powerful means of the Holy Spirit, the very gospel and its proclamation through which he brings life to us and to the world.

The Condition of the Heart Demonstrates Its Rightness

17 **"Judah's sin is engraved with an iron tool,**
inscribed with a flint point,
on the tablets of their hearts
and on the horns of their altars.
2 Even their children remember
their altars and Asherah poles
beside the spreading trees
and on the high hills.
3 My mountain in the land
and your wealth and all your treasures
I will give away as plunder,
together with your high places,
because of sin throughout your country.

4Through your own fault you will lose
the inheritance I gave you.
I will enslave you to your enemies
in a land you do not know,
for you have kindled my anger,
and it will burn forever."

By repeated and persistent habit the people of Judah had made sin a way of life. Jeremiah used a picture to drive this truth home. With the hardest tools known to them, iron and flint, they had engraved their sins upon the equally hard tables of their hearts. So deep were the grooves, so accustomed to sinning they had become, that now they found it difficult to change.

The evidences were everywhere. Their children gave ample testimony to their idolatry. Everywhere, in every suitable location, even in the temple (2 Kings 23:7), they had set up shrines to Baal and his consort Asherah. She was the mother of the gods. They worshiped her by raising up sacred wooden poles near her shrines. To honor her they wove sacred clothes as gifts. Through these widespread practices they had turned their hearts from the Lord. Because of that sin, through their own fault, the Lord would surrender them and his temple and all its treasures to the enemy.

5This is what the LORD says:
"Cursed is the one who trusts in man,
who depends on flesh for his strength
and whose heart turns away from the LORD.
6He will be like a bush in the wastelands;
he will not see prosperity when it comes.
He will dwell in the parched places of the desert,
in a salt land where no one lives.
7"But blessed is the man who trusts in the LORD,
whose confidence is in him.

8He will be like a tree planted by the water
that sends out its roots by the stream.
It does not fear when heat comes;
its leaves are always green.
It has no worries in a year of drought
and never fails to bear fruit."

Jeremiah shows the real problem. It lies in the heart of the people. He contrasts the two ways—the way of unbelief and the way of faith. The real difference comes out in the long term. Cursed is the person who puts his hope for the future in something human, who looks for ultimate security in other human beings. The person referred to in this passage parallels the young strong person, or one like him, in the full possession and use of his all of his powers. John refers to this feeling of confidence as "boasting of what he has and does" (1 John 2:16). This refers to the unshakable confidence that there is nothing we are unable to do, no problem that in the end we cannot solve, no force we cannot master and turn to our use. This confidence is the pride that grows from all our accomplishments, the gleaming monuments of our technology.

But what is the foundation of all this hope? Man and flesh. Man was made from dust and shall return to dust. The end of the one who trusts in flesh will be empty and fruitless. Jeremiah described this condition in terms very familiar to his hearers. To the east of Jerusalem lay the Judean wastelands, hard country in which even a scraggly juniper bush had to struggle to live. A little further lay a wilderness in which nothing green lived, the land of salt along the Dead Sea.

What a contrast with the blessedness of the person who trusts the Lord! This person places his hope, his faith, his confidence for all things in the Lord. Using the figures of Psalm 1, Jeremiah pictures this person as a tree planted by a source of water that does not fail. Therefore it is always green and fruit-bearing. It does not have to fear even in the hardest and hottest times.

Such is the figure of the believer. He lives by the stream of living water, flowing from Scripture, giving him fellowship with God himself. Because of this living-giving water, this fountain of life, he can stand up under the toughest times. Jeremiah, no doubt, wants the reader to understand that he too had found such strength in the Lord. It was his faith alone, sustained and nourished from the Word, that enabled him to be true to his calling and to stand up under the fierce opposition he encountered.

9 The heart is deceitful above all things
and beyond cure.
Who can understand it?
10 "I the LORD search the heart
and examine the mind,
to reward a man according to his conduct,
according to what his deeds deserve."
11 Like a partridge that hatches eggs it did not lay
is the man who gains riches by unjust means.
When his life is half gone, they will desert him,
and in the end he will prove to be a fool.

Reflecting upon the sin of Judah, Jeremiah, the physician of souls, diagnoses the disease that accounts for all the problems. The heart, the inner self, is the problem. It deceives even itself. It is knotted and twisted like a hopelessly tangled knot. Every attempt to untie it frustrates.

The heart is in such a condition at birth. Jeremiah declares that it is hopelessly incurable. The real problem of man then springs from inside. As the Lord said, "out of the heart come evil thoughts . . ." (Matthew 15:19). No solution can begin to address this problem until it recognizes the depth and nature of the problem. Changing external behavior cannot solve the problem. Every imagination of man's heart is evil from his childhood (Genesis 8:21). Only by transforming the heart, the inner self, can a remedy have any chance.

But who can understand it? No one. By nature all of us deny the evil at work within us. We refuse to recognize it. We draw back at the evil of the human heart. Like the layers of an onion, we peel back the coverings of the heart, hoping to find some good in man, the good our society tells us lies in every man. But in the end we find only self, self, and more self. We discover selfish, evil motives that drive us, and we stand before God without excuse. No wonder no one wants to know his own heart! Those who have peered into the recesses of the heart have despaired. Introspection, looking into oneself, can never bring happiness.

Without the revelation of Scripture we could never know the disease that deforms and maims us all. In the Smalcald Articles Martin Luther writes, "The hereditary sin is so deep and horrible a corruption of nature that no reason can understand it, but it must be learned and believed from the revelation of Scriptures . . ." (Part III, Art. I). Without knowing this doctrine, we can never know ourselves. Blaise Pascal, the French philosopher, said that nothing jolts us more rudely than this doctrine, and yet, but for the mystery, the most incomprehensible of all, we remain incomprehensible to ourselves. Without this knowledge we cannot know ourselves. Without this knowledge we are prey to all the quacks who promise to explain and cure the diseases of the human condition. And like the woman with the issue of blood (Mark 5:24-26), we will exhaust ourselves and never find the cure.

Who can understand it? "I the Lord search the heart. . . ." The Lord knows. Nothing is hidden to him. As the Scripture says, "The LORD does not look at the things man looks at. Man looks at the outward appearance, but the LORD looks at the heart" (1 Samuel 16:7). Through his Word and by his Spirit the Lord penetrates to the depths of the inner self, ". . . even to dividing soul and spirit, joints and marrow; it judges the thoughts and attitudes of the heart" (Hebrews 4:12). According to your heart and by the conduct and deeds it produces, you will be judged. Who can face such a judgment? Who can turn it aside? None of us. Only because of the perfect life and the innocent death of Christ, supplied as a covering for our evil hearts, will we be able to stand before the all-knowing judge.

Nowhere does the heart betray the evil within it more than in its attitude toward possessions or wealth. Covetousness and idolatry always go together. This particular form of sin had fastened its firm grip upon Judah. Jeremiah compares the situation with the example of the partridge. The partridge who hatches eggs she didn't lay—birds of another kind—would experience her strange brood deserting her. Similarly, riches unjustly gained will desert the greedy person.

As the proverb goes, you can't take it with you. But judging from the way many live, they imagine they can. In the end, like the rich man (Luke 12:13-21) who thought he had it made, the covetous person dies a fool.

12 A glorious throne, exalted from the beginning,
is the place of our sanctuary.
13 O LORD, the hope of Israel,
all who forsake you will be put to shame.
Those who turn away from you
will be written in the dust
because they have forsaken the LORD,
the spring of living water.

14Heal me, O LORD, and I will be healed;
save me and I will be saved,
for you are the one I praise.
15They keep saying to me,
"Where is the word of the LORD?
Let it now be fulfilled!"
16I have not run away from being your shepherd;
you know I have not desired the day of despair.
What passes my lips is open before you.
17Do not be a terror to me;
you are my refuge in the day of disaster.
18Let my persecutors be put to shame,
but keep me from shame;
let them be terrified,
but keep me from terror.
Bring on them the day of disaster;
destroy them with double destruction.

In a high and holy moment, Jeremiah lifts his eyes to what is not fleeting and insecure—the Lord, who had come to dwell among his people, who had given them great and precious promises. As the prophet gazes at the temple, he rejoices in the Hope of Israel, the one who will not fail, but will provide an unfailing source of strength and help. That help was close by. For through the covenant promise the Lord had provided the means by which he had sealed his love to his people.

To those promises and for that speedy help Jeremiah now turns in prayer. In these next few chapters, we witness much stronger and more open attacks upon the prophet. In the face of bolder opposition, Jeremiah prayed for strength. He wanted to be healed—healed of the doubt, the distrust, the lack of hope, the questioning he had about the Lord's ways. He also wanted to be saved, kept safe from the dangers that surrounded him. He was confident that he would be healed and saved, for when the Lord undertakes to do some work, then one knows it will be done.

His opponents threw Jeremiah's words in his face. If what you have spoken is the Lord's Word, the truth, then where is the fulfillment? In this way they laughed at God's threatened judgment and Jeremiah's work of proclaiming it. This constant attack surely worked to discourage the prophet. Despite it, however, he confessed to God that he had been faithful to his calling and that he had not wished for or taken any pleasure in the disaster that was about to come. He asked the Lord to stand by him, for, after all, the cause was not his, but the Lord's. For that reason too, he begged the Lord to keep his word and turn the tables on those who opposed him and the Lord. Such a prayer the Lord could not fail to answer.

Keeping the Sabbath Holy

**[19]This is what the LORD said to me: "Go and stand at the
gate of the people, through which the kings of Judah go in and
out; stand also at all the other gates of Jerusalem. [20]Say to
them, 'Hear the word of the LORD, O kings of Judah and all
people of Judah and everyone living in Jerusalem who come
through these gates. [21]This is what the LORD says: Be careful
not to carry a load on the Sabbath day or bring it through the
gates of Jerusalem. [22]Do not bring a load out of your houses or
do any work on the Sabbath, but keep the Sabbath day holy, as
I commanded your forefathers. [23]Yet they did not listen or pay
attention; they were stiff-necked and would not listen or respond to discipline. [24]But if you are careful to obey me, declares
the LORD, and bring no load through the gates of this city on
the Sabbath, but keep the Sabbath day holy by not doing any
work on it, [25]then kings who sit on David's throne will come
through the gates of this city with their officials. They and
their officials will come riding in chariots and on horses, ac-**

companied by the men of Judah and those living in Jerusalem, and this city will be inhabited forever. [26]People will come from the towns of Judah and the villages around Jerusalem, from the territory of Benjamin and the western foothills, from the hill country and the Negev, bringing burnt offerings and sacrifices, grain offerings, incense and thank offerings to the house of the LORD. [27]But if you do not obey me to keep the Sabbath day holy by not carrying any load as you come through the gates of Jerusalem on the Sabbath day, then I will kindle an unquenchable fire in the gates of Jerusalem that will consume her fortresses.' "

Jeremiah shows us how Judah's practical idolatry, its love for possessions, had taken concrete form. To picture the spiritual rest God would give his people through the Messiah, he had commanded them, "Remember the Sabbath day by keeping it holy." They were to do no work on the Sabbath. It was to be a day of rest and above all a day on which they were to think about the goodness of the Lord in delivering them from Egypt and making them his people. The Lord had promised his people he would not let them suffer economically if they abstained from working on the Sabbath.

Unfortunately the Israelites broke the Sabbath; they did not trust the promises of the Lord. The Lord here gives the present generation another opportunity to take him at his word. Jeremiah told the leaders of the people, especially the king and his court, for they set the example, to keep the Sabbath.

Jeremiah proclaimed this message at each gate of the city. The gates served as the centers of commercial activity. They were busy highways in the morning and evening as people went about their business, leaving and returning to the city. Jeremiah announced: "The Lord will keep his covenant promise. If you keep the Sabbath, you will be richly blessed;

abundance will crown your labor. If, however, you refuse to listen, the Lord will enforce his own rest upon you by sending a judgment that will close down the city and its business." They had heard the Word of the Lord. The choice was now theirs.

The Object Lessons of the Clay Jars

18 This is the word that came to Jeremiah from the LORD:
2"Go down to the potter's house, and there I will give
you my message." 3So I went down to the potter's house, and I
saw him working at the wheel. 4But the pot he was shaping
from the clay was marred in his hands; so the potter formed it
into another pot, shaping it as seemed best to him.
5Then the word of the LORD came to me: 6"O house of Israel,
can I not do with you as this potter does?" declares the LORD.
"Like clay in the hand of the potter, so are you in my hand, O
house of Israel. 7If at any time I announce that a nation or
kingdom is to be uprooted, torn down and destroyed, 8and if
that nation I warned repents of its evil, then I will relent and
not inflict on it the disaster I had planned. 9And if at another
time I announce that a nation or kingdom is to be built up and
planted, 10and if it does evil in my sight and does not obey me,
then I will reconsider the good I had intended to do for it.

Jeremiah was to teach the people of Judah by means of yet another object lesson. This lesson would come in two parts. First, the prophet was sent to that part of the city where the potters worked. Directed by the Lord, he went to one special potter. As the prophet observed that potter at work, molding and shaping the clay with his hands on the wheel, one pot did not take shape. So the potter shaped the clay into a different kind of pot. The potter had the right to do with the clay as he pleased. He owned it. It was for his own purpose that he had bought it.

The Lord, like the potter, owned the house of Israel. It was a vessel he had made for his glory and for his purposes. Ancient Israel was the custodian of God's written Word. It was to be the cradle of the Savior. In God's plan Israel was to be a display case showing the nations of the world how blessed is that nation whose God is the Lord. The Lord had the right to do with Israel as he pleased. For he is the creator of all, the almighty God, the omnipotent one who controls all things according to his power and purpose. Nothing restrains or constrains his actions. He is free to do whatever he pleases. As the psalmist says, "Our God is in heaven; he does whatever pleases him" (Psalm 115:3). He is subject neither to the stars nor to any of the laws of nature. No creature can give anything to him that he does not already possess. Since nothing can constrain or control him, and since he is omnipotent, whatever he does, he does out of pure freedom. Of God alone can it be said that he is free.

Though he has the power and the freedom to do whatever he pleases and though he owes us nothing, God does not act in an arbitrary way toward us. Rather he deals with us according to his Word and promise. The all-powerful God, by a solemn oath and by grace, bound himself in a covenant to Israel and to us. He calls us to repentance in his Word. If he should threaten destruction as he did with Nineveh, and if we should repent, then he will act according to his own promise and forgive and relent. If we should persist in impenitence, then he will withhold his forgiveness and not relent.

11"Now therefore say to the people of Judah and those living in Jerusalem, 'This is what the LORD says: Look! I am preparing a disaster for you and devising a plan against you. So turn from your evil ways, each one of you, and reform your ways and your actions.' 12But they will reply, 'It's no use. We will

continue with our own plans; each of us will follow the stubbornness of his evil heart.' "

13Therefore this is what the LORD says:

"Inquire among the nations:
Who has ever heard anything like this?
A most horrible thing has been done by Virgin Israel.
14Does the snow of Lebanon
ever vanish from its rocky slopes?
Do its cool waters from distant sources
ever cease to flow?
15Yet my people have forgotten me;
they burn incense to worthless idols,
which made them stumble in their ways
and in the ancient paths.
They made them walk in bypaths
and on roads not built up.
16Their land will be laid waste,
an object of lasting scorn;
all who pass by will be appalled
and will shake their heads.
17Like a wind from the east,
I will scatter them before their enemies;
I will show them my back and not my face
in the day of their disaster."

The Lord does not hide what he is doing. For that very reason he sent the prophets and revealed himself in the Scriptures so that all might know. He told the people of Judah what lay ahead for them, so that each one of them might repent. If they refused to repent, they would be without excuse.

The Lord revealed to Jeremiah the answer he could expect, an answer that might surprise us. "It's no use. We give up. We can't change. We are what we are." What an insult to the Lord! He forgives the wrongs of the past and offers and gives the power to change. But the Israelites refuse. The reason was not that they could not change. No, they did not want to change. They enjoyed what they were doing. Their lifestyle pleased them. With grim determination in the stubbornness of their hearts, they continued on their march to their own destruction.

How unbelievable unbelief is! The Lord asked Jeremiah: "Have you ever seen anything like this?" No nation gives up its god, but that's exactly what Judah had done. The Virgin of Israel, the one dearly loved by him, the one betrothed and solemnly promised to him had left him. She was straying on new paths, far from the main road, paths that led her nowhere, except to ruin. Mount Hermon in Lebanon, the highest mountain in the country, visible from almost all of the holy land, hardly ever loses its snow cap. No one could imagine the mountain without its cover. Similarly, what Judah was doing was contrary to nature.

Again the Lord foretold the destruction of the land. All who would see the devastation would be appalled. What a waste! How useless and unnecessary! As wind from the east, the hot sirocco of summer, marks the end of the growing season by drying up all green with its searing blast off the Arabian Desert, so the Lord will allow the enemies of Judah to consume her. He will not help her in the critical hour. When we are angry with someone, when we do not want to talk about the matter, when the issue is closed, we turn away. In the same way the Lord will turn his face, his love and help and grace, away from Judah. He will cut her off because she had cut him off. Jeremiah's hearers did not take kindly to this harsh message.

18They said, "Come, let's make plans against Jeremiah; for the teaching of the law by the priest will not be lost, nor will

counsel from the wise, nor the word from the prophets. So come, let's attack him with our tongues and pay no attention to anything he says."

19Listen to me, O LORD;
hear what my accusers are saying!
20Should good be repaid with evil?
Yet they have dug a pit for me.
Remember that I stood before you
and spoke in their behalf
to turn your wrath away from them.
21So give their children over to famine;
hand them over to the power of the sword.
Let their wives be made childless and widows;
let their men be put to death,
their young men slain by the sword in battle.
22Let a cry be heard from their houses
when you suddenly bring invaders against them,
for they have dug a pit to capture me
and have hidden snares for my feet.
23But you know, O LORD,
all their plots to kill me.
Do not forgive their crimes
or blot out their sins from your sight.
Let them be overthrown before you;
deal with them in the time of your anger.

These words of the people of Judah show that they were driven—but not to repentance. Instead, they were driven to plan some way to rid themselves of the prophet and blunt his message. How like their descendants! In the face of Jesus' miracles and words, the leaders in Jerusalem did not repent but only tried all the harder to catch Jesus in his words, so they might kill him.

In the same way their ancestors had attacked Jeremiah's message. Once again employing the ancient strategy of the devil, they denied everything the prophet said. In addition to their direct attack, by constant word, they aimed to undermine his message, until finally no one would pay any attention to what he had said. The devil counts it the greatest success when no one pays any attention to the Word. Then he has gained the victory.

As the bees buzzed around him even more wildly, Jeremiah once again turned to the Lord. He asked the Lord to keep the promise he had made to him. He begged God for protection from all the attempts his opponents would make against him. He asked God to carry out his judgment, to keep his word.

Jeremiah was deeply hurt by the impenitence of his people, but even more hurt by their unfair charge that he enjoyed announcing God's condemnation and that he longed for God's judgment to come. Surely this charge was the most cruel cut of all! How often the lonely prophet stood as intercessor, speaking to God on behalf of the people of Judah! How little they realized that, but for him and the other believers, the very salt of the land, the Lord might already have destroyed Judah! So Jeremiah lashed out against them. They had driven him to keep the Lord's command to him, "Do not pray for this people. . . ." Now he did not pray for them but against them. What could now postpone the day of judgment?

19 This is what the LORD says: "Go and buy a clay jar
from a potter. Take along some of the elders of the peo-
ple and of the priests
2and go out to the Valley of Ben Hinnom,
near the entrance of the Potsherd Gate. There proclaim the
words I tell you,
3and say, 'Hear the word of the LORD, O kings
of Judah and people of Jerusalem. This is what the LORD
Almighty, the God of Israel, says: Listen! I am going to bring a
disaster on this place that will make the ears of everyone who
hears of it tingle.
4For they have forsaken me and made this a
place of foreign gods; they have burned sacrifices in it to gods

**that neither they nor their fathers nor the kings of Judah ever
knew, and they have filled this place with the blood of the innocent. 5They have built the high places of Baal to burn their
sons in the fire as offerings to Baal—something I did not command or mention, nor did it enter my mind. 6So beware, the
days are coming, declares the LORD, when people will no
longer call this place Topheth or the Valley of Ben Hinnom,
but the Valley of Slaughter.**

**7" 'In this place I will ruin the plans of Judah and
Jerusalem. I will make them fall by the sword before their enemies, at the hands of those who seek their lives, and I will give
their carcasses as food to the birds of the air and the beasts of
the earth. 8I will devastate this city and make it an object of
scorn; all who pass by will be appalled and will scoff because
of all its wounds. 9I will make them eat the flesh of their sons
and daughters, and they will eat one another's flesh during the
stress of the siege imposed on them by the enemies who seek
their lives.'**

Jeremiah now made a second application and delivered another object lesson with clay jars. God commanded him to take witnesses, some of the elders and some of the priests. With them he was to go to the Potsherd Gate, also known as the Potters' Gate or the Dung Gate. This gate stood at the southeast corner of the main wall of the city where the two valleys, Hinnom and Kidron met. This immediate area was also known as Topheth. Ever since the reign of Manasseh a half century earlier, this area had been a hotbed of Baal worship.

Having purchased a clay jar from a potter, Jeremiah with the elders and priests as witnesses, delivered his message, holding out the jar in his hands. He condemned his countrymen for adopting the religion and ritual practices of their Canaanite neighbors. The people of Judah had adopted the contemptible worship of Baal and his consorts, the queens of heaven. Both women and men offered themselves as sacred prostitutes in the name of the gods.

Even more abhorrent and repulsive was their practice of human sacrifice. (An example of such sacrifice by the Moabites can be found in 2 Kings 3:27.) To Baal and the god Moloch, they offered their own young children, throwing them into the fire to gain the favor of the god. So they filled Topheth and the Valley of Hinnom with idolatry and the blood of their own innocent children.

The Lord announced judgment in proportion to the sin. He would send their enemies upon them. The slaughter would be so great that there would be no one to bury them. As their corpses lay upon the blood-soaked earth, the birds and beasts of the field, the scavengers, would consume them. During the siege of Jerusalem their distress would be so great that they would do the unthinkable—they would eat the flesh of their own children and of one another. We have another example of this sort of thing from the siege of Samaria (2 Kings 6:24-30).

10"Then break the jar while those who go with you are
watching, 11and say to them, 'This is what the LORD Almighty
says: I will smash this nation and this city just as this potter's
jar is smashed and cannot be repaired. They will bury the dead
in Topheth until there is no more room. 12This is what I will do
to this place and to those who live here, declares the LORD. I
will make this city like Topheth. 13The houses in Jerusalem and
those of the kings of Judah will be defiled like this place,
Topheth—all the houses where they burned incense on the
roofs to all the starry hosts and poured out drink offerings to
other gods.' "

14Jeremiah then returned from Topheth, where the LORD
had sent him to prophesy, and stood in the court of the LORD's
temple and said to all the people, 15"This is what the LORD

Almighty, the God of Israel, says: 'Listen! I am going to bring on this city and the villages around it every disaster I pronounced against them, because they were stiff-necked and would not listen to my words.'"

At this point in his sermon Jeremiah broke the clay jar. As the pieces flew they joined a large pile of other such broken pieces (this was the place where the potters threw all their scraps). As he broke the jar, Jeremiah told the delegation of priests and elders with him that the Lord would utterly smash the nation, leaving so many dead that the Valley of Hinnom would not have enough room to bury them all. This is how the Lord would bring their abominable and vile practices to an end. He himself would make the place unfit for any kind of worship at all. Jeremiah then returned to the temple court and repeated his stern message for a wider audience to hear.

Jeremiah and Pashhur

**20 When the priest Pashhur son of Immer, the chief officer
in the temple of the LORD, heard Jeremiah prophesying
these things, [2]he had Jeremiah the prophet beaten and put in
the stocks at the Upper Gate of Benjamin at the LORD's temple. [3]The next day, when Pashhur released him from the stocks,
Jeremiah said to him, "The LORD's name for you is not Pashhur, but Magor-Missabib. [4]For this is what the LORD says: 'I
will make you a terror to yourself and to all your friends; with
your own eyes you will see them fall by the sword of their enemies. I will hand all Judah over to the king of Babylon, who
will carry them away to Babylon or put them to the sword. [5]I
will hand over to their enemies all the wealth of this city—all
its products, all its valuables and all the treasures of the kings
of Judah. They will take it away as plunder and carry it off to
Babylon. [6]And you, Pashhur, and all who live in your house**

will go into exile to Babylon. There you will die and be buried, you and all your friends to whom you have prophesied lies.' "

". . . because they would not listen to my words." We have a good example in the action of Pashhur, chief officer in the temple. Using his police and judicial authority, he had Jeremiah put in stocks at the Upper Gate of Benjamin. No doubt he acted with the approval of the high priest and the authorities. This gate, immediately to the north of the temple court, was also known as the Sheep Gate. It was heavily used, and we can only imagine the glee of Jeremiah's enemies and their contempt at the public humiliation of their hapless victim.

The next day, having made his point, Pashhur released Jeremiah from the stocks. Pashhur may have confined Jeremiah, but he had not silenced him. In the name of the Lord, Jeremiah announced God's punishment on him and on those who had authorized his action.

Signifying the new situation that would mark Pashhur's life, at the Lord's command Jeremiah gave Pashhur a new name, Magor-Missabib, "TERROR ON EVERY SIDE", for that is what he would experience. In the siege of Jerusalem he would soon be surrounded by death. He would drink the cup of suffering to the last drop. He would have to watch as Jerusalem was laid waste. The temple he guarded would be stripped of its wealth, desecrated, and torched. (Read Psalm 74:3-7.) With his own eyes Pashhur would witness the death of many near and dear to him, but he would not be so fortunate as to die. With family and friends he would be taken as a slave to Babylon. There he would live in shame until death finally took him in a land a thousand miles from home. And Pashhur would not be the only one. His end would be the end of them all . . . "because they would not listen to my words."

Jeremiah's Complaint

7 O LORD, you deceived me, and I was deceived;
you overpowered me and prevailed.
I am ridiculed all day long;
everyone mocks me.
8 Whenever I speak, I cry out
proclaiming violence and destruction.
So the word of the LORD has brought me
insult and reproach all day long.
9 But if I say, "I will not mention him
or speak any more in his name,"
his word is in my heart like a fire,
a fire shut up in my bones.
I am weary of holding it in;
indeed, I cannot.
10 I hear many whispering,
"Terror on every side!
Report him! Let's report him!"
All my friends
are waiting for me to slip, saying,
"Perhaps he will be deceived;
then we will prevail over him
and take our revenge on him."

11 But the LORD is with me like a mighty warrior;
so my persecutors will stumble and not prevail.
They will fail and be thoroughly disgraced;
their dishonor will never be forgotten.
12 O LORD Almighty, you who examine the righteous
and probe the heart and mind,
let me see your vengeance upon them,
for to you I have committed my cause.

13 Sing to the LORD!
Give praise to the LORD!
He rescues the life of the needy
from the hands of the wicked.

14 Cursed be the day I was born!
May the day my mother bore me not be blessed!
15 Cursed be the man who brought my father the news,
who made him very glad, saying,
"A child is born to you—a son!"
16 May that man be like the towns
the LORD overthrew without pity.
May he hear wailing in the morning,
a battle cry at noon.
17 For he did not kill me in the womb,
with my mother as my grave,
her womb enlarged forever.
18 Why did I ever come out of the womb
to see trouble and sorrow
and to end my days in shame?

You can imagine that Jeremiah's message was a difficult one for him to preach. The prophet ended his long discourse, a summary of his preaching to the people of Judah, with a bitter cry of grief, bordering on despair. As he reflected on his prophetic office he grieved over the astounding impenitence of his hearers, the people and leaders of Judah. His grief welled up out of a profound love for souls. In the end his grief was too much for him.

Those whose love is deep also grieve deeply. Jeremiah grieved like Samuel (1 Samuel 15:35) who mourned for the fallen Saul. Jeremiah grieved like Paul (Romans 9:2) who could have wished himself cursed and cut off from Christ for the sake of his fellow Jews. Jeremiah grieved most of all like our Lord (Luke 19:40-44) who, when approaching Jerusalem, wept over it because it did not recognize the day of the Lord's coming and because he saw the destruction that would soon come upon the city.

Jeremiah grieved because all his preaching had failed to produce repentance, any kind of turning toward the Lord. He knew that the Lord would keep his word and destroy the city. Because the people of Jerusalem had turned away, nothing could stop its destruction. As he had experienced the increasingly bitter opposition of his countrymen, he learned with sorrow that God's law does work wrath (Romans 4:15). It drives the impenitent into even more ferocious hatred for God. Jeremiah had learned, to his sorrow, that for some the promise, the gospel itself, becomes "the smell of death" (2 Corinthians 2:16).

In his struggle with his grief, the prophet lashed out at the Lord. Grief may lead people to lash out at even those they love. Jeremiah complained that despite all his preaching and proclamation, not one word had been fulfilled. Consequently, he faced insults and taunts day after day. He tried to stop preaching, but he could not. The living Word within overpowered him and compelled him. He felt as Paul later would feel: "I am compelled to preach. Woe to me if I do not preach the gospel! . . . I am simply discharging the trust committed to me" (1 Corinthians 9:16,17).

Continuing his struggle with grief, the prophet grasped the promises God had made to him. Even his friends were waiting to snare him in his words. His every word was under the closest scrutiny. One slip and they would be all over him. But deep down he knew he was not alone. The Lord was his ever-present help and stay. He would not allow Jeremiah to be overcome. Quickly he would come to help. Momentarily the prophet's spirit lifted. He knew he was right with the Lord. A hymn of praise sprang to his lips as he exulted in the rescue the Lord would bring him.

But suddenly his joyous trust gave way to deep despondency. The storm of grief burst in upon him and swept everything before it with raging blackness. "Cursed be the day I was born!" He hurled into the Lord's face the question,

"Why did I ever come out of the womb to see trouble and sorrow and to end my days in shame?" The Lord remained silent. For intense grief, words must wait. The Lord allowed the prophet's grief to pass. He knew his prophet rested upon the solid rock of his promises. He knew that in the end Jeremiah would stand firm and continue with the work to which the Lord had called him. Perhaps, too, God was silent because the prophet's grief was also his own.

JUDAH'S BEHAVIOR EXPOSES HER IMPENITENCE

JEREMIAH 21—29

God Rejects Zedekiah's Request

**21 The word came to Jeremiah from the LORD when King
Zedekiah sent to him Pashhur son of Malkijah and the
priest Zephaniah son of Maaseiah. They said: 2"Inquire now of
the LORD for us because Nebuchadnezzar king of Babylon is
attacking us. Perhaps the LORD will perform wonders for us as
in times past so that he will withdraw from us."**

**3But Jeremiah answered them, "Tell Zedekiah, 4'This is what
the LORD, the God of Israel, says: I am about to turn against
you the weapons of war that are in your hands, which you are
using to fight the king of Babylon and the Babylonians who are
outside the wall besieging you. And I will gather them inside
this city. 5I myself will fight against you with an outstretched
hand and a mighty arm in anger and fury and great wrath. 6I
will strike down those who live in this city—both men and animals—and they will die of a terrible plague. 7After that, declares the LORD, I will hand over Zedekiah king of Judah, his
officials and the people in this city who survive the plague,
sword and famine, to Nebuchadnezzar king of Babylon and to
their enemies who seek their lives. He will put them to the
sword; he will show them no mercy or pity or compassion.'**

In the first twenty chapters of his prophecy we have a comprehensive overview of the messages Jeremiah had delivered to the people and leaders of Judah during the course of his prophetic ministry. In those chapters he made few references to any specific historical events. Certainly the reader sensed that as Jeremiah delivered his message over the years, opposition to his message grew increasingly bitter. Still, someone might have wondered whether Judah's impenitence and stubbornness of heart were as bad as they seemed to be. Could the Lord have spared them?

To answer any lingering doubts about the condition of the heart of the nation, Jeremiah in the next nine chapters (21—29), again reviewed the history of his ministry, this time in greater detail. He cited incidents that demonstrate quite clearly Judah's total impenitence. In its royal house and nobility, in its priests, in its prophets, and in the man on the street, from the greatest to the least—everywhere one turned one found impenitence. After Jeremiah finished his historical review, no one could dispute the rightness of the Lord's judgment.

Jeremiah began his review near the end of the nation's life, sometime near the beginning of Nebuchadnezzar's final siege against the city of Jerusalem (589/588). King Zedekiah, last of the dynasty of David to sit on the throne of Judah, sent two advisors to Jeremiah to find out whether there was any hope of delivery from this siege. "Perhaps. . . ." Would the Lord again work a great miracle as he had often done in the past (for example, Isaiah 37:36,37)?

The question ignored the continued sin and impenitence of those who asked it. The questioners acted as if they had no word from the Lord. "Perhaps. . . ." There is no "perhaps" with the Lord. He had told them that their impenitence would bring down his judgment, and they remained impenitent. The only answer the prophet could give them was the answer he had given them all along: because of their sin the city would fall. Because God was their real enemy, most of them would die.

[8]"Furthermore, tell the people, 'This is what the LORD says: See, I am setting before you the way of life and the way of

death. [9]Whoever stays in this city will die by the sword, famine or plague. But whoever goes out and surrenders to the Babylonians who are besieging you will live; he will escape with his life. [10]I have determined to do this city harm and not good, declares the LORD. It will be given into the hands of the king of Babylon, and he will destroy it with fire.'

For the city of Jerusalem there was no longer any hope. But for individuals there still was hope for escape, hope for saving their lives. Such hope, however, depended upon believing the Lord's Word, something which most in Judah had simply refused to do. God's message was clear: believe my Word and you will live; disbelieve my Word and you will die. Surrender to the Babylonians and your life will be spared; stay in the city and you will die.

The Lord set before them the way of life and the way of death. He gave them a test, a choice, to show what lay in their hearts. Those who believed his Word would live. Because of this kind of advice, many in the city labeled Jeremiah a traitor and used these words to try to discredit his ministry and end his life.

[11]"Moreover, say to the royal house of Judah, 'Hear the word of the LORD; [12]O house of David, this is what the LORD says:

" 'Administer justice every morning;
rescue from the hand of his oppressor
the one who has been robbed,
or my wrath will break out and burn like fire
because of the evil you have done—
burn with no one to quench it.
[13]I am against you, Jerusalem,
you who live above this valley
on the rocky plateau,
declares the LORD—

you who say, "Who can come against us?
Who can enter our refuge?"
14I will punish you as your deeds deserve,
declares the LORD.
I will kindle a fire in your forests
that will consume everything around you.'"

The Lord urged the king and nobility to govern justly, to stop the social injustice rampant in Jerusalem. But he cut his message short. Further talk was pointless. For nearly forty years Judah's leaders had refused God's message from Jeremiah, and they would not change now. Once again, therefore, the Lord warned them that Jerusalem would fall to the armies of Babylon. Jerusalem's boast of invincibility would prove empty. Their boast seemed to have some merit, for Jerusalem was a strong city, hard to attack. Her defensive position made her almost invulnerable. But the Lord said, "I am against you. . . ." She would fall.

This was the message God used Jeremiah to deliver to Zedekiah, king of Judah at the time Jerusalem fell. In the chapter ahead God reviewed some earlier history and announced judgment on three earlier kings.

Judgment Against Evil Kings

22 This is what the LORD says: "Go down to the palace of
the king of Judah and proclaim this message there:
2'Hear the word of the LORD, O king of Judah, you who sit on
David's throne—you, your officials and your people who come
through these gates. 3This is what the LORD says: Do what is
just and right. Rescue from the hand of his oppressor the one
who has been robbed. Do no wrong or violence to the alien, the
fatherless or the widow, and do not shed innocent blood in this
place. 4For if you are careful to carry out these commands,
then kings who sit on David's throne will come through the

gates of this palace, riding in chariots and on horses, accompanied by their officials and their people. 5But if you do not obey these commands, declares the LORD, I swear by myself that this palace will become a ruin.' "

6For this is what the LORD says about the palace of the king of Judah:

"Though you are like Gilead to me,
like the summit of Lebanon,
I will surely make you like a desert,
like towns not inhabited.
7I will send destroyers against you,
each man with his weapons,
and they will cut up your fine cedar beams
and throw them into the fire.

8"People from many nations will pass by this city and will ask one another, 'Why has the LORD done such a thing to this great city?' 9And the answer will be: 'Because they have forsaken the covenant of the LORD their God and have worshiped and served other gods.' "

Jeremiah begins his review of Judah's national history with an examination of her three most recent kings. No clearer measure of a people is to be found than in the attitude of its rulers, for the leaders set the tone. Perhaps early in the reign of Josiah or shortly after his death, Jeremiah delivered a general set of instructions and promises to the kings of Judah.

In these instructions Jeremiah urged them to be good kings according to the commands God himself had given them through Moses (Deuteronomy 17:14-20). According to Moses, the king of the nation was to be one of them, both in blood and spirit. He was not to consider himself superior to his subjects but their helper and servant. He was not to boast about how much wealth he had in horses, gold, and wives; he was daily and closely to read God's Word, to impress it upon his heart, and to follow it. Above all, he was to act as judge and protector for those who were the most vulnerable—the alien, the fatherless, the widow, and the person who had no one else to whom to appeal. If the kings of Judah did these things, in a sense the lesser things of the law, then surely they would keep the greater things of the covenant which had to do with worship and the Lord.

To seal the promises made in this section of the prophecy, the Lord took an awesome oath. He swore by himself. If they followed God's law in their royal duties, he would abundantly bless them. If, however, they disobeyed the covenant, he would bring them to ruin. No matter how much he loved Judah, he would keep his threat. Even if they were as dear to him as the fertile pastures of Gilead and the stately forests of Mt. Hermon were to the shepherd and his flock, yet he would destroy them. For what reason? Only because they had forsaken him and worshiped other gods.

10 Do not weep for the dead king or mourn his loss;
rather, weep bitterly for him who is exiled,
because he will never return
nor see his native land again.

11 For this is what the LORD says about Shallum son of Josiah, who succeeded his father as king of Judah but has gone from this place: "He will never return. 12 He will die in the place where they have led him captive; he will not see this land again."

Jeremiah begins his review of the three most recent kings with Jehoahaz (also known as Shallum) who succeeded his father Josiah in 609 B.C. (2 Kings. 23:31-35; 2 Chronicles 36:2-4).

Egypt's Pharaoh Neco, who had defeated and killed Josiah in battle in 609 B.C., considered Jehoahaz out of touch with his own larger aims. So three months after Jehoahaz began his rule, the pharaoh deposed him, took him as a hostage to Egypt, and put Jehoahaz's brother on the throne. Jehoahaz never saw his palace or his homeland again. Jeremiah, therefore, urged the people not to mourn for the dead Josiah but for the ex-king living in exile.

13 "Woe to him who builds his palace by unrighteousness,
his upper rooms by injustice,
making his countrymen work for nothing,
not paying them for their labor.
14 He says, 'I will build myself a great palace
with spacious upper rooms.'
So he makes large windows in it,
panels it with cedar
and decorates it in red.

15 "Does it make you a king
to have more and more cedar?
Did not your father have food and drink?
He did what was right and just,
so all went well with him.
16 He defended the cause of the poor and needy,
and so all went well.
Is that not what it means to know me?"
declares the LORD.
17 "But your eyes and your heart
are set only on dishonest gain,
on shedding innocent blood
and on oppression and extortion."

18 Therefore this is what the LORD says about Jehoiakim son of Josiah king of Judah:

"They will not mourn for him:
'Alas, my brother! Alas, my sister!'
They will not mourn for him:
'Alas, my master! Alas, his splendor!'

19 He will have the burial of a donkey—
dragged away and thrown
outside the gates of Jerusalem."

20 Go up to Lebanon and cry out,
let your voice be heard in Bashan,
cry out from Abarim,
for all your allies are crushed.
21 I warned you when you felt secure,
but you said, 'I will not listen!'
This has been your way from your youth;
you have not obeyed me.
22 The wind will drive all your shepherds away,
and your allies will go into exile.
Then you will be ashamed and disgraced
because of all your wickedness.
23 You who live in 'Lebanon,'
who are nestled in cedar buildings,
how you will groan when pangs come upon you,
pain like that of a woman in labor!

The first mark of this king was selfishness and greed. His only concern was to provide for himself. He planned the biggest and most well-furnished and well-stocked palace anyone could imagine. And he did not care how he paid for it. Even if he had to extort money from his own workmen, he would have the best. He ignored the blessing the Lord had heaped upon his father who defended the cause of the poor and needy. Greed consumed him, and he paid its price.

The second mark of Jehoiakim, Jehoahaz's successor, was stubborn disobedience. During his entire reign he attacked the Lord and his prophets. He burned the scroll containing the prophecy of Jeremiah (Jeremiah 36:20-32). He tried to kill Jeremiah and succeeded in killing another of the Lord's prophets. He rejected advice given to him by the prophets not to try to secure his kingdom against the Babylonians through alliances, especially with Egypt. He refused to listen, for as the Lord said, "This has been your way from your youth." He inspired little respect and no love. All his plans were failures, and he met a disgraceful end.

Pharaoh Neco put Jehoiakim on the throne of Judah in 609 B.C. (2 Kings 23:36,37; 2 Chronicles 36:5-8). He hoped that this man would be a more pliant ally than his brother, Jehoahaz, and he guessed correctly. Jehoiakim ruled from 609 until 598/597 B.C. As a loyal Egyptian puppet, he constantly opposed Nebuchadnezzar, even against his own self interests. In 605 B.C. he supported the pharaoh and his allies in the battle against Babylon at Carchemish, the battle that decided the balance of power in the Middle East. Jehoiakim was on the losing side. As a result, Nebuchadnezzar made Judah a vassal of Babylon and took some hostages, perhaps Daniel among them, away to Babylon.

Not having learned his lesson, Jehoiakim rebelled against Nebuchadnezzar in 602 B.C. Because Nebuchadnezzar was busy elsewhere, he sent raiding parties to ravage the land of Judah. Finally in 598/597 Nebuchadnezzar put an end to the Jewish problem. He entered Jerusalem and deported 3023 high-placed Jews back to Babylon.

[24]"As surely as I live," declares the LORD, "even if you, Jehoiachin son of Jehoiakim king of Judah, were a signet ring on my right hand, I would still pull you off. [25]I will hand you over to those who seek your life, those you fear—to Nebuchadnezzar king of Babylon and to the Babylonians. [26]I will hurl you and the mother who gave you birth into another country, where neither of you was born, and there you both will die. [27]You will never come back to the land you long to return to."

[28]Is this man Jehoiachin a despised, broken pot,
an object no one wants?

Why will he and his children be hurled out,
cast into a land they do not know?
29 O land, land, land,
hear the word of the LORD!
30 This is what the LORD says:
"Record this man as if childless,
a man who will not prosper in his lifetime,
for none of his offspring will prosper,
none will sit on the throne of David
or rule anymore in Judah."

The mark of Jehoiachin, third of Judah's recent kings, was oblivion. He succeeded to the throne upon his father's death in 597 B.C. (2 Kings 24:1-17; 2 Chronicles 36:9,10). Nebuchadnezzar did not put up with this nuisance for long. After only three months Nebuchadnezzar deposed Jehoiachin and took him, his mother, and 10,000 nobles, fighting men, and skilled workers away to Babylon. In his place Nebuchadnezzar put Jehoiachin's uncle Zedekiah on the throne. Jeremiah would have plenty to say later about the character of Zedekiah.

The end of Jehoiachin's reign also marked the end of the father-to-son succession to the throne of Judah by the house of David. How far the house of David had fallen! The Lord told the prophet to announce Jehoiachin's punishment: "Record this man as if childless."

The Righteous Branch

23 "Woe to the shepherds who are destroying and scattering the sheep of my pasture!" declares the LORD.
2 Therefore this is what the LORD, the God of Israel, says to the shepherds who tend my people: "Because you have scattered my flock and driven them away and have not bestowed care on them, I will bestow punishment on you for the evil you have

done," declares the LORD. 3 "I myself will gather the remnant of
my flock out of all the countries where I have driven them and
will bring them back to their pasture, where they will be fruit-
ful and increase in number. 4 I will place shepherds over them
who will tend them, and they will no longer be afraid or terri-
fied, nor will any be missing," declares the LORD.

5 "The days are coming," declares the LORD,
"when I will raise up to David
a righteous Branch,
a King who will reign wisely
and do what is just and right in the land.
6 In his days Judah will be saved
and Israel will live in safety.
This is the name by which he will be called:
The LORD Our Righteousness.

7 "So then, the days are coming," declares the LORD, "when
people will no longer say, 'As surely as the LORD lives, who
brought the Israelites up out of Egypt,' 8 but they will say, 'As
surely as the LORD lives, who brought the descendants of
Israel up out of the land of the north and out of all the coun-
tries where he had banished them.' Then they will live in their
own land."

The Lord makes a final comment about the kings, here called shepherds, and a passing comment about Zedekiah (whose name, ironically, means "The Lord is righteous"). Since Judah's kings had utterly failed to carry out their divine assignment, the Lord would get rid of them and replace them with shepherds after his own heart, faithful shepherds who would do the job that the Lord had called them to do.

The prophecy that follows, as is often the case in the Old Testament, brings together prophecies both about the return from exile and about the Messianic age and the Messiah himself. The Lord promises to perform a great miracle. He gives his people hope for the future. Though the Lord announced the effective end of the rule of the house of David, yet he was not about to forget the promises he had made to David (2 Samuel 7:11-16). From his offspring would come the Messiah, the great and good King of his people.

Jeremiah uses the imagery of Isaiah 11:1, "A shoot will come up from the stump of Jesse; from his roots a Branch will bear fruit." The prophet Zechariah later also would use this imagery to name the coming Messiah (3:8). From a stump that was dead and lifeless, the Lord would cause life to sprout up. These words, "The days are coming . . . ," are always a reference to a future time of the Lord's personal intervention in the life of his people, sometimes to judge them, but more often to save them, especially with reference to the time of Christ. Since Judah's kings had failed, the Lord himself would step in as Savior.

Jeremiah then gives us the richest gospel promise of his entire prophecy. There is no comparison between this Branch of David and the last fruitless branches of David's house who had been occupying the throne in Jerusalem. The "Branch" of whom Jeremiah writes would be righteous. He would be righteous, not just in obeying the law or in some external sense, but in every way. He would be righteousness in and of himself, because he would be without sin. Jesus challenged the Jews, "Can any of you prove me guilty of sin?" (John 8:46).

He would not only be righteous in and of himself, but he would rule righteously. He would bring about and exercise righteousness in all that he did and said. In all of his activity he would show a genuine understanding of the law's righteousness. Hence we see Jesus in the Gospels, perfectly fulfilling the whole law according to God's intention. Because Jesus would give God the perfect obedience God demands of every human being, his righteousness would win approval from God. He would supply the righteousness before God which every other human being lacks. In Jeremiah's words, Christ would be "The LORD Our Righteousness."

The effect of his rule of righteousness would be dramatic. Judah would be saved; Israel would dwell in safety. These are pictures of confidence, certainty, and peace. Such security and well-being are conveyed along with the righteousness of Christ, the forgiveness of sins given to every penitent sinner. This picture describes the peace that the work of Christ brings to the believing child of God. The believer has peace because of the final word of this promise.

The cause of his peace and its guarantee, its true character, are revealed by the name which the Lord gives to the Messiah: The LORD Our Righteousness. Here the whole gospel, the whole message of Scripture, is summed up in a few precious words. The Lord himself is our righteousness. For that to be true, the Lord himself must have become one of us, having taken all that we are upon himself.

These words point us to the miracle of the incarnation, the Word made flesh. But they also point to that most comforting truth: not only is the Messiah righteous in himself, but through his perfect life of obedience, his suffering and death and rising to life, he won for us justification, reconciliation with God, the forgiveness of sins. What he is and what he has and what he has done, he has done for us. He has given to us a gift, the gift of righteousness, a righteousness which we could never have gained for ourselves. Here is the door that opens heaven and keeps it open: The Lord is our righteousness, yes, the Lord is my righteousness. What he did, he did for me. He has made me his own. This is my certainty, my hope, my confidence: the Son of God who loved me and gave himself for me.

Lying Prophets

9 Concerning the prophets:

My heart is broken within me;
all my bones tremble.
I am like a drunken man,
like a man overcome by wine,
because of the LORD
and his holy words.
10 The land is full of adulterers;
because of the curse the land lies parched
and the pastures in the desert are withered.
The prophets follow an evil course
and use their power unjustly.
11 Both prophet and priest are godless;
even in my temple I find their wickedness,"
declares the LORD.
12 "Therefore their path will become slippery;
they will be banished to darkness
and there they will fall.
I will bring disaster on them
in the year they are punished,"
declares the LORD.

13 "Among the prophets of Samaria
I saw this repulsive thing:
They prophesied by Baal
and led my people Israel astray.
14 And among the prophets of Jerusalem
I have seen something horrible:
They commit adultery and live a lie.
They strengthen the hands of evildoers,
so that no one turns from his wickedness.
They are all like Sodom to me;
the people of Jerusalem are like Gomorrah."

15Therefore, this is what the LORD Almighty says concerning the prophets:

"I will make them eat bitter food
and drink poisoned water,
because from the prophets of Jerusalem
ungodliness has spread throughout the land."

Jeremiah now turns his attention to two other groups of leaders among God's ancient people. He speaks to the prophets, who were to function as God's mouthpieces, and to the priests, who were to serve as mediators between the sinner and God. Even though their kings had failed to live up to God's plan, one might have hoped that Judah's prophets and priests would have resisted the turn to evil and unbelief. Such was not the case.

Jeremiah speaks to the priests indirectly since they had failed in their duty to test and control the false prophets, but instead had approved of them, worked with them, and allowed their message to spread. Jeremiah recoiled at what he had to say. He knew something about the cost of being a prophet. He knew the burden and the awesome responsibility of one who speaks in the name of the Lord. Like a man overcome with wine, he felt numbed and paralyzed at the fearsome judgment of the Lord, for it is to the Lord that the prophet must give an account of what he has done.

None of Judah's false prophets had done any good. Jeremiah describes them as adulterers. They had left the Lord for false gods and practiced the temple prostitution common to Canaanite worship. They followed an evil course. They were godless. They had embraced Baal worship, even allowing it in the Lord's temple. They had lived the lie. All of these practices had sad consequences.

For one thing, the land was cursed by the Lord. What had been productive and alive became parched and withered, even the grass most toughened to the heat. But the worst thing they had done was to strengthen the hand of evildoers. For this they would be punished most severely. By their prophecies they had emptied the Lord's Word, the law, of its meaning. They allowed anyone to make his own convenient interpretation, an interpretation suited to cover his own self-chosen, sinful actions. The result was that no one heard or heeded God's call to repentance. Feeling confident in the assurance the false prophets had given, everyone continued on in sin. From the false prophets ungodliness had spread over the whole land. Such failure to fulfill their high calling, a calling so vital to the lives of the people, merited the severest judgment. Without knowing what was happening, they would slip and fall. They would eat the bitter and poisonous fruit of their own making.

16 This is what the LORD Almighty says:
"Do not listen to what the prophets
are prophesying to you;
they fill you with false hopes.
They speak visions from their own minds,
not from the mouth of the LORD.
17 They keep saying to those who despise me,
'The LORD says: You will have peace.'
And to all who follow the stubbornness
of their hearts
they say, 'No harm will come to you.'
18 But which of them has stood in the council of the LORD
to see or to hear his word?
Who has listened and heard his word?
19 See, the storm of the LORD
will burst out in wrath,
a whirlwind swirling down
on the heads of the wicked.

[20]The anger of the LORD will not turn back
until he fully accomplishes
the purposes of his heart.
In days to come
you will understand it clearly.
[21]I did not send these prophets,
yet they have run with their message;
I did not speak to them,
yet they have prophesied.
[22]But if they had stood in my council,
they would have proclaimed my words to my people
and would have turned them from their evil ways
and from their evil deeds.

The Lord's advice is direct and simple, still the best advice when one is confronted by dubious spiritual messengers and their advice—"do not listen to them. . . ." The prophets in Judah were not preaching messages from the Lord. That was plain to see, for what they were saying contradicted everything the Lord had said in the rest of his Word.

The false prophets gave false hope to those who despised and refused to believe the Lord's Word. They encouraged the sinner in his sin by making it seem less sinful. They dismissed God's threatened judgment with the words, "no harm will come to you"—hell and damnation are mere delusions. They gave false hope because they left the impenitent with the impression that sin does not matter and is no big thing. Hence, there was no reason to worry about repentance.

Had these prophets been close to or stood in the council of the Lord, then they surely would have grasped the heart of the Lord's message, the center of all Scripture: Repent! The Lord means what he says, "The soul that sins shall surely die." Salvation and righteousness are found in the Lord alone and in the Word which brings his forgiveness.

The prophets occupied such a central place in the Lord's blueprint for ancient Israel; it was through their preaching that souls were saved or damned. They therefore bore a special measure of responsibility. For their failure they would receive the harshest judgment. The Lord will not spare the one who perverts his Word, for that Word is life. If it is obscured and its message is distorted, then the only means God has given to save sinners is lost. The Lord therefore solemnly pledged that his anger would not stop until the false prophets had paid the full measure of punishment. Let their judgment serve as a warning to all who treat the Word or any part of it as though it did not matter.

To the believer and the prophet Jeremiah, who wonder about this, the Lord says, "In the days to come you will understand it clearly." The Lord says in other words: "Put it into my hands. Be sure that my purposes are being accomplished. In days to come you will understand clearly."

23"Am I only a God nearby,"
declares the LORD,
"and not a God far away?
24Can anyone hide in secret places
so that I cannot see him?"
declares the LORD.
"Do not I fill heaven and earth?"
declares the LORD.

25I have heard what the prophets say who prophesy lies in my name. They say, 'I had a dream! I had a dream!' 26How long will this continue in the hearts of these lying prophets, who prophesy the delusions of their own minds? 27They think the dreams they tell one another will make my people forget my name, just as their fathers forgot my name through Baal worship. 28Let the prophet who has a dream tell his dream, but let the one who has my word speak it faithfully. For what has

straw to do with grain?" declares the LORD. 29"Is not my word like fire," declares the LORD, "and like a hammer that breaks a rock in pieces?

The false prophets in Israel had waged a vigorous campaign against the truthfulness of the Lord and his Word. They had not only attacked that Word directly, but they had also undermined it by limiting the Lord and making his Word less important or applicable. But the Lord will not be limited nor his Word despised. He shows that there is no comparison between his Word and that of the false prophets. He shows this lack of comparison to encourage those who believe to trust in the power of his Word and to be confident in its use. He also rejects the more subtle attacks leveled against him and his Word.

God bursts the limits with which the false prophets tried to hedge him in. They had suggested that God was limited in his reach, that he was only a local deity, and that he could not see all that they were doing. One could hide from him. These suggestions led to the further implication that God did not care and that even if he did care, he was really quite powerless to do anything about it. With a word God swept aside such wishful prattle, "Do not I fill heaven and earth?" He is all-powerful and all-knowing. Nothing and no one escape his notice and his judgment. He calls everyone to account for his life.

The Lord rejected the attempts of the false prophets to put their dreams on a par with his Word. In so doing he exposed the real source of their message. "I have dreamed! I have dreamed!" they cried. They attributed to God whatever thought had arisen from the fevered hotbed of their own imaginations. They believed that if they just kept repeating the message, by sheer volume they could move God's people away from him. They believed they could make Judah lose sight of the Lord who was their Savior and turn the people to themselves. They had some hope of success in this, because a century earlier the prophets of Samaria had done the same thing successfully with the people of Israel. False prophecy's power to mislead is potent.

Yet, there is no comparison between the word of the false prophet and the Lord's Word. It's like comparing the value of chaff—the husks and the straw—with the grain—the food. So let the dreamer dream, let the prophet of the Lord speak God's Word faithfully, counting on that Word to do the work the Lord intends. That Word is powerful. It is fire to consume the fragile tissue of our own righteousness; it is fire to purify us for the Lord. It is a hammer to shatter even the hardest hearts so that they might be created anew.

To wield power, to have strength, to achieve success as the Lord counts success, to get real comfort and help, to reach people and save them, one need only use the Lord's Word. May nothing tempt or turn us aside from it.

False Oracles and False Prophets

**30"Therefore," declares the LORD, "I am against the prophets
who steal from one another words supposedly from me. 31"Yes,"
declares the LORD, "I am against the prophets who wag their
own tongues and yet declare, 'The LORD declares.' 32Indeed, I
am against those who prophesy false dreams," declares the
LORD. "They tell them and lead my people astray with their
reckless lies, yet I did not send or appoint them. They do not
benefit these people in the least," declares the LORD.**

**33"When these people, or a prophet or a priest, ask you,
'What is the oracle of the LORD?' say to them, 'What oracle? I
will forsake you, declares the LORD.' 34If a prophet or a priest
or anyone else claims, 'This is the oracle of the LORD,' I will
punish that man and his household. 35This is what each of you
keeps on saying to his friend or relative: 'What is the LORD's**

**answer?' or 'What has the LORD spoken?' 36But you must not
mention 'the oracle of the LORD' again, because every man's
own word becomes his oracle and so you distort the words of
the living God, the LORD Almighty, our God. 37This is what you
keep saying to a prophet: 'What is the LORD's answer to you?'
or 'What has the LORD spoken?' 38Although you claim, 'This is
the oracle of the LORD,' this is what the LORD says: You used
the words, 'This is the oracle of the LORD,' even though I told
you that you must not claim, 'This is the oracle of the LORD.'
39Therefore, I will surely forget you and cast you out of my
presence along with the city I gave to you and your fathers. 40I
will bring upon you everlasting disgrace—everlasting shame
that will not be forgotten."**

The false prophets were not wholly to blame. They found a ready audience. The people of Judah were in a frenzy. They appeared pious as they badgered and pestered the prophets for an oracle from the Lord. They asked not in faith, even as the Pharisees of Jesus' time demanded a sign not because they believed, but because they did not believe. With itching ears, not satisfied with what the Lord had already told them, Jeremiah's countrymen kept on demanding oracles until they received one that suited them. The lust for the novel and new filled them.

Because they had so misused the words, the Lord forbade anyone to use the phrase, "an oracle of the Lord." Their constant demands for new revelations encouraged the false prophets more and more to supply an ever-increasing stream of new oracles, new "words" from the Lord. These new "words" overshadowed the Word of the Lord already delivered and blunted its truth. They had distorted the Lord's Word. In the end, because of all this wicked activity, the false prophets and their "oracles" did not benefit the hearers in the least. In fact, the false prophets did the people the greatest harm, for they confused the people and led them away from the Lord.

Because these "prophets" spread lies in the name of the Lord and abused their prophetic office and corrupted the Word, the Lord pronounced his judgment. The false prophets would lose their city and be disgraced forever. Everyone who reads Jeremiah's prophecy knows how this divine threat was carried out.

Two Baskets of Figs

24 After Jehoiachin son of Jehoiakim king of Judah and the officials, the craftsmen and the artisans of Judah were carried into exile from Jerusalem to Babylon by Nebuchadnezzar king of Babylon, the LORD showed me two baskets of figs placed in front of the temple of the LORD. [2]One basket had very good figs, like those that ripen early; the other basket had very poor figs, so bad they could not be eaten.

[3]Then the LORD asked me, "What do you see, Jeremiah?"

"Figs," I answered. "The good ones are very good, but the poor ones are so bad they cannot be eaten."

[4]Then the word of the LORD came to me: [5]"This is what the LORD, the God of Israel, says: 'Like these good figs, I regard as good the exiles from Judah, whom I sent away from this place to the land of the Babylonians. [6]My eyes will watch over them for their good, and I will bring them back to this land. I will build them up and not tear them down; I will plant them and not uproot them. [7]I will give them a heart to know me, that I am the LORD. They will be my people, and I will be their God, for they will return to me with all their heart.

[8]" 'But like the poor figs, which are so bad they cannot be eaten,' says the LORD, 'so will I deal with Zedekiah king of Judah, his officials and the survivors from Jerusalem, whether they remain in this land or live in Egypt. [9]I will make them abhorrent and an offense to all the kingdoms of the earth, a re-

proach and a byword, an object of ridicule and cursing, wherever I banish them. [10]I will send the sword, famine and plague against them until they are destroyed from the land I gave to them and their fathers.' "

Shortly after King Jehoiachin had been led off into exile (about 597 B.C.), the Lord gave Jeremiah a vision. Jeremiah introduced the vision at this point to answer some questions that surely troubled him and other believers who remained behind. What would happen to the exiled Jews? Would they lose their identity in far-off Babylon? Would they lose their religion and faith? Jeremiah recorded this vision in part also to prove that the Lord keeps his word. He had promised: "In days to come you will understand it clearly." This vision provided Jeremiah with the beginning of such understanding.

In the vision two baskets of figs appeared to Jeremiah before the temple of the Lord. These baskets of figs were offerings to the Lord. The account of Cain and Abel and their sacrifices comes to mind. The contents of the two baskets were very different. The one basket contained very good figs, perhaps those picked at the beginning of the season. The other basket contained rotten figs, not fit to eat.

God explained that the good figs represented the exiles recently removed to Babylon. The Lord promised to watch over them. He promised to restore them to the promised land. Because of their experience and their repentance, they would grow stronger in their faith in the Lord and his Word. Once again they would truly be his people, who wholly leaned upon him and took him at his word. He would be their God. The Lord and his faithful people would once again share a happy communion. Despite the harsh judgment rendered against them and Jerusalem, something good would come of it. Those who were exiled would learn their lesson and return with all their hearts to the Lord, offering him a pleasing sacrifice.

The poor figs, not fit for an offering to the Lord, represented Zedekiah and those who chose to stay in Jerusalem and fight to the end. Their hearts remained stubborn and hardened. They had learned nothing from the lesson God was teaching them. Because their impenitence remained unchanged, they would fall under the Lord's judgment. They would be destroyed, even if they tried to escape it by fleeing to Egypt.

Seventy Years of Captivity

**25 The word came to Jeremiah concerning all the people
of Judah in the fourth year of Jehoiakim son of Josiah
king of Judah, which was the first year of Nebuchadnezzar
king of Babylon. [2]So Jeremiah the prophet said to all the people of Judah and to all those living in Jerusalem: [3]For twenty-
three years—from the thirteenth year of Josiah son of Amon
king of Judah until this very day—the word of the LORD has
come to me and I have spoken to you again and again, but you
have not listened.**

**[4]And though the LORD has sent all his servants the prophets
to you again and again, you have not listened or paid any attention. [5]They said, "Turn now, each of you, from your evil
ways and your evil practices, and you can stay in the land the
LORD gave to you and your fathers for ever and ever. [6]Do not
follow other gods to serve and worship them; do not provoke
me to anger with what your hands have made. Then I will not
harm you."**

**[7]"But you did not listen to me," declares the LORD, "and you
have provoked me with what your hands have made, and you
have brought harm to yourselves."**

The time is 605/604 B.C. The destroyer of Israel, Nebuchadnezzar, had succeeded his father on the throne of Babylon. Some in Judah thought that perhaps this change in rulers would transform the whole power structure of the Middle East and make it possible for Judah to pursue a more independent course. Adopting this viewpoint, Jehoiakim continued to provoke the Babylonians and followed his course on a headlong path to ruin.

Jeremiah had now served as God's prophet to the people of Judah for twenty-three years. What had he accomplished? Here he reviews a quarter century of ministry. Other prophets had delivered the same message as he had. Still, after all that time, the people of Judah had remained unmoved. They continued to break the First Commandment and follow after other gods. Clearly, the Lord was justified when he brought judgment upon them. Jeremiah introduced these words to show that even though a righteous God brought judgment against Judah, yet he set a limit to the extent of that judgment. "In the days to come you will understand it clearly."

With the words of this chapter the Lord gives a partial answer to the challenge Jeremiah had raised with the Lord earlier (Jeremiah 12). Jeremiah had asked: "Why do the righteous suffer and the wicked seem to prosper? Why, though Judah is evil, should she be punished when the nations around her, including those who will administer the punishment, are even worse?" Here Jeremiah received some answers to those questions.

8Therefore the LORD Almighty says this: "Because you have not listened to my words, 9I will summon all the peoples of the north and my servant Nebuchadnezzar king of Babylon," declares the LORD, "and I will bring them against this land and its inhabitants and against all the surrounding nations. I will completely destroy them and make them an object of horror and scorn, and an everlasting ruin. 10I will banish from them the sounds of joy and gladness, the voices of bride and bride-

groom, the sound of millstones and the light of the lamp. 11This
whole country will become a desolate wasteland, and these na-
tions will serve the king of Babylon seventy years.
12"But when the seventy years are fulfilled, I will punish the
king of Babylon and his nation, the land of the Babylonians,
for their guilt," declares the LORD, "and will make it desolate
forever. 13I will bring upon that land all the things I have spo-
ken against it, all that are written in this book and prophesied
by Jeremiah against all the nations. 14They themselves will be
enslaved by many nations and great kings; I will repay them
according to their deeds and the work of their hands."

The Lord would use Nebuchadnezzar as his servant or instrument to administer his punishment upon Judah. The surrounding nations, who might think themselves better or more fortunate, would not escape either. The devastation would be complete. There would be nothing but grinding poverty. No marriages would be celebrated. The millstones would be silent because there would be no grain to grind. The lamps would sit dust-covered and dark because there would be no olive oil to burn.

But God would set a limit to the tragedy about to fall on the Jewish nation. For the first time Jeremiah announced that God's judgment would last for seventy years. This number is a very sacred number in Scripture. It represents seven, the number always used in connection with God, and ten, the number of completeness. So at God's appointed time, according to his own deciding, he would free Judah from exile. At the same time he would punish the Babylonians for their own wickedness. His prophecies against Babylon are presented, together with those against other nations, in the final chapters of this book. The Babylonians forgot the lesson administered to Nebuchadnezzar (Daniel 4). They were great and powerful, not because of anything good in them, but because God chose to use them to serve his greater purpose.

The Cup of God's Wrath

**15This is what the LORD, the God of Israel, said to me: "Take
from my hand this cup filled with the wine of my wrath and
make all the nations to whom I send you drink it. 16When they
drink it, they will stagger and go mad because of the sword I
will send among them."**
**17So I took the cup from the LORD's hand and made all the
nations to whom he sent me drink it: 18Jerusalem and the
towns of Judah, its kings and officials, to make them a ruin
and an object of horror and scorn and cursing, as they are today; 19Pharaoh king of Egypt, his attendants, his officials and
all his people, 20and all the foreign people there; all the kings of
Uz; all the kings of the Philistines (those of Ashkelon, Gaza,
Ekron, and the people left at Ashdod); 21Edom, Moab and Ammon; 22all the kings of Tyre and Sidon; the kings of the coastlands across the sea; 23Dedan, Tema, Buz and all who are in
distant places; 24all the kings of Arabia and all the kings of the
foreign people who live in the desert; 25all the kings of Zimri,
Elam and Media; 26and all the kings of the north, near and far,
one after the other—all the kingdoms on the face of the earth.
And after all of them, the king of Sheshach will drink it too.**

God's judgment on his enemies is pictured as a cup filled with a vile brew, the wrath of God himself. He would first of all use the Babylonian superpower to make the nations drink that cup. Then he would compel the Babylonians themselves to drink that cup to the last drop. Through his preaching, Jeremiah announced to the nations that they would drink this cup. To confirm the truth of his message, Jeremiah may have delivered the Lord's judgments against the nations, written on scrolls, to their embassies in Jerusalem. Jeremiah collected these prophecies against the various nations in the last chapters of this book (46—51). All must drink that cup; no one would escape.

God's judgment would begin with Judah and Jerusalem. From there it would spread in an ever-widening circle throughout the whole Middle East. Egypt is mentioned next because many, including many Jews, fled the power of Nebuchadnezzar, hoping to find safety in Egypt. But Egypt would offer no escape, for it too would fall to Nebuchadnezzar's invading armies. The lands immediately surrounding Judah: Uz (perhaps located in the Arabian desert), Edom, Moab, Ammon, Philistia, Tyre, and Sidon—all would fall. Nebuchadnezzar's might would be felt by those in the north, the south (deserts of Arabia), and the east—even Elam and Media, lands east of Babylon. In the end Babylon, the destroyer, would itself drink the cup it had forced so many others to drink, for the Lord is the one who controls all the nations and is bringing judgment. No flesh can boast before him.

27"Then tell them, 'This is what the LORD Almighty, the God
of Israel, says: Drink, get drunk and vomit, and fall to rise no
more because of the sword I will send among you.' 28But if they
refuse to take the cup from your hand and drink, tell them,
'This is what the LORD Almighty says: You must drink it! 29See,
I am beginning to bring disaster on the city that bears my
Name, and will you indeed go unpunished? You will not go un-
punished, for I am calling down a sword upon all who live on
the earth, declares the LORD Almighty.'

30"Now prophesy all these words against them and say to
them:

" 'The LORD will roar from on high;
he will thunder from his holy dwelling
and roar mightily against his land.
He will shout like those who tread the grapes,
shout against all who live on the earth.

31 The tumult will resound to the ends of the earth,
for the LORD will bring charges against the nations;
he will bring judgment on all mankind
and put the wicked to the sword,' "
declares the LORD.

32 This is what the LORD Almighty says:

"Look! Disaster is spreading
from nation to nation;
a mighty storm is rising
from the ends of the earth."

33 At that time those slain by the LORD will be everywhere — from one end of the earth to the other. They will not be mourned or gathered up or buried, but will be like refuse lying on the ground.

34 Weep and wail, you shepherds;
roll in the dust, you leaders of the flock.
For your time to be slaughtered has come;
you will fall and be shattered like fine pottery.
35 The shepherds will have nowhere to flee,
the leaders of the flock no place to escape.
36 Hear the cry of the shepherds,
the wailing of the leaders of the flock,
for the LORD is destroying their pasture.
37 The peaceful meadows will be laid waste
because of the fierce anger of the LORD.
38 Like a lion he will leave his lair,
and their land will become desolate
because of the sword of the oppressor
and because of the LORD's fierce anger.

Kicking and screaming like a child refusing to take some bitter medicine, nations would resist the judgment of the Lord. With all their power and scheming, they would struggle to set it aside. But "you must drink it!" says the Lord. If he had to punish Jerusalem, the city in which he had chosen to reveal himself and which carried his name, how much more must those nations who had not the slightest claim to his favor feel his wrath. As Peter was later to write (1 Peter 4:17,18), "It is time for judgment to begin with the family of God; and if it begins with us, what will the outcome be for those who do not obey the gospel of God? And, 'If it is hard for the righteous to be saved, what will become of the ungodly and the sinner?' "

Jeremiah's vision broadens from the judgment of the Lord administered by Nebuchadnezzar against the surrounding nations, and finally against the Babylonians themselves, and merges into a vision of God's final judgment against the whole world. With unstoppable power the Lord will carry out his will. Jeremiah heaps image upon image to drive home the certainty and terror of the final judgment. The Lord will use the power of his Word, his mighty voice to accomplish his purpose.

Like those exuberantly shouting and crushing the juice out of the grapes, so the Lord's judgment will smash the life out of the nations and break their resistance. Weeping and wailing, the rulers of the nations, the shepherds, will stand powerless before it. Like a young lion determined to find prey, the Lord will pursue his judgment to its bitter conclusion. No one will escape. The wicked, so prosperous in their own eyes and the eyes of others, will pay the price of wickedness to the last penny. The Lord opened the eyes of Jeremiah to see clearly and to understand the end of the wicked.

From Jerusalem and Judah to the ends of the earth in an ever spreading and irresistible flood tide, the judgment of the Lord moved. But the day would come when that flood tide of judgment would become a life-giving flood of good news. In the coming days, the Lord would act in grace in Christ and bring life to the nations. As he was about to ascend into heaven, our Savior told his disciples, "You will receive power when the Holy Spirit comes on you; and you will be my witnesses in Jerusalem, and in all Judea and Samaria, and to the ends of the earth" (Acts 1:8). By the Lord's mercy we today with our prayers, our gifts, and our witness may help to swell that flood tide of life which is spreading the good news to the nations, before the Lord returns to judge the earth.

Jeremiah Threatened With Death

**26 Early in the reign of Jehoiakim son of Josiah king of
Judah, this word came from the LORD: 2"This is what
the LORD says: Stand in the courtyard of the LORD's house and
speak to all the people of the towns of Judah who come to worship in the house of the LORD. Tell them everything I command you; do not omit a word. 3Perhaps they will listen and
each will turn from his evil way. Then I will relent and not
bring on them the disaster I was planning because of the evil
they have done. 4Say to them, 'This is what the LORD says: If
you do not listen to me and follow my law, which I have set before you, 5and if you do not listen to the words of my servants
the prophets, whom I have sent to you again and again
(though you have not listened), 6then I will make this house
like Shiloh and this city an object of cursing among all the nations of the earth.' "**

The time is shortly after the death of Josiah, early in the reign of Jehoiakim, 609/608 B.C. At the Lord's command Jeremiah repeated a message he had first delivered some time during the reign of Josiah (Jeremiah 7). Jeremiah was to make the point to a new administration that the Lord stood by what he had said. The message contained both a threat and a promise. The threat: If the people of Judah did not repent, the temple would suffer the same end as the worship center at Shiloh. The promise: If they repented, the Lord would not carry out his judgment.

The Lord again displayed his great love and patience. He offered Judah and all its people another chance. Jeremiah delivered the message in the courtyard of the temple, so that the greatest number of worshipers might hear it. Then if they failed to listen, they would be without excuse.

The prophet told them exactly what God had commanded, for the message was not his but the Lord's. The cause was not his but the Lord's. Duty to his calling, fear of the Lord, and love compelled him to deliver the whole message. Jeremiah was faithful to his calling, doing everything he could for the benefit of his hearers.

In his last words to the Ephesian elders, the apostle Paul confesses that this is the solemn duty of a man of God: "You know that I have not hesitated to preach anything that would be helpful to you but have taught you publicly and from house to house. Therefore, I declare to you today that I am innocent of the blood of all men. For I have not hesitated to proclaim to you the whole will of God" (Acts 20:20,26,27). The only hope for Jeremiah's listeners lay in knowing their true situation. And Jeremiah was not alone; many others had delivered the same message.

**7The priests, the prophets and all the people heard Jeremiah
speak these words in the house of the LORD. 8But as soon as
Jeremiah finished telling all the people everything the LORD
had commanded him to say, the priests, the prophets and all
the people seized him and said, "You must die! 9Why do you
prophesy in the LORD's name that this house will be like Shiloh
and this city will be desolate and deserted?" And all the people
crowded around Jeremiah in the house of the LORD.**

**10When the officials of Judah heard about these things, they
went up from the royal palace to the house of the LORD and**

took their places at the entrance of the New Gate of the LORD's house. [11]Then the priests and the prophets said to the officials and all the people, "This man should be sentenced to death because he has prophesied against this city. You have heard it with your own ears!"

[12]Then Jeremiah said to all the officials and all the people: "The LORD sent me to prophesy against this house and this city all the things you have heard. [13]Now reform your ways and your actions and obey the LORD your God. Then the LORD will relent and not bring the disaster he has pronounced against you. [14]As for me, I am in your hands; do with me whatever you think is good and right. [15]Be assured, however, that if you put me to death, you will bring the guilt of innocent blood on yourselves and on this city and on those who live in it, for in truth the LORD has sent me to you to speak all these words in your hearing."

The response of Jeremiah's hearers, unfortunately, was predictable. Out of their hearts they spoke; out of their hearts they acted. The Lord had rightly evaluated their hearts. They were wholly impenitent from top to bottom, from the priests and prophets, to all the people. Without hesitation they arrested Jeremiah. In the legal hearing that followed they pronounced a death sentence on him: "You must die." As if they did not already know, further proving their stubbornness, they asked, "Why do you prophesy . . . ?" The priests, who were chiefly responsible for seeing that God's covenant was kept, led the charge.

The uproar reached the palace, the royal apartments, the court of the king himself. Perhaps some of the king's officials had men assigned to keep track of Jeremiah's activities. The chief officers hurried from the palace, which bordered the temple immediately to the south, and assembled in the New Gate. The location of the New Gate is uncertain, but it may have been a gate built to afford the king and his officers quick and easy access to the temple area. Having assembled, they were ready to hear the case against Jeremiah. The priests and prophets and others sympathetic to them leveled the charge: "He has prophesied against this city." They accused Jeremiah not of false doctrine or of being a false prophet, but of treason.

Jeremiah seized the chance to respond by repeating the thrust of his previous sermon. Their problem was with the Lord; he was only the Lord's messenger. They were furious with Jeremiah because he had convicted them of their sin.

Many an impenitent sinner has acted in the same way toward one sent to call him to account for his sin. It is as Jesus said, "If I had not come and spoken to them, they would not be guilty of sin. Now, however, they have no excuse" (John 15:22). The unbelieving world conspires to silence the call to repentance any way it can, for it will not face up to its sin.

Jeremiah did not flinch. He answered his accusers, "Do with me as you will, but know that to silence me will change nothing. You will only make your case worse, for you will pollute the city and make it unclean by shedding innocent blood. The Lord sent me."

16Then the officials and all the people said to the priests and the prophets, "This man should not be sentenced to death! He has spoken to us in the name of the LORD our God."

17Some of the elders of the land stepped forward and said to the entire assembly of people, 18"Micah of Moresheth prophesied in the days of Hezekiah king of Judah. He told all the people of Judah, 'This is what the LORD Almighty says:

" 'Zion will be plowed like a field,
Jerusalem will become a heap of rubble,
the temple hill a mound overgrown with thickets.'

**[19]"Did Hezekiah king of Judah or anyone else in Judah put
him to death? Did not Hezekiah fear the LORD and seek his favor? And did not the LORD relent, so that he did not bring the
disaster he pronounced against them? We are about to bring a
terrible disaster on ourselves!"**

**[20](Now Uriah son of Shemaiah from Kiriath Jearim was an-
other man who prophesied in the name of the LORD; he prophesied the same things against this city and this land as Jeremiah did. [21]When King Jehoiakim and all his officers and officials
heard his words, the king sought to put him to death. But Uriah heard of it and fled in fear to Egypt. [22]King Jehoiakim, however, sent Elnathan son of Acbor to Egypt, along with some
other men. [23]They brought Uriah out of Egypt and took him to
King Jehoiakim, who had him struck down with a sword and
his body thrown into the burial place of the common people.)**

**[24]Furthermore, Ahikam son of Shaphan supported Jeremiah,
and so he was not handed over to the people to be put to death.**

After hearing Jeremiah's defense, the officials and the people overruled the verdict pronounced by the prophets and the priests. Perhaps many of the people were awed by the presence of authority. It may even have been that many of them at first had no idea what the uproar was all about. In any case, the reversal of the verdict spared the life of the prophet and proved that some in Judah had taken his words to heart and were following in the path of good King Josiah. Many of the officials, though not all, had probably received their offices from Josiah and held views similar to his.

In support of reversing the death verdict, the elders advanced a precedent from the reign of Hezekiah a century earlier. At that time Micah the prophet had spoken the same kind of message (Micah 3:12). At that time Hezekiah took no action against Micah. In fact, Hezekiah had listened, taken Micah's words to heart, and repented. His repentance led the

Lord to delay the judgment he had announced. Furthermore, the elders exclaimed, "We will bring a terrible disaster on ourselves." The reversal was also supported by some very powerful men. Ahikam, son of Shaphan, who served as secretary in the palace, prevented the priests from carrying out their death sentence.

Jeremiah includes an aside, a bit of information that had nothing to do directly with his case. This footnote shows that Jehoiakim was willing to kill prophets. The threat to Jeremiah's life was no pretense. Uriah (not mentioned elsewhere in the Bible) had also preached a message similar to Jeremiah's. Wicked King Jehoiakim tried to kill him, but being forewarned Uriah escaped to Egypt. That escape did not save him. Jehoiakim dragged Uriah back from Egypt, had him killed, and had him buried in a pauper's grave. To preach as Jeremiah preached took courage, even though the price for such preaching could very well be death.

No wonder Jesus said that the leaders who opposed him were true children of their fathers.

Judah to Serve Nebuchadnezzar

27 Early in the reign of Zedekiah son of Josiah king of Ju-
dah, this word came to Jeremiah from the LORD: 2This is
what the LORD said to me: "Make a yoke out of straps and
crossbars and put it on your neck. 3Then send word to the kings
of Edom, Moab, Ammon, Tyre and Sidon through the envoys
who have come to Jerusalem to Zedekiah king of Judah. 4Give
them a message for their masters and say, 'This is what the
LORD Almighty, the God of Israel, says: "Tell this to your mas-
ters: 5With my great power and outstretched arm I made the
earth and its people and the animals that are on it, and I give it
to anyone I please. 6Now I will hand all your countries over to
my servant Nebuchadnezzar king of Babylon; I will make even
the wild animals subject to him. 7All nations will serve him and

his son and his grandson until the time for his land comes; then many nations and great kings will subjugate him.

The time was early in the reign of Zedekiah, 593 B.C. Zedekiah and his immediate neighbors were planning strategy and scheming how they might blunt the power of Babylon and remain free and independent. Zedekiah stubbornly continued to pursue the ill-fated policy of independence of his brother Jehoiakim. Despite its certain failure, the king still doggedly pursued it. Acting as the Lord's spokesman, Jeremiah had foretold its failure, which had already been evident in the several deportations from Jerusalem.

The Lord reinforced his previous warnings with another object lesson proclaimed in the person of the prophet. The reaction of the nation, especially the priests and false prophets, would again show that Judah was impenitent and deserved the Lord's judgment. God told Jeremiah to construct a home-made, loose-fitting yoke and to wear it on the back of his neck. He was to go about in public wearing that yoke.

What a sight Jeremiah must have presented—wearing the yoke for several months or even longer! Punctuating his message with the yoke, he delivered a warning to Zedekiah's allies through their ambassadors.

The message was clear and simple (much the same as he had delivered before, in Jeremiah 25): "I, the Lord, made the earth and everything on it. It belongs to me. I control it all. I do as I please, whatever I will. Now I please to give it all to Nebuchadnezzar, who will carry out my judgment. I will allow Babylon to have dominion until it suits my purpose to take it away. Nebuchadnezzar's empire will last through three generations (it came to an end in 539 B.C.) and then I will take it from them."

8" ' "If, however, any nation or kingdom will not serve Neb-
uchadnezzar king of Babylon or bow its neck under his yoke, I
will punish that nation with the sword, famine and plague, de-
clares the LORD, until I destroy it by his hand. 9So do not listen
to your prophets, your diviners, your interpreters of dreams,
your mediums or your sorcerers who tell you, 'You will not
serve the king of Babylon.' 10They prophesy lies to you that will
only serve to remove you far from your lands; I will banish you
and you will perish. 11But if any nation will bow its neck under
the yoke of the king of Babylon and serve him, I will let that
nation remain in its own land to till it and to live there, de-
clares the LORD." ' "

The nations that would resist Babylon faced a painful choice in the face of the inevitable victory of Nebuchadnezzar. They could surrender and freely put themselves under his rule. That choice would at least allow them to remain in their own land and to continue their way of life as before. Or they could resist and try to fight him. But they could not win, so they would pay the price of resistance. They would only make it worse for themselves. They would serve him in any case. But in the latter case their service would be much harder. Nebuchadnezzar would, as was the customary policy of the great world powers of that era, forcibly deport them to a different location and erase their culture.

Countless voices urged them to follow the course they liked. When anybody determines to go against God's Word or to sidestep it, he will find plenty of help. Deceivers more than he can count will be there to tell him what he wants to hear. The Lord warned the nations not to listen to such deceivers.

In addition to false prophets there were the diviners—those who looked at signs in earth and sky and inside the entrails of animals to predict the future. Besides the diviners, there were interpreters of dreams—those who used the dreams of the kings to foretell the future course of events. Beside the interpreters of dreams stood the mediums—those who called forth the spirits of the dead to provide insight into the future. Beside the mediums stood the sorcerers—those who through astrology and other black arts tried to peer into the future. Beside them all stood the father of lies, their master, Satan himself. "Listen to them, listen to him, listen to lies!"

[12]I gave the same message to Zedekiah king of Judah. I said, "Bow your neck under the yoke of the king of Babylon; serve him and his people, and you will live. [13]Why will you and your people die by the sword, famine and plague with which the LORD has threatened any nation that will not serve the king of Babylon? [14]Do not listen to the words of the prophets who say to you, 'You will not serve the king of Babylon,' for they are prophesying lies to you. [15]'I have not sent them,' declares the LORD. 'They are prophesying lies in my name. Therefore, I will banish you and you will perish, both you and the prophets who prophesy to you.' "

The Lord assured the nations that he had given Zedekiah the same message that he gave to them (verse 11). Zedekiah's opposition to Babylon was senseless and suicidal. The Lord could not understand why they preferred death to life. The false prophets were bringing death to Judah and its people with their lies. Did these false prophets actually imagine that they could frustrate the will of God, that somehow they could control world events and make them turn out differently than the Lord wanted? Opposing God is stupidity.

[16]Then I said to the priests and all these people, "This is what the LORD says: Do not listen to the prophets who say, 'Very soon now the articles from the LORD's house will be brought back from Babylon.' They are prophesying lies to you. [17]Do not listen to them. Serve the king of Babylon, and you will

**live. Why should this city become a ruin? [18]If they are prophets
and have the word of the LORD, let them plead with the LORD
Almighty that the furnishings remaining in the house of the
LORD and in the palace of the king of Judah and in Jerusalem
not be taken to Babylon. [19]For this is what the LORD Almighty
says about the pillars, the Sea, the movable stands and the other furnishings that are left in this city, [20]which Nebuchadnezzar
king of Babylon did not take away when he carried Jehoiachin
son of Jehoiakim king of Judah into exile from Jerusalem to
Babylon, along with all the nobles of Judah and Jerusalem—
[21]yes, this is what the LORD Almighty, the God of Israel, says
about the things that are left in the house of the LORD and in
the palace of the king of Judah and in Jerusalem: [22]'They will
be taken to Babylon and there they will remain until the day I
come for them,' declares the LORD. 'Then I will bring them
back and restore them to this place.' "**

Before all the priests and people, to their faces, Jeremiah attacked the attractive lie put forward by the false prophets. "Soon what was taken from the temple will be returned. Everything will be fine, just as it always was." The false prophets were holding out hope for the future, but it was a hope that lay in the shadows of a future they themselves did not know.

Making promises is easy. One can say almost anything about the future. Such empty promises came easily from the lips of the false prophets. How wrong they were! They were creating a future but not the one they were predicting, for what they said was not true. Whatever of value that was still left in the temple, palace, and city would be taken away to Babylon. If they had been true prophets of the Lord, if they had really known him, they should have prayed with all their might that he would spare Jerusalem—its people and its temple.

The Babylonians Destroy the Bronze Basin

People like to listen to false prophets, because they speak what people's itching ears want to hear. Because of the disobedience of the people, everything left in Jerusalem would be removed to Babylon. There it would stay until the time of the Lord's choosing. He is the only one who can make promises about the future and keep them. He decides; we can only yield and trust and obey. Hope for return and restoration of the temple and the city lay not in the hot air blown around by the false prophets but in the sure promise of the Lord. Those who believe have every good reason to hope.

The False Prophet Hananiah

**28 In the fifth month of that same year, the fourth year,
early in the reign of Zedekiah king of Judah, the
prophet Hananiah son of Azzur, who was from Gibeon, said to
me in the house of the LORD in the presence of the priests and
all the people: 2"This is what the LORD Almighty, the God of Israel, says: 'I will break the yoke of the king of Babylon. 3With-
in two years I will bring back to this place all the articles of the
LORD's house that Nebuchadnezzar king of Babylon removed
from here and took to Babylon. 4I will also bring back to this
place Jehoiachin son of Jehoiakim king of Judah and all the
other exiles from Judah who went to Babylon,' declares the
LORD, 'for I will break the yoke of the king of Babylon.'"**

**5Then the prophet Jeremiah replied to the prophet Hanani-
ah before the priests and all the people who were standing in
the house of the LORD. 6He said, "Amen! May the LORD do so!
May the LORD fulfill the words you have prophesied by bringing the articles of the LORD's house and all the exiles back to
this place from Babylon. 7Nevertheless, listen to what I have to
say in your hearing and in the hearing of all the people: 8From
early times the prophets who preceded you and me have
prophesied war, disaster and plague against many countries
and great kingdoms. 9But the prophet who prophesies peace**

will be recognized as one truly sent by the LORD only if his prediction comes true."

Chapter 28 is a sequel to chapter 27. Jeremiah carried his action-prophecy of the yoke to its conclusion. He expanded on the technique of those prophets who opposed him and revealed the apathy, yes, even the unbelief of the priests and the people of Judah. He pointed to a specific example of the sort of opposition he had to face. Not only did the false prophets speak without restraint, but the priests and people tolerated their lies with unseemly readiness to hear and believe them. They were so far removed from the truth that in the name of fairness and tolerance they approved of the lie.

The prophet Hananiah, whose name means "the Lord has been gracious," used the first and oldest deception in the world. He directly and boldly denied everything the Lord had said through Jeremiah. He spoke a message that would find immediate and favorable reception in the hearts of the hearers. Hananiah proclaimed that what Jeremiah had said was not true. He even went further. In two years Nebuchadnezzar would no longer bother Judah. In fact, his humiliation would be so great and his position so weak that he would have to give back all that his armies had stolen from Jerusalem.

Under public attack, with his honor and the Lord's honor at stake, Jeremiah gave a public answer. Using irony, he replied: "Nothing would make me happier than if what you say were true! May it really come to pass! Neither I nor the Lord wish the final and total destruction of Judah."

Employing Scripture and logic, Jeremiah continued: "Look at what all the prophets who came before have said. They have spoken the very opposite of what you have just said. The God of Israel does not lie or change his mind. He is faithful to his Word and promises. He does not contradict himself. His faithfulness is the very foundation of the covenant and of all we believe. His Word is consistent with itself. To accept what you say, we would have to deny the Lord. The weight of Scripture is against you. Only if and when the peace you have promised actually comes will your words deserve a hearing. But that peace will not come." Jeremiah provided both his hearers and us a profitable lesson in evaluating all teaching in the light of Scripture.

10Then the prophet Hananiah took the yoke off the neck of
the prophet Jeremiah and broke it, 11and he said before all the
people, "This is what the LORD says: 'In the same way will I break the yoke of Nebuchadnezzar king of Babylon off the neck of all the nations within two years.'" At this, the prophet Jeremiah went on his way.

12Shortly after the prophet Hananiah had broken the yoke off the neck of the prophet Jeremiah, the word of the LORD
came to Jeremiah: 13"Go and tell Hananiah, 'This is what the
LORD says: You have broken a wooden yoke, but in its place
you will get a yoke of iron. 14This is what the LORD Almighty,
the God of Israel, says: I will put an iron yoke on the necks of all these nations to make them serve Nebuchadnezzar king of Babylon, and they will serve him. I will even give him control over the wild animals.'"

15Then the prophet Jeremiah said to Hananiah the prophet, "Listen, Hananiah! The LORD has not sent you, yet you have
persuaded this nation to trust in lies. 16Therefore, this is what
the LORD says: 'I am about to remove you from the face of the earth. This very year you are going to die, because you have preached rebellion against the LORD.'"

17In the seventh month of that same year, Hananiah the prophet died.

Hananiah responded to Jeremiah's rebuke with foolish obstinacy. With his own hands he broke the yoke off Jeremiah's neck. He dismissed the prophet's words with contempt. He reaffirmed his own prophecy, at the same time calling the Lord a liar. By his actions he encouraged the priests and people of Judah to follow him. Unfortunately, his action didn't disturb any of those who saw it. They had believed his false promises or at least agreed enough to give him an equal hearing. Dumb like Israel at Mount Carmel before the prophet Elijah (1 Kings 18), they waited to see what would happen. Their indifference betrayed their own lukewarmness and unbelief.

At first Jeremiah did not respond. He walked away silently, perhaps stricken with grief at the depths to which even the priests had fallen, or perhaps because at this point the Lord had not given him anything to say. He was, however, not silent for long. God didn't want his momentary silence construed as approval. The Lord watches over his Word. No one can despise it and get away with it.

Soon a response came from the Lord. Hananiah had made it all the worse for Judah and the other nations. He had incited them to continue in their headlong rush to ruin. Instead of a mere yoke of wood, they would now wear a yoke of iron. This revolt against the Lord, the Almighty, the God of Israel, would doom them. Who can fight against God and win? Nebuchadnezzar would rule.

Hananiah had committed a grievous sin, the most grievous sin of all, and the people had done nothing but look on. They had God's clear instructions in this matter. In the book of Deuteronomy Moses had given them a very clear command about testing false prophets and about dealing with them. In the course of that instruction he had told them, "That prophet or dreamer must be put to death, because he preached rebellion against the LORD your God . . . he has tried to turn you from the way the LORD your God commanded you to follow. You must purge the evil from among you" (Deuteronomy 13:5).

Since the priests and the people had done nothing and had refused to carry out God's command, the Lord himself acted. He refused to allow the false prophet's message to go unchallenged. Hananiah had predicted that in two years the vessels of the temple and the exiles would return to Jerusalem. The Lord said that in this very year Hananiah would die. Two months later, in the seventh month, Hananiah the prophet died.

A Letter to the Exiles

**29 This is the text of the letter that the prophet Jeremiah
sent from Jerusalem to the surviving elders among the
exiles and to the priests, the prophets and all the other people
Nebuchadnezzar had carried into exile from Jerusalem to
Babylon. 2(This was after King Jehoiachin and the queen mother, the court officials and the leaders of Judah and Jerusalem,
the craftsmen and the artisans had gone into exile from
Jerusalem.) 3He entrusted the letter to Elasah son of Shaphan
and to Gemariah son of Hilkiah, whom Zedekiah king of Judah
sent to King Nebuchadnezzar in Babylon. It said:**

**4This is what the LORD Almighty, the God of Israel,
says to all those I carried into exile from Jerusalem to
Babylon: 5"Build houses and settle down; plant gardens
and eat what they produce. 6Marry and have sons and
daughters; find wives for your sons and give your daughters in marriage, so that they too may have sons and
daughters. Increase in number there; do not decrease.
7Also, seek the peace and prosperity of the city to which I
have carried you into exile. Pray to the LORD for it, because if it prospers, you too will prosper." 8Yes, this is
what the LORD Almighty, the God of Israel, says: "Do not
let the prophets and diviners among you deceive you. Do**

not listen to the dreams you encourage them to have.
9They are prophesying lies to you in my name. I have not
sent them," declares the LORD.

The time was early in the reign of Zedekiah. Zedekiah had sent a diplomatic mission to the court of Nebuchadnezzar in far-off Babylon. Jeremiah used someone in the diplomatic corps whom he could trust to deliver a written message to the leaders among the exiles. Jeremiah wrote the message so that it would carry more weight and so that there could be no doubt about its authenticity.

Doubt and uncertainty were troubling the exiles. They were not certain just how they were to feel about their exile. Most of the problem lay once again in hearts that were inclined away from the Lord. Their wavering increased as false prophets agitated them. Jeremiah later mentioned some of the confused exiles by name. How hard it was even for those who had experienced personally the fulfillment of the Lord's Word to accept what the Lord had done! They provided easy targets for the false prophets!

Jeremiah dispels any uncertainty about how they were to live in exile. Instead of hankering for a speedy return to Jerusalem, they were to accept the Lord's judgment patiently and believe his Word that it would be several generations (seventy years) before they would return. The Lord had given them a second chance. So Jeremiah exhorted them: "Settle down; make this land your home." Above all they were to make sure that their numbers did not decrease, for when the time for return came, they would need all the people they had to rebuild their desolate homeland.

Since Babylon would be their home for a long time, the Lord commanded the exiles to pray for the well-being of Babylon. That command must have been especially galling to the exiles. But the Lord wanted them to recognize that if things went well for Babylon, they too would prosper.

We are not unlike these exiles. As the people of Christ, we too are strangers and pilgrims. But again and again the apostles of the Lord urge us to pray for the good of the land in which we live. If it prospers, we too will prosper. Peace and prosperity enable us better to do his work and reach more people with the gospel.

To accept what Jeremiah advised was hard for the Jews in exile. It went against the deepest yearnings of the Israelites' hearts. How they wanted to return! With their talk and their dreams about return, they fed the fires of the imaginations of the false prophets, who continued to tell them, not the truth, but what they wanted to hear. The continuing lie made their adjustment to the new way of life all the harder.

10This is what the LORD says: "When seventy years are completed for Babylon, I will come to you and fulfill my gracious promise to bring you back to this place. 11For I know the plans I have for you," declares the LORD, "plans to prosper you and not to harm you, plans to give you hope and a future. 12Then you will call upon me and come and pray to me, and I will listen to you. 13You will seek me and find me when you seek me with all your heart. 14I will be found by you," declares the LORD, "and will bring you back from captivity. I will gather you from all the nations and places where I have banished you," declares the LORD, "and will bring you back to the place from which I carried you into exile."

15You may say, "The LORD has raised up prophets for us in Babylon," 16but this is what the LORD says about the king who sits on David's throne and all the people who remain in this city, your countrymen who did not go with you into exile—17yes, this is what the LORD Almighty says: "I will send the sword, famine and plague against them

and I will make them like poor figs that are so bad they cannot be eaten. [18]I will pursue them with the sword, famine and plague and will make them abhorrent to all the kingdoms of the earth and an object of cursing and horror, of scorn and reproach, among all the nations where I drive them. [19]For they have not listened to my words," declares the LORD, "words that I sent to them again and again by my servants the prophets. And you exiles have not listened either," declares the LORD.

Gently and with the sweetest and most beautiful of gospel promises, the Lord nourished the tender sprout of faith that he had planted in the hearts of many of the exiles. He gave them something to nourish them, rich and abundant soil in which faith could grow. He had set the time limit of their exile—seventy years; they could count on that. He reminded them that they were in exile only because he chose to lead them there. Nebuchadnezzar served merely as his instrument. When the Lord chose, he would bring them back.

By the time of their return they would have learned the lesson of exile. They would no longer trust in themselves and their cunning and power to maintain their national strength. They would have learned to seek the Lord with all their hearts and found that the Lord blesses those who lean wholly upon him. Once again they would enjoy the most intimate fellowship with the Lord.

In the face of greater disasters yet to come, crises of mind and spirit which could shake their very faith, the Lord gave them a promise designed by its very scope and sweep to show them the limitless horizons of his love. To those whose vision would be blurred by tears, to those whose hearts would be torn and convulsed with grief, to those whose bodies would be racked with pain, to those whose hopes would be shattered by disappointment, to those whose loss would leave them empty, God said: "I know the plans I have for you. . . ." The Lord of their fathers, the Lord who throughout their history had proved his love and his power to save them again and again, spoke this word. He had plans for them, plans growing out of his infinite wisdom. These plans were laid in the foundation of his eternal love for them.

He had prepared these plans with great care. His mind does not know the word "chance." He had omitted no detail because it was "too small." He had planned out what he would do, and it was all for their good. His purpose and his goal was, "not to harm you, but to prosper you." His desire was to give them a future and hope, a lively expectation of something good to come, the good he himself had promised. No matter how dark the hour, no matter how distant and obscure the object of their hope might seem, they could say as Paul later wrote, "We know that in all things God works for the good of those who love him. . . " (Romans 8:28). With determined step and sure confidence the exiles could face the future. With such faith they could make the future theirs, for God had promised them hope and a future.

The exiles' first reaction to Jeremiah's words was negative. They had listened to many prophets who told them a different story. They did not realize just how the Lord had blessed them by plucking them out of Jerusalem. Here they were safe with a second chance to build new lives and renew their relationship with the Lord. Those living in Jerusalem would pay the price of protracted disobedience. From afar the exiles would witness and feel the humiliation of Judah and Jerusalem. All the nations would laugh and mock, "Where is the God in whom you have boasted?" They would feel the shame and the loss keenly, but the Lord would keep them so that they might arise anew, a people of God once again.

**[20]Therefore, hear the word of the LORD, all you exiles
whom I have sent away from Jerusalem to Babylon. [21]This
is what the LORD Almighty, the God of Israel, says about
Ahab son of Kolaiah and Zedekiah son of Maaseiah, who
are prophesying lies to you in my name: "I will hand
them over to Nebuchadnezzar king of Babylon, and he
will put them to death before your very eyes. [22]Because of
them, all the exiles from Judah who are in Babylon will
use this curse: 'The LORD treat you like Zedekiah and
Ahab, whom the king of Babylon burned in the fire.' [23]For
they have done outrageous things in Israel; they have
committed adultery with their neighbors' wives and in
my name have spoken lies, which I did not tell them to do.
I know it and am a witness to it," declares the LORD.**

Jeremiah now supplies more detail about the false prophets who had made a name for themselves among the exiles. Their resistance to the Lord's Word knew no bounds. Despite the lash of the exile, the false prophets hardened themselves against the Lord and tried to persuade others to follow. So brazen and open was their opposition that it could not go unpunished. The Lord was not going to let them get away with this. Those who denied his Word and put themselves in his place would pay, for they fanned the fires of false hope in the hearts of the exiles. Left unchecked these fires would completely consume them. Judah's very existence was at stake.

Jeremiah singled out two false prophets by name, Ahab and Zedekiah. They had made themselves stand out. Not only had they broken the First and Second Commandments, but, puffed up with presumptuous arrogance, they had used their position and power to commit adultery with the wives of their own countrymen. Once pride like this seizes the heart, sin knows no limit or shame. Sin had utterly possessed them. "'I know it and am a witness to it,' declares the LORD."

Theirs was a fearsome judgment. For whatever reason, their activity would come to the attention of Nebuchadnezzar. Perhaps he viewed it as treason. No matter his reason, he would act with utmost severity and cruelty. He would have them burned to death, thereby giving them the punishment due them because of their rebellion against the Lord. Their names would live on among the exiles but only as a curse.

Message to Shemaiah

[24]Tell Shemaiah the Nehelamite, [25]"This is what the LORD Almighty, the God of Israel, says: You sent letters in your own name to all the people in Jerusalem, to Zephaniah son of Maaseiah the priest, and to all the other priests. You said to Zephaniah, [26]'The LORD has appointed you priest in place of Jehoiada to be in charge of the house of the LORD; you should put any madman who acts like a prophet into the stocks and neck-irons. [27]So why have you not reprimanded Jeremiah from Anathoth, who poses as a prophet among you? [28]He has sent this message to us in Babylon: It will be a long time. Therefore build houses and settle down; plant gardens and eat what they produce.' "

[29]Zephaniah the priest, however, read the letter to Jeremiah the prophet. [30]Then the word of the LORD came to Jeremiah: [31]"Send this message to all the exiles: 'This is what the LORD says about Shemaiah the Nehelamite: Because Shemaiah has prophesied to you, even though I did not send him, and has led you to believe a lie, [32]this is what the LORD says: I will surely punish Shemaiah the Nehelamite and his descendants. He will have no one left among this people, nor will he see the good things I will do for my people, declares the LORD, because he has preached rebellion against me.' "

Just when you think you have seen and heard it all, when you think it can't get any worse, it does. A man named Shemaiah stood head and shoulders above the other false prophets in his pride. On his own authority he ordered Zephaniah, a priest in Jerusalem, to act against his superior and depose the high priest, Jehoiada, and take his place. Then, as high priest, Zephaniah was to lock up Jeremiah. Shemaiah dismissed Jeremiah as a madman, a raving lunatic. By having Jeremiah locked up, Shemaiah hoped to destroy the effectiveness of the prophet and the credibility of his message.

Shemaiah picked the wrong man. Not all of the priests were unbelievers. Some heard the word of the prophet and believed what he had said. Zephaniah was one who believed, and he read the letter to Jeremiah. Shemaiah's plot failed; he had overstepped his bounds. He would be proven wrong and lose all respect among the exiles. The Lord would bring him down and punish him.

Shemaiah had preached rebellion against the Lord. The punishment for this crime was death. The Lord ordered the death of Shemaiah. He would not share in the many good things the Lord had promised to the exiles. He had shut himself out of grace. He had brought punishment not only upon himself but upon his family. In the end no one would survive him. His family would die off, and their name and place in Israel would be lost forever. Unbelief cuts anyone off from God's blessing. Unbelief would be the death of Jerusalem.

A few believed the solemn message of Jeremiah. The Lord's Word does its work and accomplishes his purposes; it does not return to him empty. But those few were not enough. The Lord could not find "the ten righteous" needed to save the city (Genesis 18). From top to bottom its residents took their stand against the Lord. In the palace, among the officials around the king and in the temple, among the priests and the prophets, unbelief ran wild. Like a deadly virus, its symptoms sometimes hidden, its progress sometimes quiet, again and again unbelief steadily progressed among the people of Judah and Jerusalem. It gripped their hearts and lives. Its impenitence choked the life out of them.

The Lord had no choice—they had not left him any choice—but to destroy this city and its people. Judah deserved punishment. The Lord would use that punishment to purge and cleanse them of every trace of the disease. Now nothing was left but a fearful waiting for judgment and for the final curtain to fall.

THE LORD REMAINS FAITHFUL

JEREMIAH 30—33

Restoration of Israel

**30 This is the word that came to Jeremiah from the LORD:
2"This is what the LORD, the God of Israel, says: 'Write
in a book all the words I have spoken to you. 3The days are
coming,' declares the LORD, 'when I will bring my people Israel and Judah back from captivity and restore them to the land I gave their forefathers to possess,' says the LORD."**

The impenitence of Judah was plain to see. She had brought the severest judgment upon herself, a judgment so great that the ears of those who heard about it would tingle. Jeremiah was about to describe the fall of the final curtain over the doomed city. In the last verses of this chapter he describes the Lord's anger as pent up and about to burst with all its fury. Once unleashed, that anger would not cease until Jerusalem lay in ruins.

Before describing the final events in Jerusalem's life, before the curtain of the Lord's anger falls on the city, Jeremiah invites the reader to pause and step aside. If we were to see that sight without the words of these next chapters, we might not be able to bear it. Who could? To enable us to bear this sorrow, the prophet first draws together in a little book of comfort some of the promises the Lord had given to him during his long prophetic ministry. One suspects that this little book of comfort was the secret of Jeremiah's strength. One can imagine how often the prophet himself retreated to his little book, to these promises. Here he drank of the stream of living water flowing from the heart of God. Here he refreshed himself, cleansing himself of his own sin and doubt, renewing his hope for the future.

The Lord had commanded him to put all the words of this book into writing. The occasion may be the same as that described in chapter 36. In both places the prophet was commanded to put his words into writing. In chapter 36 the emphasis was on the threats of the Lord. The purpose, however, seems to be different in this instance. In this chapter the emphasis lies on the promises of the Lord. Jeremiah may, however, have been presenting the same command from two different perspectives.

The words of verse three supply the theme for this little book of comfort. The words "The days are coming . . ." point to the future. They are first a promise of return from captivity into which the impenitence of the Jews would have led them. But it would be a mistake to limit God's promises only to the return from captivity. God promises much more than that. He speaks of the ultimate fulfillment of the promise he had made to Abraham centuries earlier: "Through your offspring all the nations of the earth will be blessed. . . ." In this little book the Lord shows how great and far-reaching his plan is. His love would reach out first to the people of Judah and from them to the ends of the earth.

4These are the words the LORD spoke concerning Israel and Judah: 5"This is what the LORD says:

" 'Cries of fear are heard—
terror, not peace.
6Ask and see:
Can a man bear children?
Then why do I see every strong man
with his hands on his stomach like a woman in labor,
every face turned deathly pale?
7How awful that day will be!
None will be like it.

It will be a time of trouble for Jacob,
but he will be saved out of it.
8 " 'In that day,' declares the LORD Almighty,
'I will break the yoke off their necks
and will tear off their bonds;
no longer will foreigners enslave them.
9 Instead, they will serve the LORD their God
and David their king,
whom I will raise up for them.
10 " 'So do not fear, O Jacob my servant;
do not be dismayed, O Israel,'
declares the LORD.
'I will surely save you out of a distant place,
your descendants from the land of their exile.
Jacob will again have peace and security,
and no one will make him afraid.
11 I am with you and will save you,'
declares the LORD.
'Though I completely destroy all the nations
among which I scatter you,
I will not completely destroy you.
I will discipline you but only with justice;
I will not let you go entirely unpunished.'

Before being restored to her homeland, Judah would face an unparalleled judgment, a time of indescribable terror. Judah's pain would render the strongest person weak. Jeremiah said that strong men would be bent over with their hands on their stomachs as if in the hardest labor pains. Searing pain would take all their strength and make them appear sick and anemic. Whatever strength of will or inner reserve they had would disappear. Who could imagine that any good could come of it or that anyone could escape it? Yet the Lord says, ". . . he will be saved out of it." The Lord promised to preserve a remnant of his people.

The chosen people would suffer greatly. They had to, if they were to be purged of their impenitence and their self-reliance. But the Lord would limit their punishment. He would also bring it to an end. From all the places he had scattered them he would lead them back. He would bring them back to their own land where they could again live in safety and prosperity.

When the Israelites experienced times of trial, when their spirits were crushed, when they couldn't take another step, when they couldn't even see tomorrow (to say nothing of a glorious future), then they had this word from the Lord to hold on to: "I am with you and will save you." It's as if God were saying: "Keep on repeating this promise to yourselves; the promise is true; it will enable you to stand up under all that comes."

At the center of the promise, at its very heart, stands David their king. The Lord promised to raise up David their king. In him and because of him they would dwell in safety. Now King David had been dead for four centuries. But one greater than David was coming, David's greater son, Jesus Christ. Jeremiah pointed to him because in him and upon him all the promises of God rest and are secured. In Christ all the promises of God are "yes and amen" (2 Corinthians 1:18-20). For that reason the words of this little book show us Christ directly and clearly. To see Christ is to know God, to understand that his promises are sure, and to know that all is well.

12"This is what the LORD says:

" 'Your wound is incurable,
your injury beyond healing.
13There is no one to plead your cause,
no remedy for your sore,
no healing for you.

14 All your allies have forgotten you;
they care nothing for you.
I have struck you as an enemy would
and punished you as would the cruel,
because your guilt is so great
and your sins so many.
15 Why do you cry out over your wound,
your pain that has no cure?
Because of your great guilt and many sins
I have done these things to you.

One thing would be certain. If the Israelites were saved, if they were restored, it would not happen because of any merit in them. They had no claim of any kind on God's mercy. Their rescue would rest in no way upon themselves or on anything that they were.

Two pictures illustrate that truth. First, no one was pleading their cause. The most skillful lawyers were silent. Theirs was an open and shut case in God's courtroom. Their advocates had nothing to work with. Because of Judah's great guilt and their many sins, they stood guilty under judgment. Second, their healers and physicians were powerless. The disease had gone too far. Their healing arts were of no help. "But where sin increased, grace increased all the more . . ." (Romans 5:20). What was impossible for man because of sin, God himself would accomplish.

16 " 'But all who devour you will be devoured;
all your enemies will go into exile.
Those who plunder you will be plundered;
all who make spoil of you I will despoil.
17 But I will restore you to health
and heal your wounds,'
declares the LORD,
'because you are called an outcast,
Zion for whom no one cares.'

18 "This is what the LORD says:

" 'I will restore the fortunes of Jacob's tents
and have compassion on his dwellings;
the city will be rebuilt on her ruins,
and the palace will stand in its proper place.
19 From them will come songs of thanksgiving
and the sound of rejoicing.
I will add to their numbers,
and they will not be decreased;
I will bring them honor,
and they will not be disdained.
20 Their children will be as in days of old,
and their community will be established before me;
I will punish all who oppress them.
21 Their leader will be one of their own;
their ruler will arise from among them.
I will bring him near and he will come close to me,
for who is he who will devote himself
to be close to me?'

declares the LORD.

22 " 'So you will be my people,
and I will be your God.' "

23 See, the storm of the LORD
will burst out in wrath,
a driving wind swirling down
on the heads of the wicked.
24 The fierce anger of the LORD will not turn back
until he fully accomplishes
the purposes of his heart.
In days to come
you will understand this.

The Great Physician promised to heal them. When all would have given up on them and imagined that no one can do anything—"Zion for whom no one cares," then the Lord would restore them as before. He would destroy their enemies. He would give them back their national health. They would once again be a people—his people.

Their prosperity would be secure because the one who ruled them would be one of their own. The reference here, of course, is to Christ. He would come from among them as the Lord had commanded about kings long ago (Deuteronomy 17). He would occupy a special place with the Lord. God would equip him with the gifts of the Spirit, to enable him to do his redeeming work. We remember that at Jesus' baptism the Spirit came upon him, and, as John testifies, Christ had that Spirit without measure. He would draw close to God to do his holy will. That would be his joy and delight, his food and drink. God would find pleasure in him and be pleased with him and all that he did.

A special kind of closeness is indicated in the last part of verse 21. The verse means something to the effect that the Savior would give his heart, give his all to be close to his heavenly Father. He would have a closeness to God unlike that of any other. Neither Moses nor any others of the high priests who entered the most holy place could be as close to God. The Savior would approach God, not with the blood of bulls and goats or the sacrifices of others, but with his own blood and with the freewill offering of his own life. In the garden of Gethsemane Jesus said, "My Father, if it is not possible for this cup to be taken away unless I drink it, may your will be done" (Matthew 26:42). So Christ would be close to God and have power with him for the benefit of all who look to him. As the writer to the Hebrews said, "By that will, we have been made holy through the sacrifice of the body of Jesus Christ once for all" (Hebrews 10:10).

31 **"At that time," declares the LORD, "I will be the God of all the clans of Israel, and they will be my people."**

2This is what the LORD says:

"The people who survive the sword
will find favor in the desert;
I will come to give rest to Israel."

3The LORD appeared to us in the past, saying:

"I have loved you with an everlasting love;
I have drawn you with loving-kindness.
4I will build you up again
and you will be rebuilt, O Virgin Israel.
Again you will take up your tambourines
and go out to dance with the joyful.
5Again you will plant vineyards
on the hills of Samaria;
the farmers will plant them
and enjoy their fruit.
6There will be a day when watchmen cry out
on the hills of Ephraim,
'Come, let us go up to Zion,
to the LORD our God.' "

Few chapters in all of Scripture are as rich in promise as this one. Jeremiah heaps promise upon promise, culminating in the promise of a new covenant. Many of the promises refer to Judah's return from exile, but a good many of them go far beyond that. They lift the eyes of the reader to the age of the Messiah. In verse one, for example, God says that he will be the God of all the clans of Israel. In this chapter, then, God's vision includes the rest of the Jews, "all the clans of Israel." He wants to reach them all. By including Israel, the Lord shows us that his outreach at the time of the Messiah would know no bounds.

The foundation of these promises, the basis for Judah's hope, lay in God's grace. Their certainty was rooted in the hidden depths of God's unfathomable love. That love springs deep from within his inner being. For the prophet says "in the past," at the time of Abraham, the Lord made his choice known. Out of all the people of the earth he chose the family of Abraham to be the family of the Messiah. Actually, God's choice had been made long before he appeared to Abraham. In eternity God chose them, freely and for no other reason than his love for them—"I have loved you with an everlasting love."

Such powerful love defies explanation. It chooses and makes its own the object of its choice so that no force in heaven or on earth can empty that choice of its power. "Who shall separate us from the love of Christ?" (Romans 8:35). Here is the certainty upon which our salvation, our life, and our hope rests. Our Savior came to us at our baptism, declaring to each of us, "I have loved you with an everlasting love."

God's choice led him to action, for the text continues, "I have drawn you with loving-kindness." His love is not momentary or passing. His love is steady. That steadiness flows from the faithfulness of God to keep all that he has promised and said. The word "loving-kindness" pictures the unshakable and unbreakable faithfulness of God. He will not and cannot break his word, for by that word he has pledged himself to the one he has chosen in a solemn covenant and promise. By that covenant and promise he made them his very own people. He seals and keeps that covenant by a solemn oath, an oath sworn by himself. As the apostle writes, "Let God be true, and every man a liar" (Romans 3:4).

Because of God's faithful love, his people could look forward to a time of joy. They would dance once again at the harvest, for there would be bumper crops. Not only would they plant, they would also enjoy the harvest. They would be so secure, so blessed, that they would be able to enjoy the grapes and new wine of the vineyards they would plant. Most farmers can plant, none of them can guarantee a future harvest. How fortunate God's people will be in restoration, for God would guarantee their harvest!

Along with physical blessings, the Lord promised spiritual blessings. The temple would be rebuilt. The watchmen would call to all of Israel, even those on the hills of Ephraim, to go to Mt. Zion for worship. Shortly after the death of Solomon, Israel was torn in two by civil war. The people of the north quickly fell into idolatry and discontinued their worship at the temple (1 Kings 12:25-33). The people of God were divided. Now God promised they would be reunited in the worship of the God who, because of his great mercy, loves them and delivers them.

7 This is what the LORD says:

"Sing with joy for Jacob;
shout for the foremost of the nations.
Make your praises heard, and say,
'O LORD, save your people,
the remnant of Israel.'
8 See, I will bring them from the land of the north
and gather them from the ends of the earth.
Among them will be the blind and the lame,
expectant mothers and women in labor;
a great throng will return.
9 They will come with weeping;
they will pray as I bring them back.
I will lead them beside streams of water
on a level path where they will not stumble,
because I am Israel's father,
and Ephraim is my firstborn son.

10 "Hear the word of the LORD, O nations;
proclaim it in distant coastlands:

'He who scattered Israel will gather them
and will watch over his flock like a shepherd.'
11 **For the Lord will ransom Jacob**
and redeem them from the hand of those stronger than they.
12 **They will come and shout for joy**
on the heights of Zion;
they will rejoice in the bounty of the Lord—
the grain, the new wine and the oil,
the young of the flocks and herds.
They will be like a well-watered garden,
and they will sorrow no more.
13 **Then maidens will dance and be glad,**
young men and old as well.
I will turn their mourning into gladness;
I will give them comfort and joy instead of sorrow.
14 **I will satisfy the priests with abundance,**
and my people will be filled with my bounty,"
declares the Lord.

How the Lord yearns for and loves all of his people! Because of their folly they sold themselves into slavery and exile. But he would buy them out of that slavery; he would ransom them and redeem them; only because of him would they be saved. Once again God embraces the apostates of the northern tribes, calling Ephraim "my firstborn son." He restores this son of Joseph who had received the inheritance of the firstborn when Jacob in his old age blessed the sons of Joseph (Genesis 47). He is their father. He could not abandon them or forget them. He holds out his hands to them, inviting them to return.

Such return would not be difficult, for he would make it easy. It would be so safe that even the blind and the lame would have no trouble. Water would be so abundant and the path so level that even pregnant women, yes, women in labor would manage easily. Obstacles that might have blocked their return, he would remove. What stood between them and him, the Savior would take away. By his grace he would ransom and redeem them. By his mercy he would wipe out their sins.

God wants his people to shout it to the nations, so that all might know that the Lord has remembered Israel. Salvation is in the Lord. Joy and bounty would overwhelm them. Tears would fill their eyes, but they would not be tears of grief. They would weep and cry at the amazing grace of God, which heaps abundance and blessing on every side. Their bounty would go beyond the material to the spiritual. They would possess the great and lasting riches, for they once again would be his people, and he once again would be their God.

15 This is what the LORD says:

"A voice is heard in Ramah,
mourning and great weeping,
Rachel weeping for her children
and refusing to be comforted,
because her children are no more."

16 This is what the LORD says:

"Restrain your voice from weeping
and your eyes from tears,
for your work will be rewarded,"
declares the LORD.
"They will return from the land of the enemy.
17 So there is hope for your future,"
declares the LORD.
"Your children will return to their own land.

18 "I have surely heard Ephraim's moaning:
'You disciplined me like an unruly calf,
and I have been disciplined.

Restore me, and I will return,
because you are the LORD my God.
19 After I strayed,
I repented;
after I came to understand,
I beat my breast.
I was ashamed and humiliated
because I bore the disgrace of my youth.'
20 Is not Ephraim my dear son,
the child in whom I delight?
Though I often speak against him,
I still remember him.
Therefore my heart yearns for him;
I have great compassion for him,"
declares the LORD.

21 "Set up road signs;
put up guideposts.
Take note of the highway,
the road that you take.
Return, O Virgin Israel,
return to your towns.
22 How long will you wander,
O unfaithful daughter?
The LORD will create a new thing on earth—
a woman will surround a man."

Nebuchadnezzar assembled those captives headed for exile in a temporary staging area at Ramah, about five miles north of Jerusalem. From there, seeing the holy land for the last time, they would go into exile. There in spirit at Ramah the prophet heard the voice of Rachel, mother of the race, weeping for her children. She who so desperately wanted children, who valued them and treasured them, would weep for the lost of Israel.

Matthew used this same picture to describe the sorrow because of the death of those slaughtered by Herod (Matthew 2:18). When Herod issued his cruel decree, Matthew once again heard Rachel weeping. She could not be comforted because her children were no more. So did all the survivors weep over the lost of the nation.

Then God told them not to weep as those who have no hope. They were to stop weeping. They would not be disappointed, for their hope was in the Lord. The exiles would return. "There is hope for your future. They will return from the land of the enemy." Surely this also pictures our hope. The Lord will not let go of those who believe in him. Though death takes them, it cannot hold them anymore than it held him. Though they go to the land of the enemy, for the last and greatest enemy is death, they will return. Our champion has overcome death and, because he lives, we too will live.

The Lord was and is ready to reach out to the penitent. After Judah, the mightiest tribe was Ephraim. Ephraim, the most numerous and prosperous tribe, was also the mightiest and foremost in committing idolatry. For this God punished it. In our text Ephraim repents. It likens itself to an unruly calf, who simply will not go to or stay in its stall. But Ephraim learned its lesson. It confessed its sin and repented. This repentance, as does that of every penitent, touched the heart of the Lord, for he has a heart brimming with forgiveness. Like a father who has waited long for a lost son, so the Lord yearned for Ephraim. Quickly the Lord acknowledged Ephraim as his dear son, the child of his delight. The Lord made the way back easy and clear. In God's treatment of Ephraim we witness how the Lord deals with every sinner that repents.

The Lord called Israel to return. He provided faithless Israel with a powerful incentive to return. The Lord promised to do something by his almighty and creative power that had never been seen before. "A woman will surround a man." These words do not seem to point to something all that new or different. But what a miracle it was when the woman Mary surrounded the mighty God, "You will . . . give birth to a son. . . . He will be great and will be called the Son of the Most High" (Luke 1:31,32). This new thing the Lord created was none other than his own incarnation, his coming in the flesh, by which he draws so close to us that we who believe may easily lay hold upon him and draw strength from him.

We need not reach up to him, groping to find Christ. He has come down to us. St. John writes, "That which was from the beginning, which we have heard, which we have seen with our eyes, which we have looked at and our hands have touched—this we proclaim concerning the Word of life. The life appeared; we have seen it and testify to it, and we proclaim to you the eternal life, which was with the Father and has appeared to us" (1 John 1:1,2). Daily, too, the believers, the church, the bride of Christ, surround him, gripping him in faith.

23 This is what the LORD Almighty, the God of Israel, says:
"When I bring them back from captivity, the people in the
land of Judah and in its towns will once again use these words:
'The LORD bless you, O righteous dwelling, O sacred moun-
tain.' 24 People will live together in Judah and all its towns—
farmers and those who move about with their flocks. 25 I will re-
fresh the weary and satisfy the faint."

26 At this I awoke and looked around. My sleep had been
pleasant to me.

27 "The days are coming," declares the LORD, "when I will
plant the house of Israel and the house of Judah with the off-
spring of men and of animals. 28 Just as I watched over them to
uproot and tear down, and to overthrow, destroy and bring

disaster, so I will watch over them to build and to plant," declares the LORD. [29]"In those days people will no longer say,

> **'The fathers have eaten sour grapes,**
> **and the children's teeth are set on edge.'**

[30]Instead, everyone will die for his own sin; whoever eats sour grapes—his own teeth will be set on edge.

Brought back together by the Lord and united in blessed fellowship and common worship centered at the temple, the people of Judah would enjoy an uncommon unity. City dwellers, farmers, and nomads would live together. Just as God had loved and forgiven them, they would love and forgive one another. Despite all their differences, they would be brought together in him. As he had formerly been against them, now he would be with them to build them up and keep them together. This, too, is a picture of all believers and the unity and fellowship they share in Christ.

God would take away any excuse to use a proverb that had become very popular in Israel. The exiles also used it, for Ezekiel records the same proverb in the eighteenth chapter of his prophecy. The Lord had often said that their fathers had sinned, and so they had. They had broken his covenant and turned from him times without number.

Following in their fathers' footsteps the children, too, had sinned. But not wanting to acknowledge their sin and wanting to blame the Lord, they threw this proverb in the Lord's face. With this proverb they accused God of being unjust and unfair. In effect, they said through this proverb, "Our fathers ate the sour grapes, but we have to suffer the bitter aftertaste." In other words, "Our fathers did the sinning, but we have to pay the price." Of course, the proverb was not true. It was not true in the past, and it certainly would not be true in the future.

Speaking of the future, the Lord says that his forgiveness would be so great, the opportunity for repentance so ample, the gracious invitation so compelling, that no one would have any excuse to use this proverb. If a person perishes because of unrepented sin, he has no one to blame but himself.

Jeremiah apparently received some of these promises in a vision while he was asleep. After having received them, he awoke. He says simply, "My sleep had been pleasant to me." Jeremiah probably had few nights of restful sleep, but this night had been different. It was a night filled with the promises of the Lord. Those promises brought him refreshment and peace and also quiet sleep. Such is the benefit of looking to the promises of the Lord and reflecting upon them. They do bring peace and well-being and the blessing of sleep.

31 "The time is coming," declares the LORD,
"when I will make a new covenant
with the house of Israel
and with the house of Judah.
32 It will not be like the covenant
I made with their forefathers
when I took them by the hand
to lead them out of Egypt,
because they broke my covenant,
though I was a husband to them,"
declares the LORD.
33 "This is the covenant I will make with the house of Israel
after that time," declares the LORD.
"I will put my law in their minds
and write it on their hearts.
I will be their God,
and they will be my people.
34 No longer will a man teach his neighbor,
or a man his brother, saying, 'Know the LORD,'

because they will all know me,
from the least of them to the greatest,"
declares the LORD.
"For I will forgive their wickedness
and will remember their sins no more."

From the ashes of the ruined city and temple would rise a new Jerusalem. From the disruption and shattering of the old covenant would rise a new and more glorious covenant. It is that covenant which lay at the heart of Israel's hope. It is that covenant about which Jeremiah now writes.

The way of salvation in both covenants, the old and the new is the same. A person is saved by faith in Christ. The believer under the old covenant looked ahead to Christ as the fulfillment of all the types and pictures of the old covenant. The believer under the new covenant looks back to the accomplished work of Christ. Because the Lord understands human nature and its weakness for sinning, the Lord provided many ways under the old covenant for the believer to receive forgiveness. Through many offerings and various sacrifices, the penitent was assured he had been reconciled with God.

The old covenant pointed to Christ as its fulfillment. By its very nature, then, it was temporary and passing. Many of its activities, the repeated animal sacrifices, for example, emphasized its transitory nature. The old covenant, announced at Mt. Sinai, also served to keep the Jewish people separate from the surrounding heathen, a unique nation, preserved intact by the regulations laid upon them by the old covenant. Their separation insured that they would remain a people until the promised Messiah would come.

Paul described this purpose of the old covenant in Galatians 3:23-25, "Before this faith came, we were held prisoners by the law, locked up until faith should be revealed. So the law was put in charge to lead us to Christ that we might be justified by faith. Now that faith has come, we are no longer under the supervision of the law."

The old covenant imposed many rules upon the Jews, rules they found impossible to observe. Hence the old covenant certainly proved that no one could be saved by keeping it. For that reason the Lord says of their fathers, "They broke my covenant." We would say: before the ink was dry they broke the covenant with the sin of the golden calf.

The covenant of Sinai left no doubt in the minds of those who tried to observe it, who tried to keep all its rules and regulations, that no one could be saved by observing the law. Of course, that was never the purpose of the old covenant. Paul underscored that truth when he wrote to the Galatians, "We who are Jews by birth and not 'Gentile sinners' know that a man is not justified by observing the law, but by faith in Jesus Christ. So we, too, have put our faith in Christ . . . and not by observing the law, because by observing the law no one will be justified" (2:15,16).

At the first council of the Christian Church, held at Jerusalem, Peter pleaded with his fellow Jews not to lay the burden of the regulations of the Sinaitic law upon Gentile believers. "Why do you try to test God by putting on the necks of the disciples a yoke that neither we nor our fathers have been able to bear? No! We believe it is through the grace of our Lord Jesus that we are saved, just as they are" (Acts 15:10,11).

The old covenant had several distinctive marks. It set out in the minutest detail how life was to be lived. Almost every aspect of Jewish life was regulated, from the kind of food one could eat to the touching of dead bodies. Two of the most prominent regulations were the Sabbath laws and the rite of circumcision. The old covenant required endless animal sacrifices, day after day and year after year, showing that it was not God's final word to the human race. The old covenant established a hereditary priesthood based on membership in one family (the family of Aaron) from one particular tribe (the tribe of Levi). No one else could minister at the Lord's altar. The old covenant conferred privileges on and was limited to only one people or nationality, the Jews.

In contrast, the new covenant is far different. "It will not be like the covenant I made with their forefathers. . . ." It contains no laws, rules, or regulations that have to be kept. It has no external mark. It does not limit the priesthood and the right to approach God to any one group. Peter wrote to all Christians: "You are a royal priesthood"(1 Peter 2:9). It invites all, regardless of nationality, to believe. It sets aside ethnic, racial, and other boundaries. The invitation is to all the world; Pentecost demonstrated that. The new covenant urges all to worship the Lord in spirit and in truth—"I will put my law in their minds and write it on their hearts." This is the miracle of conversion. Jesus told the Samaritan woman, "A time is coming and has now come when the true worshipers will worship the Father in spirit and truth, for they are the kind of worshipers the Father seeks" (John 4:23,24).

Under the new covenant the Holy Spirit, who has led us to call God "Abba, Father," can make our response to his will a child's glad "I can! I will!" This is something the message announced from Mt. Sinai could not do. All it could do was to force us to admit: "I must!"

God's new covenant is new also because the one who mediates it is one greater than Moses. The priests under the old covenant could offer only the blood of bulls and goats, for without the shedding of blood there is no forgiveness. But Christ, the Mediator of the new covenant, offers the supreme sacrifice. He offers the sacrifice that matters. He offers the once-and-for-all sacrifice that pleases God and removes sin and guilt. He offers himself. Freely and willingly, he sheds his blood and by the shedding of his blood takes away sin forever. By his sacrifice he opens the way to heaven. Nothing bars the way. The one who trusts him has a wide open approach to God. At Christ's triumphant words, "It is finished," the veil of the temple was torn from top to bottom, showing that a new and better way to God had been opened.

This new covenant proclaims a salvation complete, finished, and, above all, free for the asking. It is a salvation won in and through Christ. "For God so loved the world that he gave his one and only Son, that whoever believes in him shall not perish but have eternal life" (John 3:16).

There is no question how God saves. To see Christ is to know God's salvation. Hence "no longer will a man teach his neighbor . . . saying, 'know the Lord', because they will all know me." The promise is that through the proclamation about Christ those who hear and believe will know for themselves the salvation of God. The Samaritans who first heard the message about Christ from the woman at the well confessed, ". . . now we have heard for ourselves, and we know that this man really is the Savior of the world" (John 4:42).

This new covenant is sealed to us at our baptism. For in and through baptism God makes this new covenant with each of us. Through baptism he seals and gives to us his very Spirit and the forgiveness of our sins and the faith to believe it. In our baptism we hear God's continuing promise to each of us: "I will forgive their wickedness and will remember their sins no more."

But the marvel of the new covenant does not stop there. Heaping grace upon grace, in an equally wondrous and marvelous way, our Lord shares the meal of the new covenant with us. In that communion meal he draws us to himself. He gives us the supreme gift: with the bread, his body given on the cross; with the wine, his blood poured out on the cross. With these sacred gifts he gives to us the forgiveness of sins. With them he removes all doubts that might linger in our hearts. He comes to each of us personally and gives. We are sure. We belong to him. We are one with him. All that is his is ours.

We are united and bonded to him. But this bond goes much farther. Because we all eat of the one bread and are in him through faith, so we are joined to one another in the body of Christ, the church. Such is the vision Jeremiah saw. He saw the day of Christ and was glad. Such is the gift we taste and know.

35This is what the LORD says,

he who appoints the sun
to shine by day,
who decrees the moon and stars
to shine by night,
who stirs up the sea
so that its waves roar—
the LORD Almighty is his name:
36"Only if these decrees vanish from my sight,"
declares the LORD,
"will the descendants of Israel ever cease
to be a nation before me."

37This is what the LORD says:

"Only if the heavens above can be measured
and the foundations of the earth below be searched out
will I reject all the descendants of Israel
because of all they have done,"
declares the LORD.

38"The days are coming," declares the LORD, "when this city will be rebuilt for me from the Tower of Hananel to the Corner

**Gate. 39 The measuring line will stretch from there straight to
the hill of Gareb and then turn to Goah. 40 The whole valley
where dead bodies and ashes are thrown, and all the terraces
out to the Kidron Valley on the east as far as the corner of the
Horse Gate, will be holy to the LORD. The city will never again
be uprooted or demolished."**

To seal his promises the Lord takes a majestic oath. The maker of heaven and earth, the one who established the laws of nature and keeps them, gives his word. Only if nature itself and its laws, set in place by God, cease to function is there any possibility that the Lord will not keep his promise. Only if one could measure out the vast expanse of the heavens and the secrets of the earth below, is there any chance that God's promises could fail. But they cannot fail. The same omnipotence and might that made and upholds all things makes those promises secure. You can count on them.

The city will be rebuilt again to its full extent. Jeremiah takes us on a circuit of the city and all that it encloses. From the tower of Hananel in the north and all around in full circle to the Horse Gate in the east, the city will be rebuilt. The Lord gives his pledge. He will protect and keep it. In God's promise to protect the city of Jerusalem we hear his promise to protect the new Jerusalem, his church, so that no one will demolish it. Not even the gates of hell will prevail against it.

Jeremiah Buys a Field

**32 This is the word that came to Jeremiah from the LORD
in the tenth year of Zedekiah king of Judah, which was
the eighteenth year of Nebuchadnezzar. 2 The army of the king
of Babylon was then besieging Jerusalem, and Jeremiah the
prophet was confined in the courtyard of the guard in the royal palace of Judah.**

[3]Now Zedekiah king of Judah had imprisoned him there,
saying, "Why do you prophesy as you do? You say, 'This is
what the LORD says: I am about to hand this city over to the
king of Babylon, and he will capture it. [4]Zedekiah king of Judah will not escape out of the hands of the Babylonians but will
certainly be handed over to the king of Babylon, and will speak
with him face to face and see him with his own eyes. [5]He will
take Zedekiah to Babylon, where he will remain until I deal
with him, declares the LORD. If you fight against the Babylonians, you will not succeed.'"

[6]Jeremiah said, "The word of the LORD came to me:
[7]Hanamel son of Shallum your uncle is going to come to you
and say, 'Buy my field at Anathoth, because as nearest relative
it is your right and duty to buy it.'

[8]"Then, just as the LORD had said, my cousin Hanamel came
to me in the courtyard of the guard and said, 'Buy my field at
Anathoth in the territory of Benjamin. Since it is your right to
redeem it and possess it, buy it for yourself.'

"I knew that this was the word of the LORD; [9]so I bought the
field at Anathoth from my cousin Hanamel and weighed out
for him seventeen shekels of silver. [10]I signed and sealed the
deed, had it witnessed, and weighed out the silver on the scales.
[11]I took the deed of purchase—the sealed copy containing the
terms and conditions, as well as the unsealed copy—[12]and I
gave this deed to Baruch son of Neriah, the son of Mahseiah, in
the presence of my cousin Hanamel and of the witnesses who
had signed the deed and of all the Jews sitting in the courtyard
of the guard.

[13]"In their presence I gave Baruch these instructions: [14]'This
is what the LORD Almighty, the God of Israel, says: Take these
documents, both the sealed and unsealed copies of the deed of
purchase, and put them in a clay jar so they will last a long
time. [15]For this is what the LORD Almighty, the God of Israel,
says: Houses, fields and vineyards will again be bought in this
land.'

The time is the year 587 B.C., sometime during the final siege of Jerusalem. The Babylonians had had the city under siege for about a year and a half. Except for a couple of other powerful fortresses and Jerusalem, all the cities of Judah had surrendered to Nebuchadnezzar. Because Jeremiah had repeatedly told the king that his only hope lay in surrender, and because many of the king's advisors considered such advice and preaching treasonous, the king had placed Jeremiah under house arrest and had confined him to the courtyard of the guard in the royal palace.

During this period the Egyptians had advanced with their forces from the south in the hope of dislodging Nebuchadnezzar from his position in Palestine. Because of the Egyptian advance, the Babylonians temporarily lifted the siege of Jerusalem. This strategic and momentary shift of Babylonian forces gave the people of Judah the false hope that now Nebuchadnezzar would withdraw permanently back to the north. It also provided the Lord with the opportunity to teach Judah yet another object lesson.

Jeremiah's chance to buy land became the occasion for the lesson. The Lord revealed to Jeremiah that his cousin Hanamel was going to offer him the right to redeem some land. When the Lord had distributed the land of Israel to the people through Joshua, he intended that each family and tribe retain its inheritance, the land it had received. To enable his people to accomplish this purpose, the Lord provided laws (Leviticus 25:24ff; 27) that gave a family the right of first option on any piece of family or tribal land that was in danger of being sold outside the family.

It was such an option to buy that Hanamel would offer Jeremiah. Such an offer in the face of the imminent surrender of Jerusalem seemed completely foolish. When the Babylonians took over the land, a title deed to a piece of property would be virtually worthless to the buyer. It would be as though someone offered to sell you a piece of land recently covered by a lava flow. Jeremiah would not have seriously considered the offer unless he had received this direct command from the Lord.

Just as the Lord had said, Hanamel arrived with his offer. Jeremiah agreed to buy the land and settled on a purchase price of seventeen shekels of silver. (The shekel was a measure of weight amounting to a little more than a third of an ounce.)

Following the practice of the day, Jeremiah had a scribe, in this case his personal secretary Baruch, write up two deeds of purchase. One was a working copy for reference (unsealed) and the other the official copy (sealed). Both parties signed and sealed the deeds in the presence of witnesses, closing the deal. Jeremiah also commanded Baruch to place both copies into a clay jar and seal it. This practice was followed to preserve the documents for a long period of time. The famous Dead Sea Scrolls, discovered in the 1950's, had been preserved intact in clay jars in Palestine for two thousand years.

Jeremiah now made the Lord's application. His real estate purchase, made while the armies of Babylon were besieging Jerusalem, was not foolish. Even though the city would fall to the Babylonians, in the future the Jews would return to this land. Houses and other property would once again be bought and sold. A title deed would once again be valuable. Jeremiah's land purchase was a visible pledge by the Lord, an advance on his promise of restoration.

16"After I had given the deed of purchase to Baruch son of Neriah, I prayed to the LORD:

> **17"Ah, Sovereign LORD, you have made the heavens and the earth by your great power and outstretched arm. Nothing is too hard for you. 18You show love to thousands**

**but bring the punishment for the fathers' sins into the
laps of their children after them. O great and powerful
God, whose name is the LORD Almighty, [19]great are your
purposes and mighty are your deeds. Your eyes are open
to all the ways of men; you reward everyone according to
his conduct and as his deeds deserve. [20]You performed
miraculous signs and wonders in Egypt and have continued them to this day, both in Israel and among all
mankind, and have gained the renown that is still yours.
[21]You brought your people Israel out of Egypt with signs
and wonders, by a mighty hand and an outstretched arm
and with great terror. [22]You gave them this land you had
sworn to give their forefathers, a land flowing with milk
and honey. [23]They came in and took possession of it, but
they did not obey you or follow your law; they did not do
what you commanded them to do. So you brought all this
disaster upon them.**

**[24]"See how the siege ramps are built up to take the city.
Because of the sword, famine and plague, the city will be
handed over to the Babylonians who are attacking it.
What you said has happened, as you now see. [25]And
though the city will be handed over to the Babylonians,
you, O Sovereign LORD, say to me, 'Buy the field with silver and have the transaction witnessed.'"**

Immediately after Baruch left to put the deeds in a safe place, Jeremiah launched into a long prayer. This prayer was prayed out loud in public. Jeremiah intended that those present should hear it. It was for their benefit that he prayed it. In this prayer he addressed the doubts in the hearts of those who had witnessed his land purchase. He wanted to confirm the truth of what he had prophesied and to lead them to believe the promise the Lord had given. What the Lord had just promised seemed utterly improbable, yes, impossible. What Jeremiah had done seemed to be the act of a fool.

Jeremiah's prayer followed the pattern of great Old Testament prayers. He used two truths about God to build faith in his hearers. First, he confessed that God, their God, the God of Israel, is *all powerful.* "Nothing is too hard for you." He cited some examples of God's power. The Lord is the creator of heaven and earth. The Lord had delivered Israel from Egypt with an impressive display of power—how easily they could recite the story of their deliverance! He had broken open the way into the promised land and enabled them to take it. Again and again throughout their history he had delivered them by astounding miracles. Their national history was a history of miracles.

The second truth Jeremiah emphasized about the character of God was that he keeps his word. The God of Israel is a *faithful* God. It is the very nature of God to act justly and to do what he has promised to do. Again their national history was a chronicle of the faithfulness of God. He had promised Abraham that his descendants would inherit the land, and they did. He had promised Abraham that he would deliver his descendants from the land of bondage, and he did. He had told them that if they disobeyed him and persisted in impenitence, he would punish them, and he was now doing that. Through all of his long dealings with his ancient people God had kept his every promise and his every threat.

Now their God, the God of Israel, whom they knew to be almighty and faithful, had given them another promise. He had promised that even though the Babylonians would capture Jerusalem and devastate it and take its inhabitants into exile, they would return to their homeland and once again buy and sell houses, fields, and vineyards. What he had promised he could do. What he had promised he would do.

26Then the word of the LORD came to Jeremiah: 27"I am the LORD, the God of all mankind. Is anything too hard for me?

[28]Therefore, this is what the LORD says: I am about to hand this
city over to the Babylonians and to Nebuchadnezzar king of
Babylon, who will capture it. [29]The Babylonians who are attacking this city will come in and set it on fire; they will burn it
down, along with the houses where the people provoked me to
anger by burning incense on the roofs to Baal and by pouring
out drink offerings to other gods.
[30]"The people of Israel and Judah have done nothing but
evil in my sight from their youth; indeed, the people of Israel
have done nothing but provoke me with what their hands
have made, declares the LORD. [31]From the day it was built until now, this city has so aroused my anger and wrath that I
must remove it from my sight. [32]The people of Israel and Judah have provoked me by all the evil they have done—they,
their kings and officials, their priests and prophets, the men
of Judah and the people of Jerusalem. [33]They turned their
backs to me and not their faces; though I taught them again
and again, they would not listen or respond to discipline.
[34]They set up their abominable idols in the house that bears
my Name and defiled it. [35]They built high places for Baal in
the Valley of Ben Hinnom to sacrifice their sons and daughters to Molech, though I never commanded, nor did it enter
my mind, that they should do such a detestable thing and so
make Judah sin.
[36]"You are saying about this city, 'By the sword, famine and
plague it will be handed over to the king of Babylon'; but this
is what the LORD, the God of Israel, says: [37]I will surely gather
them from all the lands where I banish them in my furious
anger and great wrath; I will bring them back to this place and
let them live in safety. [38]They will be my people, and I will be
their God. [39]I will give them singleness of heart and action, so
that they will always fear me for their own good and the good
of their children after them. [40]I will make an everlasting
covenant with them: I will never stop doing good to them, and
I will inspire them to fear me, so that they will never turn away

from me. 41 I will rejoice in doing them good and will assuredly
plant them in this land with all my heart and soul.
42 "This is what the LORD says: As I have brought all this
great calamity on this people, so I will give them all the pros-
perity I have promised them. 43 Once more fields will be bought
in this land of which you say, 'It is a desolate waste, without
men or animals, for it has been handed over to the Babyloni-
ans.' 44 Fields will be bought for silver, and deeds will be signed,
sealed and witnessed in the territory of Benjamin, in the vil-
lages around Jerusalem, in the towns of Judah and in the towns
of the hill country, of the western foothills and of the Negev, be-
cause I will restore their fortunes, declares the LORD."

The Lord confirmed the promises he had made. To remove any remaining doubts in the hearts of the hearers, he asked, "Is anything too hard for me?" As Jesus said, "With man this is impossible, but with God all things are possible" (Matthew 19:26). All things are possible. Let that be the answer to any doubts you may have.

The Lord now summarized much of what he had said before through the prophet; what is important we repeat. Some may not listen, some may not want to listen, but this message bears repeating.

The city of Jerusalem would surely fall to the Babylonians. It would fall because of the impenitence of its citizens and for no other reason. Their evil had testified against them. They had committed every kind of perversion, from Baal worship to human sacrifice. All of them from top to bottom had joined in the sinning. Despite all the Lord's efforts to bring them around, they had turned their faces away. For these reasons and these reasons alone they were about to suffer destruction.

They deserved nothing and had no right to have any hope for the future, but the God of Israel would not desert them. In his mercy and by his power, their God would not abandon them. In his grace he promised to bring them back from their land of exile. He would be faithful to his promises. There was still more. By his working on their hearts he would make them into a new people ready to fear him and love one another. He would plant them in this land. In its farthest reaches they would settle down and buy and sell, "because I will restore their fortunes."

At first the Lord's command to buy land dumbfounded Jeremiah. Would the Lord have revealed such a thing? Once he knew it was the Lord's Word, he believed and obeyed. It is the same for us. What God does or allows in our lives sometimes seems senseless, even foolish and hopeless. It defies our logic; it disappoints our dreams; it shatters our expectations. It may lead us to challenge him and even complain against him. We may not see the reason for God's actions or understand them, but we know that it is our God and Savior who is in control. By faith we have come to understand him. By faith we come to accept what he does.

When the Lord commanded Peter to let down the nets, that command made no sense whatever to Peter (Luke 5:1-11), but he said to Jesus, "Because you say so. . . ." In the end that is the answer of faith, "Because you say so. . . ." That answer comes from a faith that has learned the greatness of God. That answer comes from a faith that knows the love of God has no limits. Faith rests in that love and power.

Promise of Restoration

**33 While Jeremiah was still confined in the courtyard of
the guard, the word of the LORD came to him a second
time: 2"This is what the LORD says, he who made the earth, the
LORD who formed it and established it—the LORD is his name:**

3“Call to me and I will answer you and tell you great and unsearchable things you do not know.’ 4For this is what the LORD,
the God of Israel, says about the houses in this city and the
royal palaces of Judah that have been torn down to be used
against the siege ramps and the sword 5in the fight with the
Babylonians: ‘They will be filled with the dead bodies of the
men I will slay in my anger and wrath. I will hide my face from
this city because of all its wickedness.

6“ ‘Nevertheless, I will bring health and healing to it; I will
heal my people and will let them enjoy abundant peace and security. 7I will bring Judah and Israel back from captivity and
will rebuild them as they were before. 8I will cleanse them from
all the sin they have committed against me and will forgive all
their sins of rebellion against me. 9Then this city will bring me
renown, joy, praise and honor before all nations on earth that
hear of all the good things I do for it; and they will be in awe
and will tremble at the abundant prosperity and peace I provide
for it.’

10“This is what the LORD says: ‘You say about this place, “It
is a desolate waste, without men or animals.” Yet in the towns
of Judah and the streets of Jerusalem that are deserted, inhabited by neither men nor animals, there will be heard once more
11the sounds of joy and gladness, the voices of bride and bridegroom, and the voices of those who bring thank offerings to the
house of the LORD, saying,

> “Give thanks to the Lord Almighty,
> for the LORD is good;
> his love endures forever.”

For I will restore the fortunes of the land as they were before,’ says the LORD.

12“This is what the LORD Almighty says: ‘In this place, desolate and without men or animals—in all its towns there will
again be pastures for shepherds to rest their flocks. 13In the
towns of the hill country, of the western foothills and of the
Negev, in the territory of Benjamin, in the villages around

Jerusalem and in the towns of Judah, flocks will again pass under the hand of the one who counts them,' says the LORD.

Jeremiah was still under house arrest in the royal palace. This incident followed shortly after he purchased the land from his cousin Hanamel. This second word from the Lord confirmed all that the Lord had promised at that time. The double revelation serves to stress the Lord's determination to keep his word, for as Joseph said to Pharaoh, ". . . the matter has been firmly decided by God. . ." (Genesis 41:32). Through this chapter the Lord used the most powerful metaphors to assure Judah of his unshakable resolve and his unwavering faithfulness in keeping his promises.

In verse three God actually invited them to search out, if they could, the greatness of his love. If they would pray for answers, he would reveal to them the plans created by his love. They would see possibilities and realities they had not even thought of. They would experience, firsthand, miracles beyond anything they could have imagined, as Jesus promised his disciples, "You shall see greater things than that" (John 1:50). For "no eye has seen, no ear has heard, no mind has conceived what God has prepared for those who love him" (1 Corinthians 2:9). "Oh, the depth of the riches of the wisdom and knowledge of God! How unsearchable his judgments, and his paths beyond tracing out!" (Romans 11:33).

These promises have found fulfillment in us. We know God's miracles and wonders, for he has revealed them to us by his Spirit and given us the mind of Christ. Our life is a daily exploration and experience of "how wide and long and deep is the love of Christ" (Ephesians 3:18). Our reward is in increasing measure "to know this love that surpasses knowledge" (Ephesians 3:19). Our confidence is in living and praying "to him who is able to do immeasurably more than all we ask or imagine" (Ephesians 3:20). We are the heirs of those who first heard this promise.

Though the Lord had given his pledged word, many locked silent unbelief in their hearts. The same people who did not believe that the Babylonians would attack Jerusalem according to the Lord's Word now doubted what the Lord promised about the future of the city. The skeptics said that it couldn't happen, that it wouldn't happen, that it was all over. They needed only to gaze at the utter desolation of the city and the surrounding territories. The defenders had used everything, every available piece of wood and stone, to resist the assault of the towering siege machines. How sorely they had underestimated the Lord! How little they knew him!

"Nevertheless . . ." The greater the desolation, the more convincing the love and might of God. What is impossible and undreamed of among men, he would accomplish. He promised, "I will restore the city and the whole country." Throngs would come to the new temple with thank offerings. They would enjoy abundance. As they approached they would sing the words of the great Hallel—the words of Psalm 118. These words were regularly sung as part of celebrations at the great festivals of the Jewish church. Flocks and shepherds would appear everywhere.

This restoration would be an act so mighty that the nations would be overawed. People would tremble with excitement at the great things God can do for his people, and they would give God the glory for what by grace he was willing to do. This vision leads us to the time of Christ and the New Testament age. For throughout the church year, the nations celebrate the wonders of God in Christ.

14" 'The days are coming,' declares the LORD, 'when I will
fulfill the gracious promise I made to the house of Israel and to
the house of Judah.

> **15 " 'In those days and at that time**
> **I will make a righteous Branch sprout**
> **from David's line;**
> **he will do what is just and right in the land.**
> **16 In those days Judah will be saved**
> **and Jerusalem will live in safety.**
> **This is the name by which it will be called:**
> **The LORD Our Righteousness.'**

17For this is what the LORD says: 'David will never fail to
have a man to sit on the throne of the house of Israel, 18nor will
the priests, who are Levites, ever fail to have a man to stand
before me continually to offer burnt offerings, to burn grain
offerings and to present sacrifices.' "

Jeremiah repeated the promise the Lord had revealed to him earlier in his ministry (chapter 23). The real marvel and wonder of God is Christ. The final words of this chapter speak about Christ and the age to follow. Jeremiah describes more fully the nature of the Righteous Branch which the Lord would raise up for David. David was dead; the Lord had written Jehoiachin off "as childless," yet he promised that one from David's line would sit eternally on the throne, ruling an eternal kingdom. To be a descendant of David he must be a man, a Jew. To rule an eternal kingdom, he must be more than a man. Since there is only one who has eternal rule, and that is God, he must also be God.

The Lord added further information about this "sprout from David's line." He would not only be a king but also a priest. For the Lord promised that the Levites would always have one to serve as priest before him. He could not be as other high priests for they served only until they died. His service would have to extend beyond the temple and its worship, for that worship would be interrupted and finally cease altogether. He would have to be the fulfillment of the promise made through David, "You are a priest forever, in the order of Melchizedek" (Psalm 110:4). (The reader may wish to read Hebrews chapters 7—9 for a fuller explanation of Jesus' high priesthood.) Christ is a priest in an extraordinary way, for the sacrifice he offered was himself, hence, he is "The Lord Our Righteousness."

What comfort these words convey! We have an eternal king whose eternal concern and rule has us as a central interest. He watches over us in all our ways to keep us safe for himself. We have a priest who has a permanent priesthood, sealed by his own blood. "Therefore he is able to save completely those who come to God through him, because he always lives to intercede for them" (Hebrews 7:25). We have the confidence that "if anybody does sin, we have one who speaks to the Father in our defense—Jesus Christ, the Righteous One. He is the atoning sacrifice for our sins, and not only for ours but also for the sins of the whole world" (1 John 2:1,2).

19The word of the LORD came to Jeremiah: 20"This is what
the LORD says: 'If you can break my covenant with the day
and my covenant with the night, so that day and night no
longer come at their appointed time, 21then my covenant with
David my servant—and my covenant with the Levites who are
priests ministering before me—can be broken and David will
no longer have a descendant to reign on his throne. 22I will
make the descendants of David my servant and the Levites
who minister before me as countless as the stars of the sky and
as measureless as the sand on the seashore.' "

23The word of the LORD came to Jeremiah: 24"Have you not
noticed that these people are saying, 'The LORD has rejected

the two kingdoms he chose'? So they despise my people and no longer regard them as a nation. [25]This is what the LORD says: 'If I have not established my covenant with day and night and the fixed laws of heaven and earth, [26]then I will reject the descendants of Jacob and David my servant and will not choose one of his sons to rule over the descendants of Abraham, Isaac and Jacob. For I will restore their fortunes and have compassion on them.' "

Jeremiah's little book of comfort or consolation ends with a glorious vision. Before Jeremiah's eyes the Lord stretched out the panorama of the whole New Testament age. He outlined the final dimensions of the new covenant. This eternal king and priest from David's line would not rule alone. His kingdom and priesthood would embrace a host of others. So the promise God made to Abraham would be fulfilled, "I will surely bless you and make your descendants as numerous as the stars in the sky and as the sand on the seashore" (Genesis 22:17).

All who believe in Christ are the descendants of Abraham. All who believe are kings, for they rule with Christ. All who believe are priests, for they approach God covered with the righteousness of Christ. All are priests, for they offer sacrifices, the sacrifices of lips and lives made new and perfect in the blood of the Lamb.

Some doubted that God could or would do what he promised. They had given up on Israel. God here challenged them. He gave absolute assurance of his intent. Only if day and night ceased, only if the fixed laws of nature were broken, was there any possibility that the Lord would fail to keep his word.

Day and night and the fixed laws of nature have not ceased. The Lord has kept his every word. His promise will not fail because it is rooted in love. His love compels him. God reminded his people that in free love, that love which lies at the center of his being, he chose Abraham, Isaac, and Jacob. Because of that love he made an oath with them that in their descendant, Jesus Christ, all the nations of the earth would be blessed. For him to break that oath, he would have had to deny the love which expresses all that he is. If he ceased loving, he would cease to be God. Then everything would dissolve into nothingness. But this has not happened, for God is love.

With this promise Jeremiah closes the little book of comfort. Certain of the love of God and of the promises he made, Jeremiah was now able to face the fall of Jerusalem. Though this event would bring about unparalleled grief and despair, he was confident of what the Lord had promised. With those promises in his pocket, he was ready to face whatever the future held for him. For "we are more than conquerors through him who loved us" (Romans 8:37).

JUDAH'S IMPENITENCE FINALLY BRINGS DOWN THE LORD'S JUDGMENT

JEREMIAH 34—39

Warning to Zedekiah

**34 While Nebuchadnezzar king of Babylon and all his
army and all the kingdoms and peoples in the empire
he ruled were fighting against Jerusalem and all its surrounding towns, this word came to Jeremiah from the LORD: 2"This
is what the LORD, the God of Israel, says: Go to Zedekiah king
of Judah and tell him, 'This is what the LORD says: I am about
to hand this city over to the king of Babylon, and he will burn
it down. 3You will not escape from his grasp but will surely be
captured and handed over to him. You will see the king of
Babylon with your own eyes, and he will speak with you face to
face. And you will go to Babylon.**

**4" 'Yet hear the promise of the LORD, O Zedekiah king of
Judah. This is what the LORD says concerning you: You will
not die by the sword; 5you will die peacefully. As people made
a funeral fire in honor of your fathers, the former kings who
preceded you, so they will make a fire in your honor and
lament, "Alas, O master!" I myself make this promise, declares the LORD.' "**

**6Then Jeremiah the prophet told all this to Zedekiah king of
Judah, in Jerusalem, 7while the army of the king of Babylon
was fighting against Jerusalem and the other cities of Judah
that were still holding out—Lachish and Azekah. These were
the only fortified cities left in Judah.**

Jeremiah gives us further insight into the last days of Jerusalem, the days leading up to the inevitable destruction of the city. To the very end, even though the Lord's every word had proved true, the people and the rulers of Judah still refused to obey the Lord's Word. Their persistent disobedience resulted in the fall of Jerusalem.

Nebuchadnezzar had returned from forcing the Egyptians to turn back. He had ended the temporary reprieve which the Egyptian advance had given Jerusalem and Judah. Once again he had tightened his grip on the city just as the Lord had predicted he would. Only two other fortified cities still held out. Lachish, which was twenty-eight miles to the southwest of Jerusalem, remained free. It was a large and impressive fortress which held the key to the defense of the south and the way from Egypt. It was to be totally destroyed before the fall of Jerusalem. Another smaller fortress, Azekah, near the king's highway about eighteen miles west of Jerusalem, was also holding out. But it too would fall shortly before the might of the Babylonians.

Zedekiah's kingdom was now reduced to three cities, and once more Jeremiah was sent to tell Zedekiah that he would be captured. According to the Lord's command, Jeremiah revealed a little more about Zedekiah's future. He would not be executed after his capture. He would die peacefully and with honor. Even in exile, his subjects would mourn him with the funeral rites suitable to his position. To assure him of this future, the Lord sealed it with a solemn oath.

Whether Zedekiah looked upon this promise as good or bad we do not know. Perhaps the Lord gave the promise to encourage Zedekiah to act with more decisiveness and follow the Lord's Word. Zedekiah was wholly inconsistent in his actions. He displayed weakness, wavering from one position to another. Whoever happened to be near him at the time seemed to have influenced his decisions. In the end he lacked the courage or strength to do what was right in the Lord's eyes.

Freedom for Slaves

**8The word came to Jeremiah from the LORD after King
Zedekiah had made a covenant with all the people in Jerusalem to proclaim freedom for the slaves. 9Everyone was to free
his Hebrew slaves, both male and female; no one was to hold a
fellow Jew in bondage. 10So all the officials and people who entered into this covenant agreed that they would free their male
and female slaves and no longer hold them in bondage. They
agreed, and set them free. 11But afterward they changed their
minds and took back the slaves they had freed and enslaved
them again.**

**12Then the word of the LORD came to Jeremiah: 13"This is
what the LORD, the God of Israel, says: I made a covenant with
your forefathers when I brought them out of Egypt, out of the
land of slavery. I said, 14'Every seventh year each of you must
free any fellow Hebrew who has sold himself to you. After he
has served you six years, you must let him go free.' Your
fathers, however, did not listen to me or pay attention to me.
15Recently you repented and did what is right in my sight: Each
of you proclaimed freedom to his countrymen. You even made
a covenant before me in the house that bears my Name. 16But
now you have turned around and profaned my name; each of
you has taken back the male and female slaves you had set free
to go where they wished. You have forced them to become your
slaves again.**

During the time Nebuchadnezzar had broken off the siege to meet the Egyptian threat, Zedekiah had shown some positive leadership. He had tried to lead the rich slaveholders of Jerusalem in a God-pleasing direction. He had persuaded them to free their Hebrew slaves, that is, their fellow countrymen who had voluntarily sold themselves into slavery. In a very solemn and impressive ceremony they had made a covenant and promise in the temple of the Lord.

Part of the covenant ceremony required the parties to the agreement to walk between animals which had been cut in two. In effect, this practice sealed the agreement with the most solemn of oaths and was a sign of the parties' intent to keep the covenant. Zedekiah recognized that this action would be God-pleasing and would show the Lord that the people of Judah were making an effort to keep the law. He hoped that this would bring a favorable response from the Lord.

The emancipation proclaimed by Zedekiah was long overdue. When God had given the law from Mt. Sinai, he had written into it a provision by which he had commanded his people to free their brothers and sisters who had been forced to sell themselves into slavery. Every seven years (the Sabbath year) and every fifty years (the year of Jubilee) God had commanded such an emancipation to take place (Exodus 21:2, Leviticus 25:39-43, and Deuteronomy 15:12-15).

The reason God gave for this practice was that the whole nation had been slaves in Egypt. God had freed them from that slavery. In truth they all belonged to him. They were, therefore, not to enslave their Israelite brothers and sisters permanently. They were further to keep these commands of the law with loving hearts, for love is the fulfillment of the law. Down through the centuries these commands about slavery had rarely been observed. The Lord praised Zedekiah and the people for following this commandment of his law.

17"Therefore, this is what the LORD says: You have not obeyed me; you have not proclaimed freedom for your fellow countrymen. So I now proclaim 'freedom' for you, declares the LORD—'freedom' to fall by the sword, plague and famine. I will make you abhorrent to all the kingdoms of the earth. 18The men who have violated my covenant and have not fulfilled the terms of the covenant they made before me, I will treat like the calf they cut in two and then walked between its pieces. 19The

leaders of Judah and Jerusalem, the court officials, the priests and all the people of the land who walked between the pieces of the calf, [20]I will hand over to their enemies who seek their lives. Their dead bodies will become food for the birds of the air and the beasts of the earth.

[21]"I will hand Zedekiah king of Judah and his officials over to their enemies who seek their lives, to the army of the king of Babylon, which has withdrawn from you. [22]I am going to give the order, declares the LORD, and I will bring them back to this city. They will fight against it, take it and burn it down. And I will lay waste the towns of Judah so no one can live there."

Very shortly after their grand gesture of freeing their slaves, the slave owners changed their minds. Without protest or any attempt to stop them, King Zedekiah went along with the reversal. Greed blinded them to their own long-term self interest. Perhaps they believed that the siege had been permanently broken and feared that they would suffer great personal financial loss if they permitted their slaves to remain free. They forgot that if Nebuchadnezzar returned and took the city, their ownership of slaves was meaningless. They themselves would be slaves.

The Lord was angry. Though he had delighted in their action of freeing their slaves, he had not compelled them to take it. Not only had they taken the action, but they also had made a great show of it. They had used the temple and a solemn oath to seal their action. Now they had broken the law and their own solemn word. They had once again revealed the real attitude of their hearts. They had proclaimed freedom. The Lord would give it to them—freedom to fall by the sword, plague, and famine. The Lord made it clear that he was in charge. As the real general in command, he issued the order for Nebuchadnezzar to return and encircle the city. By its impenitence the city had sealed its own destruction.

The Recabites

**35 This is the word that came to Jeremiah from the LORD
during the reign of Jehoiakim son of Josiah king of Judah: 2"Go to the Recabite family and invite them to come to
one of the side rooms of the house of the LORD and give them
wine to drink."**

**3So I went to get Jaazaniah son of Jeremiah, the son of
Habazziniah, and his brothers and all his sons—the whole
family of the Recabites. 4I brought them into the house of the
LORD, into the room of the sons of Hanan son of Igdaliah the
man of God. It was next to the room of the officials, which was
over that of Maaseiah son of Shallum the doorkeeper. 5Then I
set bowls full of wine and some cups before the men of the Recabite family and said to them, "Drink some wine."**

**6But they replied, "We do not drink wine, because our fore-
father Jonadab son of Recab gave us this command: 'Neither
you nor your descendants must ever drink wine. 7Also you
must never build houses, sow seed or plant vineyards; you
must never have any of these things, but must always live in
tents. Then you will live a long time in the land where you are
nomads.' 8We have obeyed everything our forefather Jonadab
son of Recab commanded us. Neither we nor our wives nor our
sons and daughters have ever drunk wine 9or built houses to
live in or had vineyards, fields or crops. 10We have lived in
tents and have fully obeyed everything our forefather Jonadab
commanded us. 11But when Nebuchadnezzar king of Babylon
invaded this land, we said, 'Come, we must go to Jerusalem to
escape the Babylonian and Aramean armies.' So we have remained in Jerusalem."**

Jeremiah now takes us back to something that happened during the reign of Jehoiakim (609–597 B.C.). After his victory at Carchemish over the Egyptians and their allies (one of whom was Judah), Nebuchadnezzar attacked Judah and Jerusalem. This attack forced the Recabite family to take refuge in the city. Jeremiah used the family history of the Recabites to teach the people of Judah still another object lesson. He showed his readers the attitude the people of Judah had toward the Word of God, an attitude that continued right up to the end of Jerusalem's existence. Nobody paid any attention to the Word. Many, in fact, were openly disrespectful and hostile toward it. Their open unbelief, including their refusal to listen to God's Word, was the chief reason for the fall of the city.

The Recabites were an old and prominent family in the land of Israel. Jonadab, the ancestor mentioned in this chapter, had allied himself with Jehu in overthrowing wicked King Ahab (2 Kings 10:15-17). This suggests that the family was important.

To enable them to pursue their trade and to keep its secrets, their ancestor Jonadab had laid down some strict family traditions. They were to stay away from wine and other alcoholic beverages. They were to live in tents and not to engage in any agricultural activity. These traditions had served the family well. For over two hundred years they had kept unbroken the traditions given them by Jonadab.

Jeremiah was now instructed to give them a public test. He invited all the male members of the Recabite family to a room off the courtyard of the temple. Such rooms provided a place of retreat for those who came to offer sacrifice and worship. In the presence of witnesses he offered the Recabites wine and urged them drink it. They refused because to drink wine would have broken the wishes of their ancestor. For their faithfulness and the example it supplied, the Lord promised the continuation of their family line even through the difficult times which lay ahead (verses 18,19).

12 Then the word of the LORD came to Jeremiah, saying:
13 "This is what the LORD Almighty, the God of Israel, says: Go
and tell the men of Judah and the people of Jerusalem, 'Will
you not learn a lesson and obey my words?' declares the LORD.
14 "Jonadab son of Recab ordered his sons not to drink wine and
this command has been kept. To this day they do not drink
wine, because they obey their forefather's command. But I
have spoken to you again and again, yet you have not obeyed
me. 15 Again and again I sent all my servants the prophets to
you. They said, "Each of you must turn from your wicked
ways and reform your actions; do not follow other gods to
serve them. Then you will live in the land I have given to you
and your fathers." But you have not paid attention or listened
to me. 16 The descendants of Jonadab son of Recab have carried
out the command their forefather gave them, but these people
have not obeyed me.'

17 "Therefore, this is what the LORD God Almighty, the God
of Israel, says: 'Listen! I am going to bring on Judah and on
everyone living in Jerusalem every disaster I pronounced
against them. I spoke to them, but they did not listen; I called
to them, but they did not answer.'"

18 Then Jeremiah said to the family of the Recabites, "This is
what the LORD Almighty, the God of Israel, says: 'You have
obeyed the command of your forefather Jonadab and have followed all his instructions and have done everything he ordered.' 19 Therefore, this is what the LORD Almighty, the God of
Israel, says: 'Jonadab son of Recab will never fail to have a
man to serve me.'"

Jeremiah now draws a conclusion. He argues from the lesser to the greater: If a family holds fast to a tradition or command laid down by a human father, how much more shouldn't God's people respect the wishes of their heavenly Father? For which is greater: the word of a man or the Word of the living God? The answer was obvious. The family of

Jonadab had kept the tradition of their forefather for over two hundred years. They could not be persuaded to disregard it. They remained faithful to the wishes of their ancestor, and their obedience had proved to be a blessing for them.

Through his prophets God had spoken continually to the people of Judah and Jerusalem. He was the Lord Almighty, their God and Father, their Savior. He had made a solemn covenant with them; that was his Word to them, his teaching, his expressed will. He had called upon them to repent. He had promised them many blessings—if only they listened.

What the Lord had to say was of far greater importance than what anyone else said. Surely God's people would listen to him more readily than the Recabites listened to their forefather. But no! The people of Judah and Jerusalem thought less of the Lord's Word than the Recabites did of their forefather's. The people of Judah and Jerusalem had rejected the divine Word and disobeyed it. As a result, they could not expect any of the blessings which faithfulness might have brought them, but only the disaster the Lord had threatened to send.

How often has this scene been repeated? Do we tend to think more of our traditions and the promises we have made than we do of God's own Word? When faced with a choice, aren't we tempted to choose the easy course and put personal considerations first? By so doing, we might forfeit the great blessings God has promised to those who are faithful to his Word and bring upon ourselves the condemnation that comes with disobedience.

Jehoiakim Burns Jeremiah's Scroll

36 In the fourth year of Jehoiakim son of Josiah king of
Judah, this word came to Jeremiah from the LORD:
2"Take a scroll and write on it all the words I have spoken to
you concerning Israel, Judah and all the other nations from

**the time I began speaking to you in the reign of Josiah till now.
3Perhaps when the people of Judah hear about every disaster I
plan to inflict on them, each of them will turn from his wicked
way; then I will forgive their wickedness and their sin."**
**4So Jeremiah called Baruch son of Neriah, and while
Jeremiah dictated all the words the LORD had spoken to him,
Baruch wrote them on the scroll. 5Then Jeremiah told Baruch,
"I am restricted; I cannot go to the LORD's temple. 6So you go
to the house of the LORD on a day of fasting and read to the
people from the scroll the words of the LORD that you wrote as
I dictated. Read them to all the people of Judah who come in
from their towns. 7Perhaps they will bring their petition before
the LORD, and each will turn from his wicked ways, for the
anger and wrath pronounced against this people by the LORD
are great."**

Jeremiah probably received this command to write down the words of his prophecy late in the year 605 B.C. and finished his work about a year later. His first edition includes all the words he had received from the Lord from a quarter-century of ministry. It might surprise us that Jeremiah was able to remember such a great amount of material. We need to remember, however, that in the days before the printing press was invented, many people had developed their ability to memorize to an extraordinary degree. Some scribes were able to recite the greater portion of the Old Testament by heart. Few people could write. So they delivered most information by word of mouth and became very good at doing that. Certainly Jeremiah also had the assistance of the Lord himself to insure completeness and accuracy.

At this point Jeremiah introduces us to his faithful helper and companion, Baruch. Baruch was a scribe by profession. Since most people could not write, scribes formed an important professional class. They did most of the writing. They transcribed important documents and proclamations into writing for greater permanence and readier reference. They used a substance known as papyrus, a paper-like material made from a reed grown in Egypt. Besides serving as Jeremiah's scribe, Baruch also helped him in other ways. In this case Baruch would also read the scroll.

Since Jeremiah had delivered his message in bits and pieces over twenty years, the purpose of the scroll was to provide a thorough overview of Jeremiah's preaching. The impact of the whole message taken at once would be more dramatic and significant. The Lord hoped that after the Jewish nation had heard the whole message they would take it to heart and repent.

Jeremiah gave the scroll to his scribe to read, since he himself could not go to the temple. Perhaps after his earlier sermon (Jeremiah 26), which had caused such an uproar, the king or temple officials had given orders barring Jeremiah from the temple, hoping to silence the prophet. In his place he sent Baruch to read the scroll. In order to gain the largest possible audience, Baruch was to read it on an important fast day. The Lord also wanted to teach the officials a lesson by having Baruch read the scroll. Though they could restrict Jeremiah's movements, they could not stop the preaching and march of the Lord's Word, for "God's word is not chained" (2 Timothy 2:9).

**8 Baruch son of Neriah did everything Jeremiah the prophet
told him to do; at the LORD's temple he read the words of the
LORD from the scroll. 9 In the ninth month of the fifth year of
Jehoiakim son of Josiah king of Judah, a time of fasting before
the LORD was proclaimed for all the people in Jerusalem and
those who had come from the towns of Judah. 10 From the room
of Gemariah son of Shaphan the secretary, which was in the
upper courtyard at the entrance of the New Gate of the temple,**

**Baruch read to all the people at the LORD's temple the words
of Jeremiah from the scroll.**
**[11]When Micaiah son of Gemariah, the son of Shaphan,
heard all the words of the LORD from the scroll, [12]he went
down to the secretary's room in the royal palace, where all the
officials were sitting: Elishama the secretary, Delaiah son of
Shemaiah, Elnathan son of Acbor, Gemariah son of Shaphan,
Zedekiah son of Hananiah, and all the other officials. [13]After
Micaiah told them everything he had heard Baruch read to
the people from the scroll, [14]all the officials sent Jehudi son of
Nethaniah, the son of Shelemiah, the son of Cushi, to say to
Baruch, "Bring the scroll from which you have read to the
people and come." So Baruch son of Neriah went to them with
the scroll in his hand. [15]They said to him, "Sit down, please,
and read it to us."**
**So Baruch read it to them. [16]When they heard all these
words, they looked at each other in fear and said to Baruch,
"We must report all these words to the king." [17]Then they
asked Baruch, "Tell us, how did you come to write all this? Did
Jeremiah dictate it?"**
**[18]"Yes," Baruch replied, "he dictated all these words to me,
and I wrote them in ink on the scroll."**
**[19]Then the officials said to Baruch, "You and Jeremiah, go
and hide. Don't let anyone know where you are."**

Baruch went to the temple as Jeremiah had commanded him. He too possessed the fearlessness he had seen in Jeremiah. Regardless of the cost, he too was ready to proclaim the Word. He went to the room of Gemariah son of Shaphan the secretary, an important government official, perhaps the man in charge of government records and archives. The family of Shaphan were God-fearing people. They were sympathetic to the aims of the Lord and his prophets. In an earlier chapter Jeremiah told us that Ahikam, Shaphan's son, had saved his life (Jeremiah 26:24).

Micaiah, the grandson of Shaphan and nephew of Ahikam, heard Baruch reading the scroll. Immediately he reported its contents to other key government officials who had also been trained under good king Josiah. Because of the possible impact of the scroll, they invited Baruch to read the scroll to them. No doubt many of them had heard various parts delivered in person over the years by the prophet himself.

The message of the scroll had its desired effect upon them. Because they believed what the Lord had said, they were afraid. They also considered this message of utmost importance to the government, because it dealt with the survival of the government and of the nation itself. Because they were sympathetic to the Lord's purpose, they resolved to take the scroll to the king himself. They showed great courage and love for their country. They knew where King Jehoiakim stood but they hoped that after hearing the message, he too would repent.

To verify the contents of the scroll, they questioned Baruch closely. Perhaps someone had started a rumor that Baruch, not Jeremiah, was chiefly responsible for the message preached by Jeremiah. We note how carefully and completely the prophet listed the names of these officials for us. Their number and identity provide a solid and reliable witness to the authorship and authenticity of the prophetic scroll. From their investigation they determined that Jeremiah had indeed authored the scroll. Jeremiah dictated and Baruch wrote.

God here gives us a firsthand account of how at least one of the books of the Bible was written. He does that so we might be sure that what we have in the Bible are his very own words. For "above all, you must understand that no prophecy of Scripture came about by the prophet's own interpretation. For prophecy never had its origin in the will of man, but men spoke from God as they were carried along by the Holy Spirit" (2 Peter 1:20,21). Realizing that the king might go into a rage after reading the scroll, the officials ordered Jeremiah and Baruch into hiding for their own safety.

**[20]After they put the scroll in the room of Elishama the secre-
tary, they went to the king in the courtyard and reported everything to him. [21]The king sent Jehudi to get the scroll, and
Jehudi brought it from the room of Elishama the secretary and
read it to the king and all the officials standing beside him. [22]It
was the ninth month and the king was sitting in the winter
apartment, with a fire burning in the firepot in front of him.
[23]Whenever Jehudi had read three or four columns of the
scroll, the king cut them off with a scribe's knife and threw
them into the firepot, until the entire scroll was burned in the
fire. [24]The king and all his attendants who heard all these
words showed no fear, nor did they tear their clothes. [25]Even
though Elnathan, Delaiah and Gemariah urged the king not to
burn the scroll, he would not listen to them. [26]Instead, the king
commanded Jerahmeel, a son of the king, Seraiah son of Azriel
and Shelemiah son of Abdeel to arrest Baruch the scribe and
Jeremiah the prophet. But the LORD had hidden them.**

After the officials had put the scroll away, they reported its contents to the king. The king sent Jehudi, one of the scribes, to fetch the scroll so that he might hear it for himself. As Jehudi finished reading three or four columns from the scroll, the king cut off the completed end and threw it into the charcoal burner which was warming his feet. (It's cold in Jerusalem in December.) In this manner the king burned up the whole scroll. His action horrified those who had alerted him to its contents, for they knew that Jeremiah's sharp message of judgment was from the Lord and that it would surely be fulfilled. Unfortunately the message

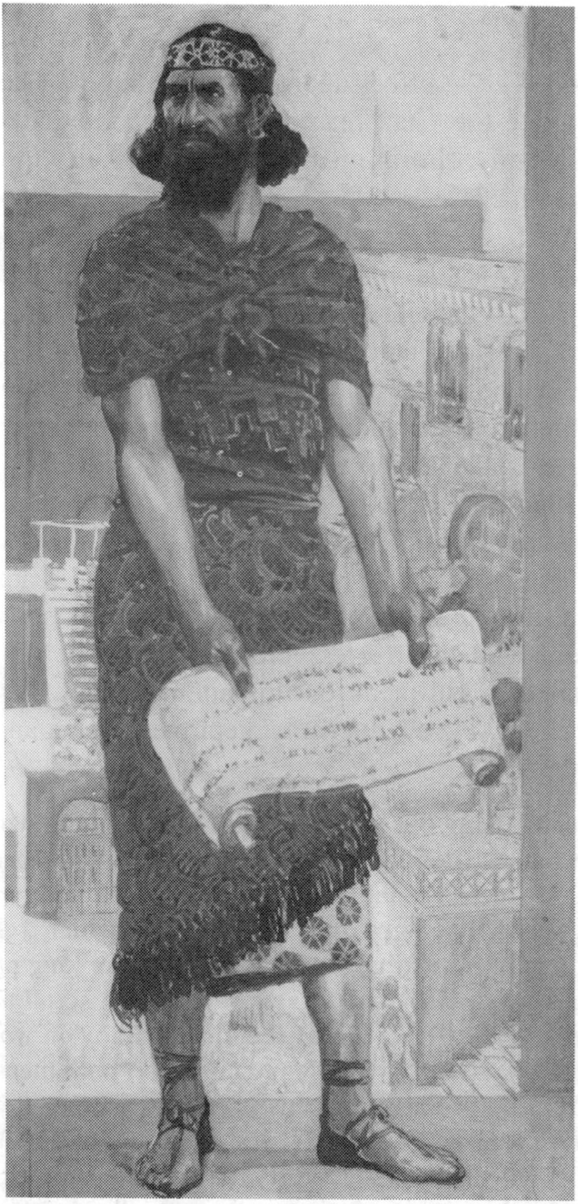

Baruch

did not have the effect upon the king they had hoped for but the one they had feared. The disobedience so characteristic of Jehoiakim had showed itself once more (Jeremiah 22:21).

The message of the scroll failed to move the king or his personal attendants to repentance. He had gathered around him men who thought the way he did. He remained impenitent and showed total contempt for God's Word. By his action he demonstrated that for him the Word was good only for warming his feet and no more meaningful than the cheap material upon which it was written.

The king's attitude was typical of the vast majority of his fellow countrymen. The people of Judah shared similar contempt for God's Word. Immediately after the reading was finished, the king ordered one of his sons and some of his personal attendants to arrest Jeremiah and Baruch. No doubt he planned to kill them, but his attempt failed. The Lord, who was the king's real enemy, kept the prophet and his attendant safe.

27 After the king burned the scroll containing the words that
Baruch had written at Jeremiah's dictation, the word of the
LORD came to Jeremiah: 28 "Take another scroll and write on it
all the words that were on the first scroll, which Jehoiakim
king of Judah burned up. 29 Also tell Jehoiakim king of Judah,
'This is what the LORD says: You burned that scroll and said,
"Why did you write on it that the king of Babylon would cer-
tainly come and destroy this land and cut off both men and an-
imals from it?" 30 Therefore, this is what the LORD says about
Jehoiakim king of Judah: He will have no one to sit on the
throne of David; his body will be thrown out and exposed to
the heat by day and the frost by night. 31 I will punish him and
his children and his attendants for their wickedness; I will
bring on them and those living in Jerusalem and the people of

Judah every disaster I pronounced against them, because they have not listened.' "

32So Jeremiah took another scroll and gave it to the scribe Baruch son of Neriah, and as Jeremiah dictated, Baruch wrote on it all the words of the scroll that Jehoiakim king of Judah had burned in the fire. And many similar words were added to them.

Because he had destroyed the scroll, the king felt good, imagining that he had won. But the Word of the Lord is not so easily set aside. The Lord stands behind his Word. He commanded Jeremiah to write another scroll with the same message. To this scroll he was to add other words which he had received from the Lord. We know that throughout the next decade or longer Jeremiah continued to add to the scroll the words of the Lord, preserving them for Judah and for all of us to read.

To the contemptuous king the Lord sent a special message. Though his son would succeed him on the throne, that son would soon be deposed and exiled. No other son would follow him. He himself would die and not be buried—no one would mourn him. Those who shared his attitude and supported him would suffer the same end as he. In fact, all those living in Judah and Jerusalem would suffer along with them, ". . . because they have not listened." The downfall of Judah and Jerusalem was brought about by their own impenitence, disobedience, and unbelief.

Through the message of Jeremiah 36 the Lord offers two words of assurance to the people of Jeremiah's day and to all who would ever read the message of the scroll. First, *the message the prophets delivered was the Lord's.* He was the author. The words were his. No one should doubt that. Every hearer and reader ought to hear and read these words as from the Lord himself. Second, *no power on earth or in heaven can set aside or destroy this Word.* The Lord watches over and protects his Word. Wicked King Jehoiakim tried to destroy Jeremiah's prophecy, but God made sure we still have it. The whole purpose of the Word is to bring its hearer and reader face to face with the living God. Our Lord has promised, "Heaven and earth will pass away, but my words will never pass away" (Luke 21:33).

Jeremiah in Prison

**37 Zedekiah son of Josiah was made king of Judah by Nebuchadnezzar king of Babylon; he reigned in place
of Jehoiachin son of Jehoiakim. 2Neither he nor his attendants nor the people of the land paid any attention to the words the LORD had spoken through Jeremiah the prophet.**

3King Zedekiah, however, sent Jehucal son of Shelemiah with the priest Zephaniah son of Maaseiah to Jeremiah the prophet with this message: "Please pray to the LORD our God for us."

**4Now Jeremiah was free to come and go among the people,
for he had not yet been put in prison. 5Pharaoh's army had
marched out of Egypt, and when the Babylonians who were besieging Jerusalem heard the report about them, they withdrew from Jerusalem.**

**6Then the word of the LORD came to Jeremiah the prophet:
7"This is what the LORD, the God of Israel, says: Tell the king of Judah, who sent you to inquire of me, 'Pharaoh's army, which has marched out to support you, will go back to its own
land, to Egypt. 8Then the Babylonians will return and attack this city; they will capture it and burn it down.'**

**9"This is what the LORD says: Do not deceive yourselves, thinking, 'The Babylonians will surely leave us.' They will not!
10Even if you were to defeat the entire Babylonian army that is attacking you and only wounded men were left in their tents, they would come out and burn this city down."**

The prophet backtracks to a time earlier in the siege of Jerusalem. A previous chapter has informed us that because an Egyptian army had advanced from Egypt, the Babylonians broke off their siege to meet this new threat. At that point Zedekiah sent messengers to Jeremiah to ask him to pray for Judah. The lifting of the siege had raised the hopes of all the people. Zedekiah wished these new hopes would prove true. To that end he asked Jeremiah to pray that God would bring a permanent end to the siege of the city.

Though Zedekiah consulted with Jeremiah often, he never really acted on what Jeremiah told him. In his heart he could never bring himself to believe what the Lord said. He followed the recommendations of his top advisors. Fear kept him from acting contrary to their wishes. He also pursued the same disastrous path as his wicked brother Jehoiakim had. Though he owed his throne to Nebuchadnezzar, he showed no loyalty to him. The pattern of disobedience and unbelief continued as before.

At this point the prophet Jeremiah was still free. In chapter 32 he had been under house arrest in the courtyard of the guard. This chapter explains how his arrest came about. Jeremiah responded to the false hopes of the king and all the citizens of Jerusalem. Nothing had changed. Their continued impenitence guaranteed the fall of the city.

To end any hopes they might have entertained, Jeremiah painted a frightening picture. Even if they were able to defeat the entire army of the Babylonians in battle, the wounded soldiers would come out of their tents to destroy Jerusalem. To all in Judah the message was clear. Just as the Lord had once saved the city from the Assyrians by destroying their army in a single night (Isaiah 37), so now he would destroy it by supporting the Babylonians. No miracle would deliver them this time, for the Lord was against them.

11After the Babylonian army had withdrawn from Jerusalem because of Pharaoh's army, 12Jeremiah started to leave the city

to go to the territory of Benjamin to get his share of the property among the people there. [13]But when he reached the Benjamin Gate, the captain of the guard, whose name was Irijah son of Shelemiah, the son of Hananiah, arrested him and said, "You are deserting to the Babylonians!"

[14]"That's not true!" Jeremiah said. "I am not deserting to the Babylonians." But Irijah would not listen to him; instead, he arrested Jeremiah and brought him to the officials. [15]They were angry with Jeremiah and had him beaten and imprisoned in the house of Jonathan the secretary, which they had made into a prison.

[16]Jeremiah was put into a vaulted cell in a dungeon, where he remained a long time. [17]Then King Zedekiah sent for him and had him brought to the palace, where he asked him privately, "Is there any word from the LORD?"

"Yes," Jeremiah replied, "you will be handed over to the king of Babylon."

[18]Then Jeremiah said to King Zedekiah, "What crime have I committed against you or your officials or this people, that you have put me in prison? [19]Where are your prophets who prophesied to you, 'The king of Babylon will not attack you or this land'? [20]But now, my lord the king, please listen. Let me bring my petition before you: Do not send me back to the house of Jonathan the secretary, or I will die there."

[21]King Zedekiah then gave orders for Jeremiah to be placed in the courtyard of the guard and given bread from the street of the bakers each day until all the bread in the city was gone. So Jeremiah remained in the courtyard of the guard.

Along with his fellow Jews Jeremiah planned to take advantage of the Babylonian withdrawal to go back home to Anathoth, in the tribal territory of Benjamin, to get whatever remained of his and his family's possessions. Jeremiah's preaching and his support of the Babylonians had made him very unpopular. Many of his countrymen regarded him as nothing more than a traitor. Up to this point, however, his enemies had been unable to hurt him in any way. Now they got their chance. As Jeremiah was leaving the city by its north gate, Irijah the captain of the guard detained him. Accusing Jeremiah of treason, Irijah arrested him.

Irijah delivered Jeremiah to his superiors, government officials who strongly opposed the prophet. This group of officials wielded great power, defying even the authority of the king. In any case, they strongly opposed Jeremiah's message and work. They took advantage of the prophet's arrest to beat him and put him in a maximum security prison. Jeremiah now was in the hands of his bitterest enemies. This harsh imprisonment broke his health and weakened his spirit.

After his armies had driven the Egyptians back to Egypt, Nebuchadnezzar tightened his merciless grip on Jerusalem. At this point Zedekiah summoned Jeremiah once again. He had the prophet brought from his prison cell to the royal palace. The wishy-washy king asked Jeremiah if he had heard any word from the Lord. Without any promise from the Lord or any change of heart, the king still looked for the slimmest shred of hope to hold on to. There was none. The word from the Lord remained the same. The city would fall, and the king would be handed over to the Babylonians.

Jeremiah was desperate and angry, so he seized this opportunity to ask for an explanation for his cruel treatment. What crime had he committed? He was not the one who deserved to be in prison. Where were all the false prophets now who had predicted that the Babylonians would never attack the city? What of their words now? Jeremiah had always spoken the truth because his word came from the Lord. He entreated the king not to return him to his former prison. Zedekiah knew that Jeremiah was right, and he ordered the prophet to be kept under protective custody in the courtyard of the guard. There he was to receive a ration of bread as long as the city's supply lasted.

Though for a moment Zedekiah had found the strength to oppose the strong men around him, he remained weak. He simply could not bring himself to repent and do what the prophet had advised him. Though he had every evidence that Jeremiah had spoken the truth, he seemed unwilling or unable to change from that course which was leading him to his own ruin. He is a prime example of the way in which unbelief works.

Jeremiah Thrown Into a Cistern

38 Shephatiah son of Mattan, Gedaliah son of Pashhur, Jehucal son of Shelemiah, and Pashhur son of Malkijah heard what Jeremiah was telling all the people when he said, 2"This is what the LORD says: 'Whoever stays in this city will die by the sword, famine or plague, but whoever goes over to the Babylonians will live. He will escape with his life; he will live.' 3And this is what the LORD says: 'This city will certainly be handed over to the army of the king of Babylon, who will capture it.' "

4Then the officials said to the king, "This man should be put to death. He is discouraging the soldiers who are left in this city, as well as all the people, by the things he is saying to them. This man is not seeking the good of these people but their ruin."

5"He is in your hands," King Zedekiah answered. "The king can do nothing to oppose you."

6So they took Jeremiah and put him into the cistern of Malkijah, the king's son, which was in the courtyard of the guard. They lowered Jeremiah by ropes into the cistern; it had no water in it, only mud, and Jeremiah sank down into the mud.

Throughout the siege Jeremiah continued to proclaim the Lord's message: "Surrender to the Babylonians!" The message did not vary, but the danger of proclaiming it grew as the siege worsened. His message urged those in the city to surrender to the Babylonians. It promised life to anyone who surrendered. It threatened capture and death to all who resisted the Babylonians.

Although Jeremiah had been confined to the courtyard of the guard, his message kept spreading, most immediately to those charged with the defense of the city. A good number of soldiers and government officials heard his message again and again. Perhaps Jeremiah's insistent preaching had led some in the military to question the wisdom of continued resistance. Some believed what the prophet had said. Surely some had followed the advice of the Lord's Word and gone over to the Babylonians.

Jeremiah's message and the freedom with which he was able to deliver it, however, enraged many powerful nobles and high government officials. His message was undermining their attempts to defend the city. These nobles, therefore, approached the king with a demand. They accused Jeremiah of treason. As a traitor, he deserved to die. Though he had always been under the suspicion of treason, the intensity of the siege made the charge even more damning. The accusers pressed the king to do something. Against better knowledge, the king surrendered Jeremiah to them. He had neither the strength nor the resolve to oppose them.

The nobles and high officials took action against Jeremiah but did not immediately take his life. Perhaps they feared the consequences that would follow such an act. Perhaps they wanted him to die a slow death. Perhaps they wanted to relieve themselves of their own guilt and shift the burden of responsibility away from themselves to Jeremiah. They used an old cistern as a makeshift dungeon. Its bottom no longer contained any water, but it oozed with mud and crawled with vermin. Into this prison they lowered the poor unfortunate prophet and left him to die.

**[7]But Ebed-Melech, a Cushite, an official in the royal
palace, heard that they had put Jeremiah into the cistern.
While the king was sitting in the Benjamin Gate, [8]Ebed-
Melech went out of the palace and said to him, [9]"My lord the
king, these men have acted wickedly in all they have done to
Jeremiah the prophet. They have thrown him into a cistern,
where he will starve to death when there is no longer any
bread in the city."**
**[10]Then the king commanded Ebed-Melech the Cushite,
"Take thirty men from here with you and lift Jeremiah the
prophet out of the cistern before he dies."**
**[11]So Ebed-Melech took the men with him and went to a room
under the treasury in the palace. He took some old rags and
worn-out clothes from there and let them down with ropes to
Jeremiah in the cistern. [12]Ebed-Melech the Cushite said to
Jeremiah, "Put these old rags and worn-out clothes under your
arms to pad the ropes." Jeremiah did so, [13]and they pulled him
up with the ropes and lifted him out of the cistern. And
Jeremiah remained in the courtyard of the guard.**

Jeremiah would have died in his pit-prison but for intervention from a most unlikely source. Ebed-Melech (his name means "servant of the king") served in the personal household of the king. His personal name remains a mystery to us. He obviously held a trusted and important position in the palace. Even more remarkable is that he was not a Jew but most likely an Ethiopian whom the king had brought to serve in his household. Such an arrangement and such servants were common in the royal households of that time.

Ebed-Melech, however, was no ordinary person. To save the prophet, he risked the embarrassment of the king, who had allowed the miscarriage of justice against Jeremiah, and he risked the anger and revenge of the powerful nobles and high officials whom he had snubbed. But he took the risk. He had heard Jeremiah's message, and he had believed it. Bold in faith, Ebed-Melech approached the king as he sat in his courtroom at the city gate, serving in his capacity as high court judge.

Ebed-Melech pointed to the cruelty with which the nobles and high officials had treated Jeremiah. He also argued that Jeremiah would die unless someone intervened. Recognizing the truth of Ebed-Melech's words, the king changed his mind once more and ordered Jeremiah's release. To see that his order was carried out, the king sent a contingent of thirty armed men with Ebed-Melech.

Immediately Ebed-Melech made preparations for the rescue. Jeremiah was so weakened by hunger, thirst, and the abuse to which he had been subjected that he could not have climbed a ladder out of the cistern or even held onto a rope to be pulled up. Ebed-Melech foresaw the problem. From a storage room under the treasury, he brought rags and old clothes. He threw these down first and had the prophet put them under his arms and then wrap the rope around himself. This extra padding kept the rope from cutting him. The soldiers pulled Jeremiah up out of the cistern, and he returned to the courtyard of the guard, where he remained under the watchful eye of Ebed-Melech until the city fell to the Babylonians.

Zedekiah Questions Jeremiah Again

14Then King Zedekiah sent for Jeremiah the prophet and had him brought to the third entrance to the temple of the LORD. "I am going to ask you something," the king said to Jeremiah. "Do not hide anything from me."

15Jeremiah said to Zedekiah, "If I give you an answer, will you not kill me? Even if I did give you counsel, you would not listen to me."

16But King Zedekiah swore this oath secretly to Jeremiah: "As surely as the LORD lives, who has given us breath, I will neither kill you nor hand you over to those who are seeking your life."

17Then Jeremiah said to Zedekiah, "This is what the LORD God Almighty, the God of Israel, says: 'If you surrender to the officers of the king of Babylon, your life will be spared and this city will not be burned down; you and your family
will live. 18But if you will not surrender to the officers of the king of Babylon, this city will be handed over to the Babylonians and they will burn it down; you yourself will not escape from their hands.' "

19King Zedekiah said to Jeremiah, "I am afraid of the Jews who have gone over to the Babylonians, for the Babylonians may hand me over to them and they will mistreat me."

20"They will not hand you over," Jeremiah replied. "Obey the LORD by doing what I tell you. Then it will go well with you, and
your life will be spared. 21But if you refuse to surrender, this is
what the LORD has revealed to me: 22All the women left in the
palace of the king of Judah will be brought out to the officials of the king of Babylon. Those women will say to you:

> **" 'They misled you and overcame you—**
> **those trusted friends of yours.**
> **Your feet are sunk in the mud;**
> **your friends have deserted you.'**

23"All your wives and children will be brought out to the Babylonians. You yourself will not escape from their hands but will be captured by the king of Babylon; and this city will be burned down."

Once more Zedekiah sent for Jeremiah. He met with him in a private place where no one could overhear their conversation. This was the last exchange between the king and the prophet. The king wavered, paralyzed by impenitence, inaction, and unbelief. The prophet was weary and worn out from his prison ordeal. Yet he tried one more time, hoping against hope that this time the king would listen.

The king demanded to know the truth. Knowing that speaking the truth had nearly killed him before, Jeremiah hesitated to tell the king the truth again, fearing that after hearing it the king might decide to kill him. Jeremiah was convinced that even if the king heard the truth again, he would not act according to it anyway. In either case there was little point to Jeremiah's saying anything. To secure an answer from Jeremiah, the king promised with a solemn oath to protect his life. He would not kill the prophet nor would he allow his nobles to kill him.

Satisfied by the king's assurance and moved by the love that still burned in his heart, Jeremiah repeated his message for the last time. If the king surrendered, he and his family would survive. His surrender would not only benefit him and his family, but the whole city would be spared from destruction. His surrender would be a heroic and courageous act, since it would save the nation.

Zedekiah had other fears and excuses. He was afraid that if he surrendered, he might be turned over to his fellow countrymen who had already surrendered, and he would be tortured. Jeremiah had promised the king one last time that if he surrendered, all would go well with him. If, however, he refused to surrender, he would be the ruin of his family, the city, and the nation. When the city fell to the Babylonians, the women in the palace, his wives and concubines, would openly mock him because of his weakness. For the moment, Jeremiah's words may have persuaded the king. The following chapter makes it clear, however, that Zedekiah decided to doubt the prophetic warning and to disobey what the Lord had told him through the prophet.

[24]Then Zedekiah said to Jeremiah, "Do not let anyone know about this conversation, or you may die. [25]If the officials hear that I talked with you, and they come to you and say, 'Tell us what you said to the king and what the king said to you; do not hide it from us or we will kill you,' [26]then tell them, 'I was pleading with the king not to send me back to Jonathan's house to die there.' "

[27]All the officials did come to Jeremiah and question him, and he told them everything the king had ordered him to say. So they said no more to him, for no one had heard his conversation with the king.

[28]And Jeremiah remained in the courtyard of the guard until the day Jerusalem was captured.

Zedekiah commanded Jeremiah not to reveal the content of this conversation to anyone. The king, fearing for his own life, knew that the powerful nobles would question the prophet. If they had the slightest inkling that the king was thinking of surrender, they might well kill him for the good of the city. In the opinion of the nobles, nothing must weaken the resolve of the city's defenders. Jeremiah gave his word to the king and promised to abide by his wishes. When the nobles questioned Jeremiah about his conversation with the king, he answered just as Zedekiah had commanded him. With that he remained in the courtyard of the guard until Jerusalem fell.

The Fall of Jerusalem

39 This is how Jerusalem was taken: [1]In the ninth year of Zedekiah king of Judah, in the tenth month, Nebuchadnezzar king of Babylon marched against Jerusalem with his whole army and laid siege to it. [2]And on the ninth day of the

**fourth month of Zedekiah's eleventh year, the city wall was bro-
ken through. 3Then all the officials of the king of Babylon came
and took seats in the Middle Gate: Nergal-Sharezer of Samgar,
Nebo-Sarsekim a chief officer, Nergal-Sharezer a high official
and all the other officials of the king of Babylon. 4When Zedekiah king of Judah and all the soldiers saw them, they fled; they
left the city at night by way of the king's garden, through the
gate between the two walls, and headed toward the Arabah.**

**5But the Babylonian army pursued them and overtook
Zedekiah in the plains of Jericho. They captured him and took
him to Nebuchadnezzar king of Babylon at Riblah in the land
of Hamath, where he pronounced sentence on him. 6There at
Riblah the king of Babylon slaughtered the sons of Zedekiah
before his eyes and also killed all the nobles of Judah. 7Then he
put out Zedekiah's eyes and bound him with bronze shackles
to take him to Babylon.**

**8The Babylonians set fire to the royal palace and the houses
of the people and broke down the walls of Jerusalem. 9Neb-
uzaradan commander of the imperial guard carried into exile
to Babylon the people who remained in the city, along with
those who had gone over to him, and the rest of the people.
10But Nebuzaradan the commander of the guard left behind in
the land of Judah some of the poor people, who owned nothing; and at that time he gave them vineyards and fields.**

In a very matter of fact way Jeremiah describes the end of the city of Jerusalem. Its end was anything but matter of fact for the prophet or any of those who lived in the city. What an iron grip Jeremiah kept on his emotions! He saved his grief for another time and another place. In the book of Lamentations he released that grief. As he here chronicles the fall of Jerusalem, he proves to all that the Lord had kept his word. The Lord had done just as he said he would.

After a siege of about a year and a half the Babylonian army finally broke down the walls of Jerusalem. Nebuchadnezzar was not present at the final break-through. He had gone north of Jerusalem about 200 miles to Riblah in Syria. At this strategic location he set up his headquarters. From here he could not only supervise the siege of Jerusalem but watch the rest of his far-reaching empire. He left his top commanders to finish the operation at Jerusalem. Among these commanders was Nergal-Sharezer of Samgar, his son-in-law. Once they had secured the city, Nebuchadnezzar's commanders set up court at the Middle Gate, probably the Valley Gate, located between the old and new parts of the city. Here they would decide the fate of their captives.

Apparently King Zedekiah and his personal guard had eluded capture up to this point. Since the king feared his fate, he fled by the southeast corner of the city along with his personal guard and other nobles and headed east toward the Jordan Valley. If he could make it across the Jordan, he'd be safe. After running for about eighteen miles, his group reached the open plains around Jericho. But there the Babylonian army overtook them. The Lord had warned him that he would be captured and taken to Babylon. Though he had many opportunities to surrender, he had refused and persisted in unbelief. Now he would pay the price for his actions.

Nebuchadnezzar made Zedekiah an example for others who might plan to rebel against him. Shortly after his arrival at Nebuchadnezzar's headquarters at Riblah, the king of Judah received his sentence. He watched as his sons died a cruel death; then all the nobles who had served him and advised him were murdered. Zedekiah had no time for tears, for then Nebuchadnezzar had Zedekiah's eyes put out. The last thing he would ever see was the death of his sons. Blind and shackled with bronze chains, he was then led away to prison in Babylon. There he would serve as a warning to any who might dream of rebelling against Nebuchadnezzar.

As the Lord had predicted, the Babylonians plundered the city and then torched it. To complete its destruction and humiliation they pulled down its walls, leaving it defenseless. After that, they took most of the Jews who were left and those who had surrendered earlier away into exile. The commander of the imperial guard left a few of the poorest people behind to serve as a warning to others and to repopulate the country. He insured their loyalty by giving them property. Since they now owed everything to the Babylonians, they would be loyal allies.

**11Now Nebuchadnezzar king of Babylon had given these or-
ders about Jeremiah through Nebuzaradan commander of the
imperial guard: 12"Take him and look after him; don't harm
him but do for him whatever he asks." 13So Nebuzaradan the
commander of the guard, Nebushazban a chief officer, Nergal-
Sharezer a high official and all the other officers of the king of
Babylon 14sent and had Jeremiah taken out of the courtyard of
the guard. They turned him over to Gedaliah son of Ahikam,
the son of Shaphan, to take him back to his home. So he remained among his own people.**

**15While Jeremiah had been confined in the courtyard of the
guard, the word of the LORD came to him: 16"Go and tell Ebed-
Melech the Cushite, 'This is what the LORD Almighty, the God
of Israel, says: I am about to fulfill my words against this city
through disaster, not prosperity. At that time they will be fulfilled before your eyes. 17But I will rescue you on that day, declares the LORD; you will not be handed over to those you fear.
18I will save you; you will not fall by the sword but will escape
with your life, because you trust in me, declares the LORD.' "**

Nebuchadnezzar had given specific orders about Jeremiah the prophet. He was to be kept safe and treated well. In fact, Jeremiah could choose what he wanted to do. Nebuchadnezzar had heard about Jeremiah's prophecy and regarded him as the Lord's man. Because of his experience with Daniel and other Jewish members of his administration, Nebuchadnezzar might have learned to respect the Lord's prophets.

The chief of the imperial guard personally released Jeremiah and placed him under the protection of Gedaliah, the new governor of Judea. Once again a member of the family of Shaphan would serve as Jeremiah's protector (see chapter 26:24). God had also blessed this faithful family in its exile. True to his promise the Lord had kept Jeremiah through all this trouble.

To finish the story, Jeremiah takes us back to the time just before the fall of the city. After Ebed-Melech had rescued the prophet from sure death, the Lord rewarded him. Though he would see the destruction of the city, he himself would be spared. Ebed-Melech knew that destruction was coming because he believed what the Lord had said through the prophet. Many would die when the city fell, but Ebed-Melech would escape alive because he had trusted the Lord. The Lord does not leave the believer helpless. And anyone who helps someone because that person is a believer will receive his reward (Matthew 10:41,42).

THE FEW SURVIVORS LEARN NOTHING FROM THE DISASTER

JEREMIAH 40—44

Jeremiah Freed

**40 The word came to Jeremiah from the LORD after Nebuzaradan commander of the imperial guard had released him at Ramah. He had found Jeremiah bound in chains among all the captives from Jerusalem and Judah who were
being carried into exile to Babylon. 2When the commander of
the guard found Jeremiah, he said to him, "The LORD your
God decreed this disaster for this place. 3And now the LORD
has brought it about; he has done just as he said he would. All this happened because you people sinned against the LORD and did not obey him.
4But today I am freeing you from the chains
on your wrists. Come with me to Babylon, if you like, and I will look after you; but if you do not want to, then don't come. Look, the whole country lies before you; go wherever you
please." 5However, before Jeremiah turned to go, Nebuzaradan
added, "Go back to Gedaliah son of Ahikam, the son of Shaphan, whom the king of Babylon has appointed over the towns of Judah, and live with him among the people, or go anywhere else you please."**

**Then the commander gave him provisions and a present and
let him go. 6So Jeremiah went to Gedaliah son of Ahikam at
Mizpah and stayed with him among the people who were left behind in the land.**

These verses expand on Jeremiah's release from captivity. He had been taken to Ramah (about five miles north of Jerusalem) with others bound for exile. The Babylonians used Ramah as a staging area and collection point to gather those whom they were going to deport to Babylon.

According to Nebuchadnezzar's order, Nebuzaradan searched for Jeremiah and found him among the captives. After releasing him, Nebuzaradan gave Jeremiah a choice. As a free man he could go wherever he pleased. If he chose to go to Babylon, he could live safely under the eye of Nebuzaradan. Or he could choose to stay behind, a riskier course. The captain of the imperial guard did not care what Jeremiah did, but he advised him that if he remained behind, he should go to Gedaliah, the new governor, and live with him.

Although Jeremiah does not reveal this directly, it seems reasonable to suppose that God advised him what he ought to do. As he wrestled with the decision of remaining behind or going to Babylon, the Lord directed him to stay behind. For this reason, then, Jeremiah joined Gedaliah at Mizpah.

It seems strange to hear Nebuzaradan, a heathen, speak Jeremiah's own prophetic words back to him. Jeremiah had warned that disaster would come to Judah and Jerusalem because of the nation's disobedience. God had fulfilled his word and brought that disaster.

Perhaps Nebuzaradan was trying to soften the numbness Jeremiah clearly felt at the nightmare that had overtaken the Jews. Certainly Jeremiah had done everything possible to bring his message home to them, but they had simply refused to listen. Nebuzaradan perhaps also felt that Jeremiah would serve Gedaliah and the remnant of the Jews well as a counselor.

Since Jeremiah did not wish to go to Babylon, Nebuzaradan urged him to go to Gedaliah. He gave Jeremiah provisions and a gift and sent him on his way. Jeremiah joined Gedaliah at Mizpah, a city about eight miles north of Jerusalem and a couple miles from Ramah. Gedaliah, the new Jewish governor, had chosen it as his temporary administrative center.

Gedaliah Assassinated

**[7]When all the army officers and their men who were still in
the open country heard that the king of Babylon had appointed Gedaliah son of Ahikam as governor over the land and had
put him in charge of the men, women and children who were
the poorest in the land and who had not been carried into exile
to Babylon, [8]they came to Gedaliah at Mizpah—Ishmael son of
Nethaniah, Johanan and Jonathan the sons of Kareah, Seraiah
son of Tanhumeth, the sons of Ephai the Netophathite, and
Jaazaniah the son of the Maacathite, and their men. [9]Gedaliah
son of Ahikam, the son of Shaphan, took an oath to reassure
them and their men. "Do not be afraid to serve the Babylonians," he said. "Settle down in the land and serve the king of
Babylon, and it will go well with you. [10]I myself will stay at
Mizpah to represent you before the Babylonians who come to
us, but you are to harvest the wine, summer fruit and oil, and
put them in your storage jars, and live in the towns you have
taken over."**

**[11]When all the Jews in Moab, Ammon, Edom and all the oth-
er countries heard that the king of Babylon had left a remnant
in Judah and had appointed Gedaliah son of Ahikam, the son
of Shaphan, as governor over them, [12]they all came back to the
land of Judah, to Gedaliah at Mizpah, from all the countries
where they had been scattered. And they harvested an abundance of wine and summer fruit.**

Slowly those who had fled from the city during the siege trickled back. Encouraged by Nebuchadnezzar's choice of Gedaliah as governor, scattered elements of the army gathered at Mizpah. Jeremiah lists their commanders. Others who had fled to neighboring countries—Moab, Ammon, and Edom—began to return. Gedaliah encouraged them to begin their lives again. By a solemn oath he pledged to do all in his power to help them start over. He offered to serve as mediator between them and their Babylonian overlords.

The Lord had not left those Jews who still remained in the area without some hope. Though the disaster was great, the timing could have been worse. They had lost the grain harvest, but many had hidden caches of grain in secret storage cisterns. Fortunately it was late summer, September or early October, and the late summer harvest was still there for the taking. They could bring in the summer fruit, chiefly the bulk of the fig crop. They could pick the grapes and make wine. They could bring in the olives and press out the oil. Gedaliah urged them to move quickly, and they followed his advice and brought in an abundant harvest. These crops were cash crops, part of which they could sell to obtain the money to buy other supplies.

13Johanan son of Kareah and all the army officers still in the open country came to Gedaliah at Mizpah 14and said to him, "Don't you know that Baalis king of the Ammonites has sent Ishmael son of Nethaniah to take your life?" But Gedaliah son of Ahikam did not believe them.

15Then Johanan son of Kareah said privately to Gedaliah in Mizpah, "Let me go and kill Ishmael son of Nethaniah, and no one will know it. Why should he take your life and cause all the Jews who are gathered around you to be scattered and the remnant of Judah to perish?"

16But Gedaliah son of Ahikam said to Johanan son of Kareah, "Don't do such a thing! What you are saying about Ishmael is not true."

Johanan, one of the army commanders, warned Gedaliah of a plot against his life. The plot was no secret. Johanan privately offered to kill the plotter in such a way that the killing could not be traced back to the governor. He made the offer because Gedaliah's death would disrupt, if not destroy, the nation just as it was starting to recover. Gedaliah refused to have anything to do with it. He refused to believe the accusation and forbade any action to stop the plot. His idealism would cost him his life.

Baalis, king of the Ammonites, was behind the plot. The Ammonites, ancient enemies of Judah and Israel had fought Israel from the time it first approached the Holy Land throughout its history. With Judah's defeat, the way opened for the Ammonites. It served Baalis's self-interest to keep Judah weak and leaderless. He hoped to use this opportunity to increase his own power and enlarge his territory. His only obstacle was Gedaliah who had rallied the Jews behind him. To get rid of him Baalis found a ready tool in Ishmael, a member of the Jewish royal house who was jealous of Gedaliah's new prominence.

**41 In the seventh month Ishmael son of Nethaniah, the son
of Elishama, who was of royal blood and had been one
of the king's officers, came with ten men to Gedaliah son of
Ahikam at Mizpah. While they were eating together there,
[2]Ishmael son of Nethaniah and the ten men who were with him
got up and struck down Gedaliah son of Ahikam, the son of
Shaphan, with the sword, killing the one whom the king of
Babylon had appointed as governor over the land. [3]Ishmael
also killed all the Jews who were with Gedaliah at Mizpah, as
well as the Babylonian soldiers who were there.**

**[4]The day after Gedaliah's assassination, before anyone knew
about it, [5]eighty men who had shaved off their beards, torn
their clothes and cut themselves came from Shechem, Shiloh
and Samaria, bringing grain offerings and incense with them
to the house of the LORD. [6]Ishmael son of Nethaniah went out
from Mizpah to meet them, weeping as he went. When he met
them, he said, "Come to Gedaliah son of Ahikam." [7]When they
went into the city, Ishmael son of Nethaniah and the men who
were with him slaughtered them and threw them into a cistern.
[8]But ten of them said to Ishmael, "Don't kill us! We have wheat
and barley, oil and honey, hidden in a field." So he let them**

**alone and did not kill them with the others. 9Now the cistern
where he threw all the bodies of the men he had killed along
with Gedaliah was the one King Asa had made as part of his
defense against Baasha king of Israel. Ishmael son of Nethaniah filled it with the dead.**

Under the pretense of friendship Ishmael sat down to eat with the unsuspecting Gedaliah. While they were eating, Ishmael assassinated Gedaliah just as Johanan had warned. He also killed the "Jews" who were there, along with a contingent of Babylonian mercenaries. Since Jeremiah survived and later mentions many other survivors, we may assume that these "Jews" were part of the provincial government Gedaliah had established at Mizpah.

Ishmael had served his master Baalis well. He had destroyed the budding provincial government and had openly challenged Babylonian authority, but he had also burned all his bridges behind him. His act was an act of rebellion sure to bring swift and certain punishment from Nebuchadnezzar.

Two motives lay at the root of Ishmael's action. First and foremost was jealousy. He was jealous because Gedaliah had received the post of governor. It galled him to see one not of the royal house ruling in Judah. Vying with jealousy in his heart was greed, an equally powerful motive.

Ishmael lured some eighty pilgrims on their way into the city to worship, and started to kill them. He spared ten of them after they offered him stores of grain, olive oil, and honey, which they had hidden away during the Babylonian occupation. This practice was very common in Israel. Throughout its history, people had hidden foodstuffs and other treasures in fields, carefully concealed in large sealed clay jars or even cisterns secretly dug for that purpose. With the threat of robbers and invaders ever present, it was the only kind of insurance people could get for themselves.

In the seven or eight months Gedaliah had governed, he had made great strides in the restoration of the Jewish people. Central to that project was the re-establishment of a worship center, which he apparently had set up at Mizpah.

The eighty men mentioned in this incident were coming to the worship center. They had shaved their beards, ceremonially torn their clothes and cut themselves. Those were signs often associated with mourning or with making a vow to the Lord. They had come to offer incense and sacrifice in the "house of the Lord." The temple had been destroyed, so a temporary place of worship must have been set up by Gedaliah, who was a pious man. He also realized how important the covenant and its exercise were to the welfare of his people.

10Ishmael made captives of all the rest of the people who were in Mizpah—the king's daughters along with all the others who were left there, over whom Nebuzaradan commander of the imperial guard had appointed Gedaliah son of Ahikam. Ishmael son of Nethaniah took them captive and set out to cross over to the Ammonites.

**11When Johanan son of Kareah and all the army officers
who were with him heard about all the crimes Ishmael son of
Nethaniah had committed, 12they took all their men and went
to fight Ishmael son of Nethaniah. They caught up with him
near the great pool in Gibeon. 13When all the people Ishmael
had with him saw Johanan son of Kareah and the army officers who were with him, they were glad. 14All the people Ishmael had taken captive at Mizpah turned and went over to Johanan son of Kareah. 15But Ishmael son of Nethaniah and eight
of his men escaped from Johanan and fled to the Ammonites.**

Ishmael's greed proved to be his undoing, for by sparing the lives of the ten pilgrims he allowed them to spread the story of the massacre. Having gathered up the treasures he had extorted from the pilgrims and taken the others whom he allowed to live, he prepared to head across the Jordan to Ammon. Jeremiah mentions especially the king's daughters, the only surviving members of the royal household. Ishmael may have dreamed of marrying one of them and trying to reestablish the royal house of Judah from a base in Ammon. Because he had so much and so many with him, he could move only very slowly.

Quickly the word of the slaughter reached Johanan and the army. Just as quickly, they moved to follow and attack Ishmael. They caught up with him at Gibeon, an historic battlefield, about five miles west of Jerusalem. The captives whom Ishmael had dragged along quickly deserted him. Ishmael escaped to the Ammonites with eight men but with no treasure. Any plans he had for gaining the throne were frustrated, and Baalis king of Ammon probably found little use for a notorious murderer.

Flight to Egypt

[16]Then Johanan son of Kareah and all the army officers who were with him led away all the survivors from Mizpah whom he had recovered from Ishmael son of Nethaniah after he had assassinated Gedaliah son of Ahikam: the soldiers, women, children and court officials he had brought from Gibeon. [17]And they went on, stopping at Geruth Kimham near Bethlehem on their way to Egypt [18]to escape the Babylonians. They were afraid of them because Ishmael son of Nethaniah had killed Gedaliah son of Ahikam, whom the king of Babylon had appointed as governor over the land.

The rescuers and the survivors did not know what to do. They were innocent of any crime, but they could not know how Nebuchadnezzar might react to Gedaliah's murder. So they headed south toward the region of Bethlehem. After pausing to regroup, they planned to head to Egypt and safety.

42 Then all the army officers, including Johanan son of Kareah and Jezaniah son of Hoshaiah, and all the people from the least to the greatest approached [2]Jeremiah the prophet and said to him, "Please hear our petition and pray to the LORD your God for this entire remnant. For as you now see, though we were once many, now only a few are left. [3]Pray that the LORD your God will tell us where we should go and what we should do."

[4]"I have heard you," replied Jeremiah the prophet. "I will certainly pray to the LORD your God as you have requested; I will tell you everything the LORD says and will keep nothing back from you."

[5]Then they said to Jeremiah, "May the LORD be a true and faithful witness against us if we do not act in accordance with everything the LORD your God sends you to tell us. [6]Whether it is favorable or unfavorable, we will obey the LORD our God, to whom we are sending you, so that it will go well with us, for we will obey the LORD our God."

As this little group camped, most agreed that the best thing they could do was to go to Egypt. They had no idea how Nebuchadnezzar would react to the death of Gedaliah but felt that in Egypt they would find refuge and security. A few of them were not nearly so sure; they wished they had a clearer direction about what they should do. Some suggested that it might be a good idea to consult the prophet Jeremiah and to ask him to pray for them. The decision to go to Egypt made the most sense, and most of the group really believed that was the best decision. But to convince the few who were uncertain and to confirm what they already believed, why not go to the prophet? Surely he would give them the same advice. So they petitioned the prophet to pray to the Lord for advice.

The entire group approached the prophet, claiming to be seeking the answer that was best for them. Their petition sounded good. To take away any doubts in the prophet's mind, they gave a solemn oath to him and to God. No matter what the outcome, however the Lord advised them, they promised to obey.

Jeremiah listened to their request, setting aside whatever reservations he may have had about their sincerity. He promised to do what they asked—he would go to the Lord on their behalf, and whatever the Lord told him, he would tell them.

7Ten days later the word of the LORD came to Jeremiah. 8So he called together Johanan son of Kareah and all the army officers who were with him and all the people from the least to the greatest. 9He said to them, "This is what the LORD, the God of Israel, to whom you sent me to present your petition, says: 10'If you stay in this land, I will build you up and not tear you down; I will plant you and not uproot you, for I am grieved over the disaster I have inflicted on you. 11Do not be afraid of the king of Babylon, whom you now fear. Do not be afraid of him, declares the LORD, for I am with you and will save you and deliver you from his hands. 12I will show you compassion so that he will have compassion on you and restore you to your land.'

Jeremiah gave the Lord's answer to the assembly of all the people. The answer came after ten days, the number of completeness, to show them that the Lord had freely and firmly decided what was the best. The Lord's answer was: "Stay in the land!" No doubt the Lord felt pity for these stubborn, misguided people. He had punished them enough. They were afraid of the king of Babylon, but they didn't have to be. Just as the Lord had used him as an instrument to punish them, so now he would use him as his instrument to save his people.

But the real guarantee of their safety lay with their God, “for I am with you and will save you.”

13“However, if you say, ‘We will not stay in this land,’ and so disobey the LORD your God, 14and if you say, ‘No, we will go and live in Egypt, where we will not see war or hear the trumpet or be hungry for bread,’ 15then hear the word of the LORD, O remnant of Judah. This is what the LORD Almighty, the God of Israel, says: ‘If you are determined to go to Egypt and you do go to settle there, 16then the sword you fear will overtake you there, and the famine you dread will follow you into Egypt, and there you will die. 17Indeed, all who are determined to go to Egypt to settle there will die by the sword, famine and plague; not one of them will survive or escape the disaster I will bring on them.’ 18This is what the LORD Almighty, the God of Israel, says: ‘As my anger and wrath have been poured out on those who lived in Jerusalem, so will my wrath be poured out on you when you go to Egypt. You will be an object of cursing and horror, of condemnation and reproach; you will never see this place again.’

19“O remnant of Judah, the LORD has told you, ‘Do not go to Egypt.’ Be sure of this: I warn you today 20that you made a fatal mistake when you sent me to the LORD your God and said, ‘Pray to the LORD our God for us; tell us everything he says and we will do it.’ 21I have told you today, but you still have not obeyed the LORD your God in all he sent me to tell you. 22So now, be sure of this: You will die by the sword, famine and plague in the place where you want to go to settle.”

They had asked the Lord for an answer, and he had given them one but not the one they wanted. God always answers those who ask of him, but these people had not asked honestly. They had already made up their minds. They were not ready to obey God’s will. Because they did not trust the Lord, they did not listen to his answer. Because they did not trust the Lord, they looked elsewhere for security. They yearned for Egypt, where they imagined they would find peace and prosperity. They forgot the most basic truth of Scripture and life. Only in the Lord does anyone find peace and security. And because they looked to themselves, they refused to do what the Lord had told them.

Because of their unbelief they felt it necessary to secure their own future, but they could not. The problems from which they were running away would find them even in Egypt. Sword, plague, and famine would dog them even there. None of them would escape; every one of them would die in Egypt. As the Lord had punished Jerusalem and they had just witnessed that punishment, so he would punish them in Egypt. Their stay would not be temporary but final. They would never see their homeland again.

Jeremiah therefore informed them that they had made a fatal mistake. They had imagined they could play games with God. They had pretended to approach him in sincerity and honesty. They had said they would put themselves under his will, but they had lied. They did not really want to know or do what the Lord said. Their minds were already made up, and their oath was meaningless. Their prayer was dishonest, for they never intended to do what God willed and said. They had condemned themselves.

Like so many others before them and like so many others since then, they had deluded themselves into thinking that the Lord's Word does not matter, that they could fake obedience. They serve as a warning. No one should pretend he is ready to do God's will if he is not. No one should pray to the Lord unless he comes with an obedient heart and is prepared to accept the answer the Lord gives. We can deceive people, but no one deceives God. No one will escape the judgment that deception brings. No one can escape the force of God's own Word. The Lord keeps his word and stands by his promises. The person who thinks he can fool God has only fooled himself.

43 When Jeremiah finished telling the people all the words
of the LORD their God—everything the LORD had sent
him to tell them—2Azariah son of Hoshaiah and Johanan son
of Kareah and all the arrogant men said to Jeremiah, "You are
lying! The LORD our God has not sent you to say, 'You must
not go to Egypt to settle there.' 3But Baruch son of Neriah is in-
citing you against us to hand us over to the Babylonians, so
they may kill us or carry us into exile to Babylon."
4So Johanan son of Kareah and all the army officers and all
the people disobeyed the LORD's command to stay in the land
of Judah. 5Instead, Johanan son of Kareah and all the army of-
ficers led away all the remnant of Judah who had come back to
live in the land of Judah from all the nations where they had
been scattered. 6They also led away all the men, women and
children and the king's daughters whom Nebuzaradan com-
mander of the imperial guard had left with Gedaliah son of
Ahikam, the son of Shaphan, and Jeremiah the prophet and
Baruch son of Neriah. 7So they entered Egypt in disobedience
to the LORD and went as far as Tahpanhes.

As soon as Jeremiah had finished delivering the Lord's message, the leaders of the remnant attacked him. Jeremiah had forcefully reminded them that this message was the very one they themselves had requested from the Lord. Led by the officers of the army, Johanan rejected what Jeremiah had said. He called Jeremiah a liar and a pawn. He charged that Baruch, Jeremiah's assistant, was behind it all. He said that Baruch had pushed Jeremiah to give them this advice. In this way they rejected the Word of the Lord. The officers hadn't wanted to consult Jeremiah in the first place, so they found a convenient excuse to disregard his message. They used this excuse to salve their own consciences and to answer the question that they had asked Jeremiah in the first place. At least they could say they had tried.

In direct disobedience to the Lord's Word the military commanders led all the people to Egypt. They allowed no one in the group any choice. They compelled everyone to go along—even Jeremiah and Baruch and perhaps other believers, too, who may have wished to follow the Lord's Word. In their unbelief, the commanders tolerated no difference of opinion. They marched south along the Mediterranean coast, entered into Egypt, and stopped at Tahpanhes (also called Daphne) in the easternmost part of the Nile delta. Pharaoh Hophra (588 to 569 B.C.) and his dynasty had built up this fortress as part of their defense system against invasion.

Nearly a thousand years after God had delivered his people from Egypt, Johanan and the others, in their disobedience had taken the whole nation back to Egypt. What an irony! They returned willingly to the land of slavery.

In the twelfth chapter of his Gospel, John reaches a climax. He had presented seven great miracles of Jesus, each one more astounding and marvelous than the previous. The last miracle John presents is about Jesus' raising Lazarus from the dead. He had also recited some of Jesus' most memorable and moving words including the great sermons he had preached to the Jews. Then John writes, "Even after Jesus had done all these miraculous signs in their presence, they still would not believe in him" (John 12:37). Johanan and the remnant had seen, how every Word of the Lord had proved true, yet they did not believe.

8In Tahpanhes the word of the LORD came to Jeremiah:
9"While the Jews are watching, take some large stones with you and bury them in clay in the brick pavement at the entrance to

Pharaoh's palace in Tahpanhes. [10]Then say to them, 'This is what the LORD Almighty, the God of Israel, says: I will send for my servant Nebuchadnezzar king of Babylon, and I will set his throne over these stones I have buried here; he will spread his royal canopy above them. [11]He will come and attack Egypt, bringing death to those destined for death, captivity to those destined for captivity, and the sword to those destined for the sword. [12]He will set fire to the temples of the gods of Egypt; he will burn their temples and take their gods captive. As a shepherd wraps his garment around him, so will he wrap Egypt around himself and depart from there unscathed. [13]There in the temple of the sun in Egypt he will demolish the sacred pillars and will burn down the temples of the gods of Egypt.' "

At the Lord's command Jeremiah gave the disobedient Jews one last object lesson. They thought that by fleeing to Egypt they had escaped war forever. While they were watching, Jeremiah took some large stones, smeared them with clay, and placed them into the roadway leading up to the palace of the pharaoh. Egypt would be no haven for the people of Judah because Nebuchadnezzar would come to Egypt and set his throne over the stones Jeremiah had placed there. Later in his reign he would invade Egypt and conquer the Egyptians. This invasion would occur in 568 B.C. As easily as a shepherd throws his loose outer garment around him, so the king of Babylon would take Egypt—as we would say, "with no sweat."

The Jewish remnant who escaped to Egypt, hoping to find safety, would be disappointed. Having left the Lord, they looked for security in Egypt and instead would find death, captivity, and the sword. They would find the gods of Egypt as worthless as the false gods they had worshiped in Judah. But they were hooked on those false gods. The simple way of faith was abhorrent to them.

Disaster Because of Idolatry

44 This word came to Jeremiah concerning all the Jews
living in Lower Egypt—in Migdol, Tahpanhes and
Memphis—and in Upper Egypt: 2"This is what the LORD
Almighty, the God of Israel, says: You saw the great disaster I
brought on Jerusalem and on all the towns of Judah. Today
they lie deserted and in ruins 3because of the evil they have
done. They provoked me to anger by burning incense and by
worshiping other gods that neither they nor you nor your fathers ever knew. 4Again and again I sent my servants the
prophets, who said, 'Do not do this detestable thing that I
hate!' 5But they did not listen or pay attention; they did not
turn from their wickedness or stop burning incense to other
gods. 6Therefore, my fierce anger was poured out; it raged
against the towns of Judah and the streets of Jerusalem and
made them the desolate ruins they are today.

7"Now this is what the LORD God Almighty, the God of Israel, says: Why bring such great disaster on yourselves by cutting off from Judah the men and women, the children and infants, and so leave yourselves without a remnant? 8Why provoke me to anger with what your hands have made, burning
incense to other gods in Egypt, where you have come to live?
You will destroy yourselves and make yourselves an object of
cursing and reproach among all the nations on earth. 9Have
you forgotten the wickedness committed by your fathers and
by the kings and queens of Judah and the wickedness committed by you and your wives in the land of Judah and the streets
of Jerusalem? 10To this day they have not humbled themselves
or shown reverence, nor have they followed my law and the decrees I set before you and your fathers.

11"Therefore, this is what the LORD Almighty, the God of Israel, says: I am determined to bring disaster on you and to
destroy all Judah. 12I will take away the remnant of Judah
who were determined to go to Egypt to settle there. They will
all perish in Egypt; they will fall by the sword or die from

famine. From the least to the greatest, they will die by sword or famine. They will become an object of cursing and horror, of condemnation and reproach.
[13]I will punish those who live in Egypt with the sword, famine and plague, as I punished Jerusalem.
[14]None of the remnant of Judah who have gone to live in Egypt will escape or survive to return to the land of Judah, to which they long to return and live; none will return except a few fugitives."

Jewish refugees had spread to all parts of Egypt. The two chief parts of Egypt are named. Their names are derived from the way the Nile river flows, from south to north. Lower Egypt is in the north where the Nile forms its great delta and empties into the Mediterranean Sea. Upper Egypt is in the south where the Nile emerges from the interior of Africa. This region is also called Pathros.

The call of the Lord went out to all the refugees, to those who lived in Migdol and Tahpanhes, the fortress cities of the eastern delta, to those who lived in the ancient city of Memphis just south of the delta, and to those who had moved deep into the south of Egypt. For all of them, no matter where they might be, the Lord had a message.

They imagined they were safe. The Lord asked them to remember the disaster they had seen with their own eyes that had overtaken their homeland because of their idolatry. The false gods whom they and their fathers worshiped had done nothing but make trouble for them. These gods had not saved them by any powerful intervention. These gods had given no evidence at all of any ability to do anything! The Jews had never gotten any help from these gods. They had totally failed those who worshiped them. Yet, despite their own experience and the warnings of generations of prophets the Lord had sent, they did not believe. Finally the Lord carried out the judgment with which he had threatened them. He laid waste the land of Judah and the city of Jerusalem. Even as God spoke these words through his prophet, their own land lay in desolate ruins. Jeremiah's hearers had seen it with their own eyes, but they ran from the hard lesson God was teaching them. They had learned nothing from it.

The Lord pleaded with them: "Why do you want to repeat the disaster? Your present course will destroy all but a few of you who have fled to Egypt. You will bring your own nation to the very brink of extinction. The ground is about to give way, swallowing you all up." But still they refused to listen. They made no attempt to change. Like boxers hit with too many blows, they had knocked themselves senseless. They no longer knew the way back to the Lord. Persistent unbelief and rejection of the Lord's Word had hardened their hearts.

They had fled to Egypt for safety and security to escape the wrath and power of Nebuchadnezzar. They would not escape his wrath for they could not escape the Lord's wrath. Even the remnant left from the ruin of Judah would be wiped out. Instead of preserving themselves by their own wisdom, they hastened their own ruin, because their wisdom was foolishness. Only a very few stragglers would survive. They would be spared, to serve as living witnesses to the certainty of the Lord's Word.

**15Then all the men who knew that their wives were burning
incense to other gods, along with all the women who were present—a large assembly—and all the people living in Lower and
Upper Egypt, said to Jeremiah, 16"We will not listen to the message you have spoken to us in the name of the LORD! 17We will
certainly do everything we said we would: We will burn incense
to the Queen of Heaven and will pour out drink offerings to her
just as we and our fathers, our kings and our officials did in the
towns of Judah and in the streets of Jerusalem. At that time we
had plenty of food and were well off and suffered no harm. 18But**

ever since we stopped burning incense to the Queen of Heaven
and pouring out drink offerings to her, we have had nothing
and have been perishing by sword and famine."
[19]The women added, "When we burned incense to the Queen
of Heaven and poured out drink offerings to her, did not our
husbands know that we were making cakes like her image and
pouring out drink offerings to her?"
[20]Then Jeremiah said to all the people, both men and wom-
en, who were answering him, [21]"Did not the LORD remember
and think about the incense burned in the towns of Judah and
the streets of Jerusalem by you and your fathers, your kings
and your officials and the people of the land? [22]When the
LORD could no longer endure your wicked actions and the detestable things you did, your land became an object of cursing
and a desolate waste without inhabitants, as it is today. [23]Be-
cause you have burned incense and have sinned against the
LORD and have not obeyed him or followed his law or his decrees or his stipulations, this disaster has come upon you, as
you now see."
[24]Then Jeremiah said to all the people, including the wom-
en, "Hear the word of the LORD, all you people of Judah in
Egypt. [25]This is what the LORD Almighty, the God of Israel,
says: You and your wives have shown by your actions what
you promised when you said, 'We will certainly carry out the
vows we made to burn incense and pour out drink offerings to
the Queen of Heaven.'
"Go ahead then, do what you promised! Keep your vows!
[26]But hear the word of the LORD, all Jews living in Egypt: 'I
swear by my great name,' says the LORD, 'that no one from Judah living anywhere in Egypt will ever again invoke my name
or swear, "As surely as the Sovereign LORD lives." [27]For I am
watching over them for harm, not for good; the Jews in Egypt
will perish by sword and famine until they are all destroyed.
[28]Those who escape the sword and return to the land of Judah
from Egypt will be very few. Then the whole remnant of Judah

**who came to live in Egypt will know whose word will stand—
mine or theirs.**

**29" 'This will be the sign to you that I will punish you in this
place,' declares the LORD, 'so that you will know that my
threats of harm against you will surely stand.' 30This is what
the LORD says: 'I am going to hand Pharaoh Hophra king of
Egypt over to his enemies who seek his life, just as I handed
Zedekiah king of Judah over to Nebuchadnezzar king of Babylon, the enemy who was seeking his life.' "**

For some reason the Jews who had fled to Egypt held a solemn assembly. During the course of this assembly Jeremiah engaged in his final dialogue with his people. After this dialogue there was nothing more he could say. During this assembly the Jews in Egypt confirmed their unbelief. Determined to sin, they grabbed at whatever cover they could to justify themselves. They did not show the slightest sign of repentance; in fact, their attitude had hardened into bold defiance.

The women, and especially the wives, cultivated the worship of the Queen of Heaven. We don't know for sure which deity is meant. Obviously they had made her their special goddess. They served her with every honor. They burned incense to her, offered drink offerings, and made little sweet cakes in her image. Their husbands and fathers had not forbidden them to serve the Queen of Heaven. No one could blame the women. In fact, they could claim innocence, for the law said that if a husband or father heard the vow of his wife or daughter and said nothing, then she had his permission to do whatever she did (Numbers 30:1-10).

The men were fully aware of what the women were doing and of their own guilt. They had accepted the evil; now they tried to justify it. They rejected outright what Jeremiah had to say. With a narrowness of vision they rewrote their history by looking at what had happened in a different light. According to their revised version of history, as long as they served the Queen of Heaven in Judah, all was well; when they stopped serving her, things went bad.

Their unbelief had blinded them. They could no longer see the truth. Wanting desperately to believe the lie, they completely deceived themselves. They did not bother to think about their reason for being in Egypt. It was because they had disobeyed the Lord and brought upon themselves his terrible judgment. Where was their "Queen of Heaven" when Nebuchadnezzar broke through the walls of Jerusalem and burned it to the ground? Jeremiah's warning fell on deaf ears. They had given up the Word of the Lord and there was no wisdom in them.

This section gives us our last glimpse of the prophet Jeremiah. We know nothing more about him for sure. He may have died in Egypt. The Lord may have rescued him and allowed him to return to the land of Judah once more. We do not know. But we do know that the Lord kept his word to Jeremiah.

Few men have served as hard a ministry as Jeremiah did. For over forty years, until his old age, and wherever the Lord sent him, he preached the Lord's Word without compromise. Sometimes he staggered under the burden, and at times he wanted to throw it off, but the Lord never failed him. Through all those years the Lord kept the promise he had made to the prophet at the very beginning, "Do not be afraid of them, for I am with you and will rescue you" (Jeremiah 1:8). In the end Jeremiah stood unbowed and unbroken, still proclaiming to his people that Word of the Lord.

By human standards, Jeremiah's long ministry was a failure. A few listened and believed, but most rejected his message. The destruction he so ardently longed to prevent fell upon the Jews because of their unbelief. In the end he stood alone. No one remembered his service or appreciated him.

Still he ranks as one of the Lord's greatest servants. For by the grace given him he was faithful to that which the Lord had called him to do. The Lord asks no more than that of his spokesmen. "Now it is required that those who have been given a trust must prove faithful" (1 Corinthians 4:2).

Jeremiah proved faithful. At the end he knew he had served him who is all in all, and Jeremiah was content with that service. Faithful to the end, he waited to receive the fulfillment of the promise made to him and every believer, "Be faithful, even to the point of death, and I will give you the crown of life" (Revelation 2:10).

A MESSAGE TO BARUCH

JEREMIAH 45

**45 This is what Jeremiah the prophet told Baruch son of
Neriah in the fourth year of Jehoiakim son of Josiah
king of Judah, after Baruch had written on a scroll the words
Jeremiah was then dictating: 2"This is what the LORD, the God
of Israel, says to you, Baruch: 3You said, 'Woe to me! The
LORD has added sorrow to my pain; I am worn out with groaning and find no rest.' "
4The LORD said, "Say this to him: 'This is what the LORD
says: I will overthrow what I have built and uproot what I
have planted, throughout the land. 5Should you then seek great
things for yourself? Seek them not. For I will bring disaster on
all people, declares the LORD, but wherever you go I will let
you escape with your life.' "**

This chapter serves as a kind of footnote explaining how it was that Baruch was able to escape destruction and be with Jeremiah to the end.

Baruch served Jeremiah as a scribe and personal assistant for at least twenty years. We hear of him first in the fourth year of Jehoiakim, the year 605 B.C. (Jeremiah 36). At that time he put Jeremiah's prophecy down in writing. He took about a year to transcribe the message of the prophet to scrolls. After he had finished, Jeremiah commanded Baruch, in his place, to read the message to all of Judah.

Baruch's reading provoked the king to rage. In that rage the king ordered the arrest of Jeremiah and Baruch. No doubt Baruch suffered indignities along with Jeremiah. Some even made him the "evil genius" behind Jeremiah (Jeremiah 43:3). Yet through all of those hard times Baruch stayed with the prophet.

At the beginning of his association with Jeremiah, Baruch seems to have thought that his work with the prophet would be a chance for him to move up to an important position. He could not have been more wrong. The Lord gently rebuked him for his ambition. His ambition was unseemly in the face of the great disaster the Lord was bringing on Judah. Instead of advancement, Baruch found pain and groaning—so much that he did not know whether he could stand it all. To strengthen Baruch for future service, the Lord promised him that he would keep him wherever he would go. Even with death all around, the Lord would preserve him.

Jeremiah includes God's promise to Baruch as he closes the narrative portion of his book, to show that the Lord keeps all of his promises. He had kept his word to Baruch in the same way he had kept it to Jeremiah. The Lord never fails those whom he has called to serve.

THE LORD'S JUDGMENT AGAINST THE NATIONS

JEREMIAH 46—51

A Message About Egypt

46 This is the word of the LORD that came to Jeremiah the prophet concerning the nations:
2 Concerning Egypt:
This is the message against the army of Pharaoh Neco king of Egypt, which was defeated at Carchemish on the Euphrates River by Nebuchadnezzar king of Babylon in the fourth year of Jehoiakim son of Josiah king of Judah:

3 "Prepare your shields, both large and small,
and march out for battle!
4 Harness the horses,
mount the steeds!
Take your positions
with helmets on!
Polish your spears,
put on your armor!
5 What do I see?
They are terrified,
they are retreating,
their warriors are defeated.
They flee in haste
without looking back,
and there is terror on every side,"
declares the LORD.
6 "The swift cannot flee
nor the strong escape.
In the north by the River Euphrates
they stumble and fall.

7 "Who is this that rises like the Nile,
like rivers of surging waters?
8 Egypt rises like the Nile,
like rivers of surging waters.
She says, 'I will rise and cover the earth;
I will destroy cities and their people.'
9 Charge, O horses!
Drive furiously, O charioteers!
March on, O warriors—
men of Cush and Put who carry shields,
men of Lydia who draw the bow.
10 But that day belongs to the Lord, the LORD Almighty—
a day of vengeance, for vengeance on his foes.
The sword will devour till it is satisfied,
till it has quenched its thirst with blood.
For the Lord, the LORD Almighty, will offer sacrifice
in the land of the north by the River Euphrates.

11 "Go up to Gilead and get balm,
O Virgin Daughter of Egypt.
But you multiply remedies in vain;
there is no healing for you.
12 The nations will hear of your shame;
your cries will fill the earth.
One warrior will stumble over another;
both will fall down together."

Jeremiah delivered these prophecies against the nations over a period of twenty-five years. He probably began with the prophecy against the Philistines (Jeremiah 47) at the end of the reign of Josiah or at the beginning of the reign of Jehoiakim (609 B.C.) and ended with his second prophecy against Egypt in 585 B.C. He may very well have spoken the last prophecy in Egypt where he had been dragged by Johanan (Jeremiah 43,44). The rest of the prophecies he wrote during the first four years of King Zedekiah's reign (597–586 B.C.).

Jeremiah gathered these prophecies in a single section of his book to show that the Lord rules and judges all nations, and that in the end he would protect and deliver his own people out of the land of their oppressors. He controls history for the good of those he loves.

Because Egypt was Israel's most ancient enemy, Jeremiah presents his prophecies against Egypt first. For more than a thousand years Egypt had been a major power in the Middle East. She had fallen under the power of Assyria in the early 600s B.C. In 655 B.C., under the leadership of a new dynasty and its pharaoh, Psammetichus I, Egypt broke free from Assyria and, under Pharaoh Neco (609–593 B.C.), began to assert her power once more. After the Assyrian empire fell before the Babylonians, Egypt's armies headed north for a showdown with Babylon to determine which of the two would be the dominant power in the Middle East. The key battle was fought at Carchemish near the Euphrates River in 605 B.C. The Egyptians and their allies, as Jeremiah had prophesied, went down to a crushing defeat, and forever after Egypt was a second-rate power.

Jeremiah's prophecy describes Egypt as confident of victory. Her troops, all spit and polish, were ready for the day of battle. Like the mighty Nile when it irresistibly surges over its banks, Egypt's conquering armies were ready to pour over the face of the earth. Her elite mercenaries led her armies into battle. Her infantry was from Cush (perhaps present-day Sudan) and from Put (probably Libya, to the west of Egypt). The men of Put were some of the most famous mercenaries of the ancient world. Her bowmen came from Lydia, in Asia Minor (modern Turkey). In the fight against Assyria and other eastern powers Lydia and Egypt were long-time allies. They continued their alliance against the rising power of Babylon. They both wanted to maintain their independence.

But Egypt's preparations did her no good. There was no healing of any kind for Egypt. Instead of victory she would suffer a bitter defeat, for ". . . that day belongs to the Lord." The Lord had determined to give Nebuchadnezzar and the Babylonians the victory so that Nebuchadnezzar might serve as the Lord's instrument to punish Judah.

13This is the message the LORD spoke to Jeremiah the prophet about the coming of Nebuchadnezzar king of Babylon to attack Egypt:

14"Announce this in Egypt,
and proclaim it in Migdol;
proclaim it also in Memphis and Tahpanhes:
'Take your positions and get ready,
for the sword devours those around you.'
15Why will your warriors be laid low?
They cannot stand, for the LORD will push them down.
16They will stumble repeatedly;
they will fall over each other.
They will say, 'Get up, let us go back
to our own people and our native lands,
away from the sword of the oppressor.'
17There they will exclaim,
'Pharaoh king of Egypt is only a loud noise;
he has missed his opportunity.'
18"As surely as I live," declares the King,
whose name is the LORD Almighty,
"one will come who is like Tabor among the mountains,
like Carmel by the sea.
19Pack your belongings for exile,
you who live in Egypt,
for Memphis will be laid waste
and lie in ruins without inhabitant.

20 "Egypt is a beautiful heifer,
but a gadfly is coming
against her from the north.
21 The mercenaries in her ranks
are like fattened calves.
They too will turn and flee together,
they will not stand their ground,
for the day of disaster is coming upon them,
the time for them to be punished.
22 Egypt will hiss like a fleeing serpent
as the enemy advances in force;
they will come against her with axes,
like men who cut down trees.
23 They will chop down her forest,"
declares the LORD,
"dense though it be.
They are more numerous than locusts,
they cannot be counted.
24 The Daughter of Egypt will be put to shame,
handed over to the people of the north."

25 The LORD Almighty, the God of Israel, says: "I am about
to bring punishment on Amon god of Thebes, on Pharaoh, on
Egypt and her gods and her kings, and on those who rely on
Pharaoh. 26 I will hand them over to those who seek their lives,
to Nebuchadnezzar king of Babylon and his officers. Later,
however, Egypt will be inhabited as in times past," declares
the LORD.

27 "Do not fear, O Jacob my servant;
do not be dismayed, O Israel.
I will surely save you out of a distant place,
your descendants from the land of their exile.
Jacob will again have peace and security,
and no one will make him afraid.
28 Do not fear, O Jacob my servant,
for I am with you," declares the LORD.

"Though I completely destroy all the nations
among which I scatter you,
I will not completely destroy you.
I will discipline you but only with justice;
I will not let you go entirely unpunished."

Jeremiah spoke this prophecy about the time he had given his last object lesson to the Jews. He had buried some large stones in the street leading up to the pharaoh's palace in Tahpanhes (Jeremiah 43:8-13). The year was about 585 B.C.

Jeremiah prophesied that Nebuchadnezzar would launch a successful attack against Egypt. His might would be like the two great mountains on either end of the Jezreel Valley in northern Israel: Mount Carmel on the coast in the west and Tabor to the east at the other end of the valley. His army would prove unstoppable. As little as a forest can halt the axmen, so little would Egypt be able to stop his advance. The invading army would be more numerous than the locusts which choked the land from time to time.

Egypt's mercenaries would run from her and leave her to herself. Egypt had made a lot of noise, but she had missed the chance to regain her position as a world power. Egypt's power was a mirage. When put to the real test, Egypt would collapse. By letting this happen, the Lord was punishing the remnant of Judah who had fled to Egypt and "relied on Pharaoh" (verse 25) for protection. Since the time of Isaiah (Isaiah 31:1) the Lord had repeatedly warned his people against relying on Egypt for any help. Once again they would learn the hard way that Egypt was a broken reed (Isaiah 36:6) and that their only real safety was in the Lord. Despite the punishment the Lord would inflict upon his disobedient people in Egypt, he promised to be with them, to save them, and to bring them back from exile (Jeremiah 30:10,11).

A Message About the Philistines

47 This is the word of the LORD that came to Jeremiah the prophet concerning the Philistines before Pharaoh attacked Gaza:

2 This is what the LORD says:

"See how the waters are rising in the north;
  they will become an overflowing torrent.
They will overflow the land and everything in it,
  the towns and those who live in them.
The people will cry out;
  all who dwell in the land will wail
3 at the sound of the hoofs of galloping steeds,
  at the noise of enemy chariots
  and the rumble of their wheels.
Fathers will not turn to help their children;
  their hands will hang limp.
4 For the day has come
  to destroy all the Philistines
and to cut off all survivors
  who could help Tyre and Sidon.
The LORD is about to destroy the Philistines,
  the remnant from the coasts of Caphtor.
5 Gaza will shave her head in mourning;
  Ashkelon will be silenced.
O remnant on the plain,
  how long will you cut yourselves?
6 " 'Ah, sword of the LORD,' you cry,
  'how long till you rest?
Return to your scabbard;
  cease and be still.'
7 But how can it rest
  when the LORD has commanded it,
when he has ordered it
  to attack Ashkelon and the coast?"

The Philistines were part of a larger migration of peoples, called the Sea People, who poured down over the eastern Mediterranean during the 1400s B.C. Because the Philistines had overrun Crete (here called Caphtor) before arriving in Palestine, they are referred to as the "remnants of Caphtor." From about 1200–1000 B.C. they were the major power in the eastern Mediterranean. For centuries they fought Israel for control of Canaan. When David became king (1010 B.C.), he thoroughly defeated them and reduced their power, so that they never again posed any great threat to Israel. By switching alliances among the major powers, the Philistines maintained their semi-independence until they were conquered by Babylon.

Most of the time the Philistines had allied themselves with the Egyptians. They fought with the Egyptians against Nebuchadnezzar at Carchemish (605 B.C.). This defeat apparently made them waver in their allegiance to Egypt, so the pharaoh attacked Gaza in 601/600 B.C. to try to secure their loyalty. This is probably the attack referred to in our text. Jeremiah warned the Philistines, however, that the real danger to them would come not from Egypt but from the north. It was the invading Babylonian army that would bring an end to the Philistine nation.

Even though their sympathies lay with Egypt, the Philistines did help Nebuchadnezzar in his attack against Judah and King Jehoiakim in 598 B.C. As a reward Nebuchadnezzar allowed them to split a portion of the southern part of Judah (also called the Negev) with his other ally Edom. The Philistines, however, made the mistake of encouraging Zedekiah in his revolt against Nebuchadnezzar in 587 B.C. As a result they were deported by Nebuchadnezzar to another part of his empire, a deportation which brought an end to Philistine national existence.

A Message About Moab

48 Concerning Moab:
This is what the LORD Almighty, the God of Israel, says:

"Woe to Nebo, for it will be ruined.
Kiriathaim will be disgraced and captured;
the stronghold will be disgraced and shattered.
2 Moab will be praised no more;
in Heshbon men will plot her downfall:
'Come, let us put an end to that nation.'
You too, O Madmen, will be silenced;
the sword will pursue you.
3 Listen to the cries from Horonaim,
cries of great havoc and destruction.
4 Moab will be broken;
her little ones will cry out.
5 They go up the way to Luhith,
weeping bitterly as they go;
on the road down to Horonaim
anguished cries over the destruction are heard.
6 Flee! Run for your lives;
become like a bush in the desert.
7 Since you trust in your deeds and riches,
you too will be taken captive,
and Chemosh will go into exile,
together with his priests and officials.
8 The destroyer will come against every town,
and not a town will escape.
The valley will be ruined
and the plateau destroyed,
because the LORD has spoken.
9 Put salt on Moab,
for she will be laid waste;
her towns will become desolate,
with no one to live in them.

10 "A curse on him who is lax in doing the LORD's work!
A curse on him who keeps his sword
from bloodshed!
11 "Moab has been at rest from youth,
like wine left on its dregs,
not poured from one jar to another—
she has not gone into exile.
So she tastes as she did,
and her aroma is unchanged.
12 But days are coming,"
declares the LORD,
"when I will send men who pour from jars,
and they will pour her out;
they will empty her jars
and smash her jugs.
13 Then Moab will be ashamed of Chemosh,
as the house of Israel was ashamed
when they trusted in Bethel.

14 "How can you say, 'We are warriors,
men valiant in battle'?
15 Moab will be destroyed and her towns invaded;
her finest young men will go down
in the slaughter,"
declares the King, whose name is
the LORD Almighty.
16 "The fall of Moab is at hand;
her calamity will come quickly.

According to the Bible the Moabites were descendants of Lot, Abraham's nephew (Genesis 19:36-38), and so were distant relatives of the Israelites. The Moabites were settled in their land east of the Dead Sea when the Israelites arrived in the Holy Land. Because they were relatives, the Lord commanded the Israelites to leave the land of Moab alone. Although they were relatives, Moab opposed the coming of the

Israelites. The Moabite king tried to have a curse pronounced on them (Numbers 22).

Later, during the period of the Judges, the Moabites under Eglon (Judges 3:14) subjugated Israel for eighteen years. David, whose ancestress Ruth was a Moabitess, finally brought Moab under the sphere of Israelite rule. That rule lasted about two hundred years. About the time of Ahab (830 B.C.) the Moabites successfully revolted and gained their independence. They remained independent until the time of Jeremiah. They assisted Nebuchadnezzar in punishing Jehoiakim for his disloyalty in 602 B.C. (2 Kings 24:2). But they too made the mistake of joining Zedekiah in his revolt against Nebuchadnezzar in 588 B.C. Some time after the fall of Jerusalem Nebuchadnezzar conquered Moab and deported most of its people to a different part of his empire. Isaiah had also prophesied this against Moab (Isaiah 15,16).

Though occasionally Moab was loosely subject to other nations, it remained free throughout most of its history. Jeremiah compares it to wine which had sat undisturbed on its dregs ever since it was fermented. "She has not gone into exile" (verse 11). Because of its secure position and good fortune Moab had grown prosperous, proud, and arrogant. It came to believe that it could never be taken. This belief and its long history of freedom made its final ruin all the more painful.

The prophet makes special mention of Moab's idolatry as another reason for God's judgment. The Moabites worshiped many gods, but Chemosh was their national god, chief among all their deities. He was the protector of Moab, the one whom they believed had given their land to them. In times of war they looked to him for help and victory. But Chemosh would fail them, and they would be ashamed of him just as the ten tribes of Israel were ashamed of their calf shrine at Bethel. When the crucial hour came, Moab's idols would do them no good.

17 Mourn for her, all who live around her,
all who know her fame;
say, 'How broken is the mighty scepter,
how broken the glorious staff!'

18 "Come down from your glory
and sit on the parched ground,
O inhabitants of the Daughter of Dibon,
for he who destroys Moab
will come up against you
and ruin your fortified cities.
19 Stand by the road and watch,
you who live in Aroer.
Ask the man fleeing and the woman escaping,
ask them, 'What has happened?'
20 Moab is disgraced, for she is shattered.
Wail and cry out!
Announce by the Arnon
that Moab is destroyed.
21 Judgment has come to the plateau—
to Holon, Jahzah and Mephaath,
22 to Dibon, Nebo and Beth Diblathaim,
23 to Kiriathaim, Beth Gamul and Beth Meon,
24 to Kerioth and Bozrah—
to all the towns of Moab, far and near.
25 Moab's horn is cut off;
her arm is broken,"
declares the LORD.

In Jeremiah's prophecy against Moab he lists twenty-one cities to emphasize just how total and widespread the destruction of Moab would be. He refers to Dibon, Moab's capital, twice. The loss of Dibon would be a painful and humbling lesson. A good number of the cities Jeremiah mentions in this group were taken from the tribe of Reuben when Moab expanded its territory in the early 800s and late 700s.

26 "Make her drunk,
for she has defied the LORD.
Let Moab wallow in her vomit;
let her be an object of ridicule.
27 Was not Israel the object of your ridicule?
Was she caught among thieves,
that you shake your head in scorn
whenever you speak of her?
28 Abandon your towns and dwell among the rocks,
you who live in Moab.
Be like a dove that makes its nest
at the mouth of a cave.

29 "We have heard of Moab's pride—
her overweening pride and conceit,
her pride and arrogance
and the haughtiness of her heart.
30 I know her insolence but it is futile,"
declares the LORD,
"and her boasts accomplish nothing.
31 Therefore I wail over Moab,
for all Moab I cry out,
I moan for the men of Kir Hareseth.
32 I weep for you, as Jazer weeps,
O vines of Sibmah.
Your branches spread as far as the sea;
they reached as far as the sea of Jazer.
The destroyer has fallen
on your ripened fruit and grapes.
33 Joy and gladness are gone
from the orchards and fields of Moab.

I have stopped the flow of wine from the presses;
no one treads them with shouts of joy.
Although there are shouts,
they are not shouts of joy.

34 "The sound of their cry rises
from Heshbon to Elealeh and Jahaz,
from Zoar as far as Horonaim and Eglath Shelishiyah,
for even the waters of Nimrim are dried up.
35 In Moab I will put an end
to those who make offerings on the high places
and burn incense to their gods,"
declares the LORD.

In addition to her arrogance and her idolatry, another reason Moab would fall was that she had defied the Lord (Jeremiah 27). The Lord warned Moab not to revolt against Nebuchadnezzar, but Moab would not listen. Now she would get what she had coming. No one would pity her. Her wealth and independence had given her a false sense of security and well-being, an overbearing attitude of pride. In that pride she had ridiculed the deportation of the ten northern tribes and the punishment of Judah by Nebuchadnezzar. Now her time would come. She had boasted about the abundant fruitfulness of her land; now that would be taken from her. Her destruction would be so great that she would never recover. Even the waters of Nimrim, a spring in the extreme south of Moab, would dry up. As Moabite fugitives fled south to escape the invading armies, they would find no water at this spring, which had always flowed continuously. That discovery would take away all hope.

36 "So my heart laments for Moab like a flute;
it laments like a flute for the men of Kir Hareseth.
The wealth they acquired is gone.
37 Every head is shaved
and every beard cut off;

every hand is slashed
and every waist is covered with sackcloth.
38 On all the roofs in Moab
and in the public squares
there is nothing but mourning,
for I have broken Moab
like a jar that no one wants,"
declares the LORD.
39 "How shattered she is! How they wail!
How Moab turns her back in shame!
Moab has become an object of ridicule,
an object of horror to all those around her."
40 This is what the LORD says:
"Look! An eagle is swooping down,
spreading its wings over Moab.
41 Kerioth will be captured
and the strongholds taken.
In that day the hearts of Moab's warriors
will be like the heart of a woman in labor.
42 Moab will be destroyed as a nation
because she defied the LORD.
43 Terror and pit and snare await you,
O people of Moab,"
declares the LORD.
44 "Whoever flees from the terror
will fall into a pit,
whoever climbs out of the pit
will be caught in a snare;
for I will bring upon Moab
the year of her punishment,"
declares the LORD.

45 "In the shadow of Heshbon
the fugitives stand helpless,
for a fire has gone out from Heshbon,
a blaze from the midst of Sihon;

it burns the foreheads of Moab,
the skulls of the noisy boasters.
46 **Woe to you, O Moab!**
The people of Chemosh are destroyed;
your sons are taken into exile
and your daughters into captivity.
47 **"Yet I will restore the fortunes of Moab**
in days to come,"
declares the LORD.

Here ends the judgment on Moab.

The destruction of Moab would be total. No one would escape. To drive that point home Jeremiah used a powerful picture. Fleeing the invading terror, the fugitive would fall into a pit. Trying to climb out, he would stumble into an iron trap. Barely escaping with his life, he would have to watch as his cities were torched, together with the wealth he had accumulated. In the end "Moab will be destroyed as a nation" (verse 42). As a nation Moab did not survive the deportation of Nebuchadnezzar in 582 B.C.

The destruction of Moab would numb those who lived there, and they would mourn as a people without hope. They would shave their heads and beards, signs of extreme shame and sorrow. They would slash their hands and wear sackcloth. But it was too late. The Lord had warned them, but they had not listened.

A Message About Ammon

49 **Concerning the Ammonites:**

This is what the LORD says:

"Has Israel no sons?
Has she no heirs?

Why then has Molech taken possession of Gad?
Why do his people live in its towns?
2 **But the days are coming,"**
declares the LORD,
"when I will sound the battle cry
against Rabbah of the Ammonites;
it will become a mound of ruins,
and its surrounding villages will be set on fire.
Then Israel will drive out
those who drove her out,"
says the LORD.
3 **"Wail, O Heshbon, for Ai is destroyed!**
Cry out, O inhabitants of Rabbah!
Put on sackcloth and mourn;
rush here and there inside the walls,
for Molech will go into exile,
together with his priests and officials.
4 **Why do you boast of your valleys,**
boast of your valleys so fruitful?
O unfaithful daughter,
you trust in your riches and say,
'Who will attack me?'
5 **I will bring terror on you**
from all those around you,"
declares the Lord, the LORD Almighty.
"Every one of you will be driven away,
and no one will gather the fugitives.
6 **"Yet afterward, I will restore the fortunes**
of the Ammonites,"
declares the LORD.

Like the Moabites (chapter 48), the Ammonites were descendants of Lot (Genesis 19:36-38), the nephew of Abraham. When Israel entered the Holy Land, God forbade them to take the territory of the Ammonites. Ammon, located directly east of the Jordan river, had its capital and political center at Rabbah, about seventeen miles east of the Jordan. The ancient site of Rabbah is the present Amman, capital of modern Jordan.

Ammon was subject to Israel during the reign of David and part of the reign of Solomon. It constantly vied with the tribe of Gad for control of the territory east of the Jordan. When Israel was deported to Assyria, the Ammonites moved into Israel's transjordanian territory. The god mentioned in verses one and three is the national god of the Ammonites. Ammon allied itself with Moab in 582 B.C. and lost its political independence to her. Before its defeat it had opposed the Jewish remnant under Gedaliah and later resisted those who returned from exile to rebuild Jerusalem (Nehemiah 4:1-12).

A Message About Edom

7 Concerning Edom:

This is what the LORD Almighty says:

"Is there no longer wisdom in Teman?
Has counsel perished from the prudent?
Has their wisdom decayed?
8 Turn and flee, hide in deep caves,
you who live in Dedan,
for I will bring disaster on Esau
at the time I punish him.
9 If grape pickers came to you,
would they not leave a few grapes?
If thieves came during the night,
would they not steal only as much as they wanted?
10 But I will strip Esau bare;
I will uncover his hiding places,
so that he cannot conceal himself.
His children, relatives and neighbors will perish,
and he will be no more.

11 Leave your orphans; I will protect their lives.
Your widows too can trust in me."

12 This is what the LORD says: "If those who do not deserve to
drink the cup must drink it, why should you go unpunished?
You will not go unpunished, but must drink it. 13 I swear by myself," declares the LORD, "that Bozrah will become a ruin and
an object of horror, of reproach and of cursing; and all its
towns will be in ruins forever."

14 I have heard a message from the LORD:
An envoy was sent to the nations to say,
"Assemble yourselves to attack it!
Rise up for battle!"

15 "Now I will make you small among the nations,
despised among men.
16 The terror you inspire
and the pride of your heart have deceived you,
you who live in the clefts of the rocks,
who occupy the heights of the hill.
Though you build your nest as high as the eagle's,
from there I will bring you down,"
declares the LORD.
17 "Edom will become an object of horror;
all who pass by will be appalled and will scoff
because of all its wounds.
18 As Sodom and Gomorrah were overthrown,
along with their neighboring towns,"
says the LORD,
"so no one will live there;
no man will dwell in it.

19 "Like a lion coming up from Jordan's thickets
to a rich pastureland,
I will chase Edom from its land in an instant.
Who is the chosen one I will appoint for this?
Who is like me and who can challenge me?
And what shepherd can stand against me?"

20 Therefore, hear what the LORD has planned
against Edom,
what he has purposed against those
who live in Teman:
The young of the flock will be dragged away;
he will completely destroy their pasture
because of them.
21 At the sound of their fall the earth will tremble;
their cry will resound to the Red Sea.
22 Look! An eagle will soar and swoop down,
spreading its wings over Bozrah.
In that day the hearts of Edom's warriors
will be like the heart of a woman in labor.

The Edomite people were descendants of Esau (Genesis 36), Isaac's son and Jacob's twin brother. They lived on a small inaccessible high plateau to the south and east of the Dead Sea. Their land was not fertile and could support only flocks. The land of Edom, however, straddled key trade routes running south to Egypt and to Elath, a port on the Gulf of Aqaba. Edomites also controlled access to the copper mines near Aqaba. As warriors and plunderers, they derived their wealth from control of these key areas. Edom's capital was Bozrah, located on a main north-south trade route. The northern part of Edom was called Teman and the southern Dedan.

For centuries, especially after the time of David, Edom lived in the shadow of Israel. About 200 years after David's death (830/820s B.C.), Edom broke free and managed to remain free until the mid 500s. It escaped Nebuchadnezzar's invasions. Because it rested on a high, hard-to-reach place, it prided itself on its magnificent defenses. It was very difficult to attack. Nevertheless, the Lord announced he would finally bring Edom down.

A Message About Damascus

23 Concerning Damascus:

"Hamath and Arpad are dismayed,
for they have heard bad news.
They are disheartened,
troubled like the restless sea.
24 Damascus has become feeble,
she has turned to flee
and panic has gripped her;
anguish and pain have seized her,
pain like that of a woman in labor.
25 Why has the city of renown not been abandoned,
the town in which I delight?
26 Surely, her young men will fall in the streets;
all her soldiers will be silenced in that day,"
declares the LORD Almighty.
27 "I will set fire to the walls of Damascus;
it will consume the fortresses of Ben-Hadad."

The ancient city of Damascus, capital of modern Syria, was one of the most ancient cities of the Middle East. It lay in some of the most fertile land in that part of the world. The rivers around it provided an abundant supply of water. Since it was situated along key north-south trade routes, its chief interests were commercial. It often fought Israel for control of those trade routes. For awhile under David it was subject to Israelite control (1 Kings 11:23-25). Several centuries later it regained its independence and warred with Israel (2 Kings 13). Ben-Hadad was one of its leaders during that golden period of the city.

Later Assyria held control of Damascus. The city managed to free itself from the Assyrians, however, and allied itself with Judah to stop the advance of the Babylonians. Two other great trading centers to the north of Damascus—Hamath and Arpad—also joined the alliance. The Lord warned Damascus, however, that its efforts would fail. Damascus fell to Nebuchadnezzar and faded from history for many centuries.

A Message About Kedar and Hazor

28 Concerning Kedar and the kingdoms of Hazor, which Nebuchadnezzar king of Babylon attacked:

This is what the LORD says:

"Arise, and attack Kedar
and destroy the people of the East.
29 Their tents and their flocks will be taken;
their shelters will be carried off
with all their goods and camels.
Men will shout to them,
'Terror on every side!'

30 "Flee quickly away!
Stay in deep caves, you who live in Hazor,"
declares the LORD.
"Nebuchadnezzar king of Babylon has plotted against you;
he has devised a plan against you.

31 "Arise and attack a nation at ease,
which lives in confidence,"
declares the LORD,
"a nation that has neither gates nor bars;
its people live alone.
32 Their camels will become plunder,
and their large herds will be booty.
I will scatter to the winds those who are in distant places
and will bring disaster on them from every side,"
declares the LORD.
33 "Hazor will become a haunt of jackals,
a desolate place forever.

No one will live there;
no man will dwell in it."

These were insignificant Bedouin settlements in northern Arabia. Because they lay in the desert and chiefly south and east of Judah, they were also called the "people of the East." These Bedouins were descendants of Ishmael, Isaac's half-brother (Genesis 25). The location of Hazor is completely unknown to us. These people were nomads who made their living off the desert. They moved with their flocks for forage throughout the area. With their camels they also plied the trade routes through Arabia to the land of Ophir, the land of gold and spices. To protect their interests, they joined Judah against the Babylonians. God announced that they would share also in Judah's defeat. The Lord of the nations judges the sin not only of superpowers but of insignificant nations as well.

A Message About Elam

34 This is the word of the LORD that came to Jeremiah the prophet concerning Elam, early in the reign of Zedekiah king of Judah:

35 This is what the LORD Almighty says:
"See, I will break the bow of Elam,
the mainstay of their might.
36 I will bring against Elam the four winds
from the four quarters of the heavens;
I will scatter them to the four winds,
and there will not be a nation
where Elam's exiles do not go.
37 I will shatter Elam before their foes,
before those who seek their lives;
I will bring disaster upon them,
even my fierce anger,"
declares the LORD.

"I will pursue them with the sword
until I have made an end of them.
38 I will set my throne in Elam
and destroy her king and officials,"
declares the LORD.

39 "Yet I will restore the fortunes of Elam
in days to come,"
declares the LORD.

Elam was an ancient country and civilization located south and east of Babylon near the Persian Gulf. It is part of present day Iran. For centuries it fought, first against the Assyrians and then the Babylonians, to maintain its independence. It allied itself with Judah under Zedekiah to try to contain the Babylonian empire. It escaped domination by Babylon, but was submerged under the onslaught of the Medes and the Persians who conquered it and the whole of the Middle East (530s B.C.). Their conquest brought an end to Elam as a nation, though many elements of its culture and civilization lived on in the Persian empire.

A Message About Babylon

50 This is the word the LORD spoke through Jeremiah the prophet concerning Babylon and the land of the Babylonians:

2 "Announce and proclaim among the nations,
lift up a banner and proclaim it;
keep nothing back, but say,
'Babylon will be captured;
Bel will be put to shame,
Marduk filled with terror.
Her images will be put to shame
and her idols filled with terror.'
3 A nation from the north will attack her
and lay waste her land.

No one will live in it;
both men and animals will flee away.

4 "In those days, at that time,"
declares the LORD,
"the people of Israel and the people of Judah together
will go in tears to seek the LORD their God.
5 They will ask the way to Zion
and turn their faces toward it.
They will come and bind themselves to the LORD
in an everlasting covenant
that will not be forgotten.

6 "My people have been lost sheep;
their shepherds have led them astray
and caused them to roam on the mountains.
They wandered over mountain and hill
and forgot their own resting place.
7 Whoever found them devoured them;
their enemies said, 'We are not guilty,
for they sinned against the LORD, their true pasture,
the LORD, the hope of their fathers.'

8 "Flee out of Babylon;
leave the land of the Babylonians,
and be like the goats that lead the flock.
9 For I will stir up and bring against Babylon
an alliance of great nations from the land
of the north.
They will take up their positions against her,
and from the north she will be captured.
Their arrows will be like skilled warriors
who do not return empty-handed.
10 So Babylonia will be plundered;
all who plunder her will have their fill,"
declares the LORD.

Jeremiah wrote this prophecy against Babylon early in the reign of Zedekiah (597/596 B.C.), to confirm the words of a prophecy he had made during the reign of Jehoiakim ten years earlier. At that time he had prophesied that Babylon would conquer all the nations of the Middle East. He had urged all those nations to surrender. He also had said that Judah would fall to Babylon and be taken into exile for seventy years. What is striking is that Jeremiah spoke these words while Babylon was on its rise to becoming a superpower in the Middle East.

In this prophecy Jeremiah also provides part of the answer to the question: "Why did Judah face judgment when so many other nations were more unrighteous than she" (Jeremiah 12)? Jeremiah supplies the insight promised by the Lord, "In days to come you will understand . . ." (Jeremiah 30:24).

In his prophecy Jeremiah drew on the work of Isaiah (Isaiah 13,14), employing many of the same pictures and images as the earlier prophet. Both agreed that the chief cause of Babylon's fall would be pride and arrogance. For the Jews and future generations of believers Babylon would become synonymous with all the enemies of the church. It would become a title for all unbelief in its opposition to Christ. St. John used this same imagery in his Revelation.

Babylon was a very ancient city situated between the Tigris and Euphrates Rivers in what is today Iraq. For over a thousand years it had been a force to be reckoned with in the Middle East. Though it suffered eclipse during the golden years of the Assyrian empire, it begin to revive in the middle 600s, as Assyria began to decline. Babylon reached its zenith under Nebuchadnezzar, who ruled for forty years. After his death his empire began a slow decline until the Medes and Persians overran it in 539 B.C. Throughout the Persian period it slipped more and more into obscurity. By the time of Christ it was only heap of ruins.

Jeremiah's oracle pronouncing God's judgment on Babylon begins by proclaiming the shame and failure of Babylon's great god Bel/Marduk. The people of Babylon and Mesopotamia had worshiped this god from ancient times. For them Bel/Marduk was the great god, the ruler and controller of the universe, the only god who mattered. As their empire spread they became more and more committed to their worship of Bel/Marduk. They acknowledged no god but him.

Perhaps it was for that reason that Nebuchadnezzar set up his image of gold and demanded that his subjects worship it (Daniel 3). But Bel/Marduk and all the false gods of Babylon would not be able to save her. Invaders from the north would wage a successful war against her and take from her all the plunder they wanted. The only way Babylon's inhabitants could save themselves would be by fleeing from the city.

With a single act of judgment God would both punish Babylon and rescue his own people. Israel had destroyed itself by worshiping idols and following the leadership of wicked kings. It had forgotten its true resting place, the only one who could help them, the Lord. Others had used Israel's sin as a convenient excuse to plunder it. Blaming everything on Israel's sin and shifting the burden from themselves, their enemies had plundered the nation, grabbing everything they could get from Israel.

God controlled the history of ancient nations, however, so that the people of Judah would learn a lesson from their bitter experience. They would come to realize how powerless idols are and how powerful and faithful the Lord is. Having learned that lesson, they would turn to him in repentance. They would once again turn to the Lord, believing the promise of return he had given. To show their new zeal and love, they would voluntarily make a new covenant with their Lord.

11 "Because you rejoice and are glad,
you who pillage my inheritance,
because you frolic like a heifer threshing grain
and neigh like stallions,
12 your mother will be greatly ashamed;
she who gave you birth will be disgraced.
She will be the least of the nations—
a wilderness, a dry land, a desert.
13 Because of the LORD's anger she will not be inhabited
but will be completely desolate.
All who pass Babylon will be horrified and scoff
because of all her wounds.

14 "Take up your positions around Babylon,
all you who draw the bow.
Shoot at her! Spare no arrows,
for she has sinned against the LORD.
15 Shout against her on every side!
She surrenders, her towers fall,
her walls are torn down.
Since this is the vengeance of the LORD,
take vengeance on her;
do to her as she has done to others.
16 Cut off from Babylon the sower,
and the reaper with his sickle at harvest.
Because of the sword of the oppressor
let everyone return to his own people,
let everyone flee to his own land.

17 "Israel is a scattered flock
that lions have chased away.
The first to devour him
was the king of Assyria;
the last to crush his bones
was Nebuchadnezzar king of Babylon."

18 **Therefore this is what the LORD Almighty, the God of Israel, says:**

> **"I will punish the king of Babylon and his land**
> **as I punished the king of Assyria.**
> 19 **But I will bring Israel back to his own pasture**
> **and he will graze on Carmel and Bashan;**
> **his appetite will be satisfied**
> **on the hills of Ephraim and Gilead.**
> 20 **In those days, at that time,"**
> **declares the LORD,**
> **"search will be made for Israel's guilt,**
> **but there will be none,**
> **and for the sins of Judah,**
> **but none will be found,**
> **for I will forgive the remnant I spare.**

Babylon would suffer defeat and ruin because she took delight in the downfall of God's chosen people. Her success led her to imagine that she deserved the credit for what she was. She did not know that she was only the Lord's instrument. Because of the Lord's anger, her defenses would crumble before the great armies that would gather to fight her. The Lord's powerful vengeance would pay back Babylon for her own evil pride, and mighty Babylon would fall as suddenly as mighty Assyria had. Her fall would serve as a reminder to all the nations that the Lord controls their destinies.

Strangely enough, the Israelites, who had been oppressed first by the Assyrians and then by the Babylonians, would survive and prosper. Like flocks quietly grazing in lush pasture, they would once again live at peace in their own land. God would grant such peace to his people, not because they deserved it but because the Lord had shown mercy. The guilt of Israel and the sin of Judah would be put out of sight, for the Lord would forgive them and give them a fresh start.

21 "Attack the land of Merathaim
and those who live in Pekod.
Pursue, kill and completely destroy them,"
declares the LORD.

"Do everything I have commanded you.
22 The noise of battle is in the land,
the noise of great destruction!
23 How broken and shattered
is the hammer of the whole earth!
How desolate is Babylon
among the nations!
24 I set a trap for you, O Babylon,
and you were caught before you knew it;
you were found and captured
because you opposed the LORD.
25 The LORD has opened his arsenal
and brought out the weapons of his wrath,
for the Sovereign LORD Almighty has work to do
in the land of the Babylonians.
26 Come against her from afar.
Break open her granaries;
pile her up like heaps of grain.
Completely destroy her
and leave her no remnant.
27 Kill all her young bulls;
let them go down to the slaughter!
Woe to them! For their day has come,
the time for them to be punished.
28 Listen to the fugitives and refugees from Babylon
declaring in Zion
how the LORD our God has taken vengeance,
vengeance for his temple.

The Lord urged Babylon's attackers to penetrate to the farthest reaches of Babylonian power. The two names he used for Babylon add insult. Merathaim was a swampy area of reeds formed by the convergence of the Tigris and Euphrates Rivers near the Persian Gulf. Even as its waters were salty and bitter, so bitter and worthless had Babylon become. Pekod refers to a tribe, the Puqudu, who lived near the same area. The root word in Hebrew means "punishment." Babylon would be punished for her pride.

The Lord was the real enemy of Babylon, and he would not allow the destruction of his temple to go unpunished. The last king of Babylon, drunk with wine and pride, ordered the temple utensils taken by Nebuchadnezzar to be used for his orgy. That order sealed his end. The Lord brought swift judgment on Babylon (Daniel 5). The Jewish fugitives who escaped from the city were instructed to spread word of the Lord's vengeance. Though Babylon was a world power, it would fall because the Lord would give strength and cunning to its attackers. The great walls of the city would prove useless. Great Babylon would fall.

29 "Summon archers against Babylon,
all those who draw the bow.
Encamp all around her;
let no one escape.
Repay her for her deeds;
do to her as she has done.
For she has defied the LORD,
the Holy One of Israel.
30 Therefore, her young men will fall in the streets;
all her soldiers will be silenced in that day,"
declares the LORD.
31 "See, I am against you, O arrogant one,"
declares the Lord, the LORD Almighty,
"for your day has come,
the time for you to be punished.

32 The arrogant one will stumble and fall
and no one will help her up;
I will kindle a fire in her towns
that will consume all who are around her."

33 This is what the LORD Almighty says:

"The people of Israel are oppressed,
and the people of Judah as well.
All their captors hold them fast,
refusing to let them go.
34 Yet their Redeemer is strong;
the LORD Almighty is his name.
He will vigorously defend their cause
so that he may bring rest to their land,
but unrest to those who live in Babylon.

35 "A sword against the Babylonians!"
declares the LORD—
"against those who live in Babylon
and against her officials and wise men!
36 A sword against her false prophets!
They will become fools.
A sword against her warriors!
They will be filled with terror.
37 A sword against her horses and chariots
and all the foreigners in her ranks!
They will become women.
A sword against her treasures!
They will be plundered.
38 A drought on her waters!
They will dry up.
For it is a land of idols,
idols that will go mad with terror.

39 "So desert creatures and hyenas will live there,
and there the owl will dwell.
It will never again be inhabited
or lived in from generation to generation.

40 As God overthrew Sodom and Gomorrah
along with their neighboring towns,"
declares the LORD,
"so no one will live there;
no man will dwell in it.

The final assault on Babylon would be successful, her devastation total. Because the Almighty by his Word called for the "sword" to strike mighty Babylon, it would do so. The sword would do what it was told to do. In the end only desert creatures would make their home in Babylon, which would become like Sodom and Gomorrah. Gradually that is exactly what happened. Under Persian rule Babylon slipped in prestige and power and never recovered. By the time of Christ five centuries later, Babylon had indeed become a heap of ruins.

All of this would turn out quite differently from what was expected. Israel, the captive, would find rest in her land. Babylon, the aggressor, would have no rest. The Lord fulfills his purposes. The fall of Babylon would serve to fulfill God's promise to restore his people. Since no one would come to the rescue of his people, the Lord would. Their redeemer is mighty and strong. He would save them and deliver them.

41 "Look! An army is coming from the north;
a great nation and many kings
are being stirred up from the ends of the earth.
42 They are armed with bows and spears;
they are cruel and without mercy.
They sound like the roaring sea
as they ride on their horses;
they come like men in battle formation
to attack you, O Daughter of Babylon.
43 The king of Babylon has heard reports about them,
and his hands hang limp.

Anguish has gripped him,
pain like that of a woman in labor.
44 **Like a lion coming up from Jordan's thickets**
to a rich pastureland,
I will chase Babylon from its land in an instant.
Who is the chosen one I will appoint for this?
Who is like me and who can challenge me?
And what shepherd can stand against me?"
45 **Therefore, hear what the LORD has planned**
against Babylon,
what he has purposed against the land
of the Babylonians:
The young of the flock will be dragged away;
he will completely destroy their pasture
because of them.
46 **At the sound of Babylon's capture the earth**
will tremble;
its cry will resound among the nations.

The great armies stationed against them would dishearten the Babylonians and their leaders. Using the same imagery he used about the fall of Edom (Jeremiah 49:19), Jeremiah pictured the helplessness of the flock of Babylon against the advance of the Lion of Judah. As a lion tears the flock and takes what he wants, so the Lord would tear the best and choicest from Babylon, leaving her with nothing. The fall of Babylon would shake the world itself. If Babylon could fall, what nation could stand? Without the Lord's permission, not one.

51 **This is what the LORD says:**
"See, I will stir up the spirit of a destroyer
against Babylon and the people of Leb Kamai.
2 **I will send foreigners to Babylon**
to winnow her and to devastate her land;
they will oppose her on every side
in the day of her disaster.

3 Let not the archer string his bow,
nor let him put on his armor.
Do not spare her young men;
completely destroy her army.
4 They will fall down slain in Babylon,
fatally wounded in her streets.
5 For Israel and Judah have not been forsaken
by their God, the LORD Almighty,
though their land is full of guilt
before the Holy One of Israel.

6 "Flee from Babylon!
Run for your lives!
Do not be destroyed because of her sins.
It is time for the LORD's vengeance;
he will pay her what she deserves.
7 Babylon was a gold cup in the LORD's hand;
she made the whole earth drunk.
The nations drank her wine;
therefore they have now gone mad.
8 Babylon will suddenly fall and be broken.
Wail over her!
Get balm for her pain;
perhaps she can be healed.

9 " 'We would have healed Babylon,
but she cannot be healed;
let us leave her and each go to his own land,
for her judgment reaches to the skies,
it rises as high as the clouds.'

10 " 'The LORD has vindicated us;
come, let us tell in Zion
what the LORD our God has done.'

Jeremiah repeats many of the same words announcing God's judgment on Babylon, whom he designates not only by name but by a Semitic cryptogram, Leb Kamai (sort of a code word for Babylon). Those for whom the message was intended needed to hear it over and over again.

To the Jews who first heard these words, they must have seemed unbelievably good news, far beyond their wildest imagination. With their own eyes they had seen Babylon's power used against them, and they saw no weakening of that power. Yet God wanted them to focus on his promise of return from captivity in Babylon. He wanted them to remember that in all of their troubles he was their real protector. He wanted them never to trust another source of power again.

The prophet spells out three reasons why the Lord would punish Babylon. First, by this punishment he would prove that he had not forsaken his own people. He was still with them. He remained faithful to his Word and promise. Secondly, by punishing Babylon he would prove that Babylon was going to pay for its sin. The Lord had used Babylon as the golden cup to make the nations drink his wrath (Jeremiah 25). Babylon, puffed up with pride, did not know it was only an instrument in the Lord's hands. Finally, he would prove to Babylon and all the other nations that he alone is God, the Almighty. He decides the rise and fall of nations.

God's judgment against Babylon would be so overwhelming that even the Jews and foreigners who had become accustomed to living in Babylon and had developed some fondness for her would flee. They would give up on Babylon's cause as hopeless. Babylon would lose her status quickly and suddenly. Her loss would be the Jews' gain. For Babylon's fall would initiate the Jews' return to the Holy Land.

11 **"Sharpen the arrows,**
take up the shields!

The LORD has stirred up the kings of the Medes,
because his purpose is to destroy Babylon.
The LORD will take vengeance,
vengeance for his temple.
12 Lift up a banner against the walls of Babylon!
Reinforce the guard,
station the watchmen,
prepare an ambush!
The LORD will carry out his purpose,
his decree against the people of Babylon.
13 You who live by many waters
and are rich in treasures,
your end has come,
the time for you to be cut off.
14 The LORD Almighty has sworn by himself:
I will surely fill you with men,
as with a swarm of locusts,
and they will shout in triumph over you.
15 "He made the earth by his power;
he founded the world by his wisdom
and stretched out the heavens by his understanding.
16 When he thunders, the waters in the heavens roar;
he makes clouds rise from the ends of the earth.
He sends lightning with the rain
and brings out the wind from his storehouses.
17 "Every man is senseless and without knowledge;
every goldsmith is shamed by his idols.
His images are a fraud;
they have no breath in them.
18 They are worthless, the objects of mockery;
when their judgment comes, they will perish.
19 He who is the Portion of Jacob is not like these,
for he is the Maker of all things,
including the tribe of his inheritance—
the LORD Almighty is his name.

One of the reasons the Lord would bring judgment upon Babylon was to take vengeance on the nation that destroyed his temple. The building was not the issue, but rather the character of the God worshiped in the building. When they destroyed the Lord's earthly dwelling place the Babylonians believed that they had put down the God of Israel. God warned them that he cannot be put down. Quoting from an earlier part of his prophecy (Jeremiah 10:12-16) Jeremiah proclaimed that the Lord is the maker of all things. He controls all things. His power is unlimited; nothing can restrain it. That almighty God here swore by himself to punish Babylon.

He would punish the Babylonians to strip them of their confidence in idols. He would destroy the powerful delusion with which idols hold men fast in their grip. After all, idols are nothing more than the products of human imagination and invention. They are the creations of the mind of man. As such, their power can never be greater than the power of their creators. Their unbounded promise of power and success is a fraud. God's judgment over Babylon would teach this lesson once more.

20 "You are my war club,
my weapon for battle—
with you I shatter nations,
with you I destroy kingdoms,
21 with you I shatter horse and rider,
with you I shatter chariot and driver,
22 with you I shatter man and woman,
with you I shatter old man and youth,
with you I shatter young man and maiden,
23 with you I shatter shepherd and flock,
with you I shatter farmer and oxen,
with you I shatter governors and officials.

24 "Before your eyes I will repay Babylon and all who live in
Babylonia for all the wrong they have done in Zion," declares
the LORD.

25 "I am against you, O destroying mountain,
you who destroy the whole earth,"
declares the LORD.
"I will stretch out my hand against you,
roll you off the cliffs,
and make you a burned-out mountain.
26 No rock will be taken from you for a cornerstone,
nor any stone for a foundation,
for you will be desolate forever,"
declares the LORD.

27 "Lift up a banner in the land!
Blow the trumpet among the nations!
Prepare the nations for battle against her;
summon against her these kingdoms:
Ararat, Minni and Ashkenaz.
Appoint a commander against her;
send up horses like a swarm of locusts.
28 Prepare the nations for battle against her—
the kings of the Medes,
their governors and all their officials,
and all the countries they rule.
29 The land trembles and writhes,
for the LORD's purposes against Babylon stand—
to lay waste the land of Babylon
so that no one will live there.
30 Babylon's warriors have stopped fighting;
they remain in their strongholds.
Their strength is exhausted;
they have become like women.
Her dwellings are set on fire;
the bars of her gates are broken.

31 One courier follows another
and messenger follows messenger
to announce to the king of Babylon
that his entire city is captured,
32 the river crossings seized,
the marshes set on fire,
and the soldiers terrified."

33 This is what the Lord Almighty, the God of Israel, says:

"The Daughter of Babylon is like a threshing floor
at the time it is trampled;
the time to harvest her will soon come."

Babylon had served the Lord well as his war club. With it he had shattered nations and all their strength. It was a destroying mountain, rising above all kingdoms. Its influence extended over the entire ancient Near East.

But now that war club itself would be shattered ". . . for all the wrong they have done in Zion." Enemies would smash Babylon so completely that no rock would be big enough or suitable enough to provide a cornerstone or a foundation stone for rebuilding its former greatness. What was true of Babylon is true of any nation. No national power, no human foundation can give any real or lasting security. "For no one can lay any foundation other than the one already laid, which is Jesus Christ" (1 Corinthians 3:11). "My hope is built on nothing less than Jesus' blood and righteousness; . . . All other ground is sinking sand" (CW 382:1).

As his instruments in Babylon's destruction the Lord would use the Medes and their allies. The Medes lived in an area south of the Caspian Sea, in what is presently northwest Iran. They were warriors who had lost their independence to the Persians but remained first in honor and rank among the allies and friends of the Persians.

Cyrus the Persian used Darius the Mede (Daniel 5:30,31) as his instrument to conqueror Babylon. Assisting the Medes were allies from the north, from the land between and immediately south of the Black and Caspian Seas, an area presently occupied by the Kurds. These fearless, fresh warriors would sweep over a tired Babylon. Messenger after messenger would bring the distressing news to the king of Babylon that his great empire was collapsing.

34 "Nebuchadnezzar king of Babylon has devoured us,
he has thrown us into confusion,
he has made us an empty jar.
Like a serpent he has swallowed us
and filled his stomach with our delicacies,
and then has spewed us out.
35 May the violence done to our flesh be upon Babylon,"
say the inhabitants of Zion.
"May our blood be on those who live in Babylonia,"
says Jerusalem.

36 Therefore, this is what the LORD says:

"See, I will defend your cause
and avenge you;
I will dry up her sea
and make her springs dry.
37 Babylon will be a heap of ruins,
a haunt of jackals,
an object of horror and scorn,
a place where no one lives.
38 Her people all roar like young lions,
they growl like lion cubs.
39 But while they are aroused,
I will set out a feast for them
and make them drunk,

so that they shout with laughter—
then sleep forever and not awake,"
declares the LORD.
40 "I will bring them down
like lambs to the slaughter,
like rams and goats.
41 "How Sheshach will be captured,
the boast of the whole earth seized!
What a horror Babylon will be
among the nations!
42 The sea will rise over Babylon;
its roaring waves will cover her.
43 Her towns will be desolate,
a dry and desert land,
a land where no one lives,
through which no man travels.
44 I will punish Bel in Babylon
and make him spew out what he has swallowed.
The nations will no longer stream to him.
And the wall of Babylon will fall.

45 "Come out of her, my people!
Run for your lives!
Run from the fierce anger of the LORD.
46 Do not lose heart or be afraid
when rumors are heard in the land;
one rumor comes this year, another the next,
rumors of violence in the land
and of ruler against ruler.
47 For the time will surely come
when I will punish the idols of Babylon;
her whole land will be disgraced
and her slain will all lie fallen within her.
48 Then heaven and earth and all that is in them
will shout for joy over Babylon,

for out of the north
destroyers will attack her,"
declares the LORD.

49 "Babylon must fall because of Israel's slain,
just as the slain in all the earth
have fallen because of Babylon.

Again and again the prophet repeated the reasons great Babylon would fall. The blood of God's people was upon her hands. The Lord had not forgotten his people and would avenge them. He would prove just how worthless idols are. He would expose the weakness of Babylon's national god Bel/Marduk. He would avenge Israel's slain. Those who persecuted God's people could not and would not escape their just punishment.

Babylon's destruction would be sweeping and total. Just when the Babylonians were at ease in the midst of feasting and drinking, when they were the fattest and the fullest, God's sword would cut them down. Amid the rumors of revolt and war, God urged his people, however, to stay calm. They would know what was coming, and they would know the outcome. They were, therefore, not to lose heart or be afraid. The Lord would protect them.

50 You who have escaped the sword,
leave and do not linger!
Remember the LORD in a distant land,
and think on Jerusalem."

51 "We are disgraced,
for we have been insulted
and shame covers our faces,
because foreigners have entered
the holy places of the LORD's house."

52 "But days are coming," declares the LORD,
"when I will punish her idols,

and throughout her land
the wounded will groan.
53 **Even if Babylon reaches the sky**
and fortifies her lofty stronghold,
I will send destroyers against her,"
declares the LORD.

54 **"The sound of a cry comes from Babylon,**
the sound of great destruction
from the land of the Babylonians.
55 **The LORD will destroy Babylon;**
he will silence her noisy din.
Waves of enemies will rage like great waters;
the roar of their voices will resound.
56 **A destroyer will come against Babylon;**
her warriors will be captured,
and their bows will be broken.
For the LORD is a God of retribution;
he will repay in full.
57 **I will make her officials and wise men drunk,**
her governors, officers and warriors as well;
they will sleep forever and not awake,"
declares the King, whose name is
the LORD Almighty.

58 **This is what the LORD Almighty says:**

"Babylon's thick wall will be leveled
and her high gates set on fire;
the peoples exhaust themselves for nothing,
the nations' labor is only fuel for the flames."

At the time the Babylonian empire collapsed, many of the exiles had made their homes in Babylon, as the Lord had instructed them (Jeremiah 29). But God here reminded them that Babylon was not their real home. They were to remember their God and his worship. God was going to bring down

Babylon for their sakes, so that they could return home. As their lives would once again be thrown into turmoil, they were to "think on Jerusalem." When the destruction came, they were to have no regrets or reservations. They were to leave the city without lingering.

Throughout his prophecy Jeremiah mentions the walls of Babylon. Again in these verses he prophesies that the walls of the city would be leveled. Babylon's walls would not give its citizens the safety they had hoped for. In the way they were constructed, the walls of Babylon might have given them or anyone who would have seen them a real sense of security. They were the best that the human mind could design. Ancient Babylon was protected by a double wall. The inner wall (21 feet thick) was separated from the outer wall by a moat 23 feet wide. Spaced along the walls were massive towers to provide additional protection. On top of the wall was a roadway wide enough for horses and chariots. This would enable defenders to move with speed to meet attacks at any point. Their defenders were hardened and seasoned soldiers who were accustomed to victory. How could anyone hope to succeed against such defenses? But Babylon's defenders did not have the Lord on their side. Their walls could not save them.

59This is the message Jeremiah gave to the staff officer Sera-
iah son of Neriah, the son of Mahseiah, when he went to Baby-
lon with Zedekiah king of Judah in the fourth year of his reign.
60Jeremiah had written on a scroll about all the disasters that
would come upon Babylon—all that had been recorded con-
cerning Babylon. 61He said to Seraiah, "When you get to Baby-
lon, see that you read all these words aloud. 62Then say, 'O
LORD, you have said you will destroy this place, so that neither
man nor animal will live in it; it will be desolate forever.'
63When you finish reading this scroll, tie a stone to it and throw
it into the Euphrates. 64Then say, 'So will Babylon sink to rise

no more because of the disaster I will bring upon her. And her people will fall.' "

The words of Jeremiah end here.

To make his point about Babylon's fall even more emphatically, Jeremiah had all these prophecies written on a scroll. He sent that scroll with Seraiah, an official who was going with King Zedekiah on a state visit to Babylon. There in far-off Babylon Seraiah was to read the scroll aloud. It was as though God were putting his truthfulness on the line. In writing and in word he had made it very clear what would happen to Babylon more than half a century later, after it had served his purpose. He wanted all the world to know that he speaks the truth. He will not back down from what he has said and written.

After reading the scroll aloud Seraiah was to tie it to a rock and throw it into the Euphrates River. The scroll tied to the rock represented Babylon. Like the scroll and rock it would sink to nothingness. Seraiah was to do this so that those who saw it would believe that God would surely do what he promised. If it seemed impossible to them, let them, "Call to me and I will answer you and tell you great and unsearchable things you do not know" (Jeremiah 33:3).

A RAY OF HOPE IN THE MIDST OF EXILE

JEREMIAH 52

The Fall of Jerusalem

52 Zedekiah was twenty-one years old when he became king, and he reigned in Jerusalem eleven years. His mother's name was Hamutal daughter of Jeremiah; she was from Libnah. 2He did evil in the eyes of the LORD, just as Jehoiakim had done. 3It was because of the LORD's anger that all this happened to Jerusalem and Judah, and in the end he thrust them from his presence.

Now Zedekiah rebelled against the king of Babylon.

4So in the ninth year of Zedekiah's reign, on the tenth day of the tenth month, Nebuchadnezzar king of Babylon marched against Jerusalem with his whole army. They camped outside the city and built siege works all around it. 5The city was kept under siege until the eleventh year of King Zedekiah.

6By the ninth day of the fourth month the famine in the city had become so severe that there was no food for the people to eat. 7Then the city wall was broken through, and the whole army fled. They left the city at night through the gate between the two walls near the king's garden, though the Babylonians were surrounding the city. They fled toward the Arabah, 8but the Babylonian army pursued King Zedekiah and overtook him in the plains of Jericho. All his soldiers were separated from him and scattered, 9and he was captured.

He was taken to the king of Babylon at Riblah in the land of Hamath, where he pronounced sentence on him. 10There at Riblah the king of Babylon slaughtered the sons of Zedekiah before his eyes; he also killed all the officials of Judah. 11Then he put out Zedekiah's eyes, bound him with bronze shackles and took him to Babylon, where he put him in prison till the day of his death.

**12On the tenth day of the fifth month, in the nineteenth year
of Nebuchadnezzar king of Babylon, Nebuzaradan commander of the imperial guard, who served the king of Babylon,
came to Jerusalem. 13He set fire to the temple of the LORD, the
royal palace and all the houses of Jerusalem. Every important
building he burned down. 14The whole Babylonian army under
the commander of the imperial guard broke down all the walls
around Jerusalem. 15Nebuzaradan the commander of the
guard carried into exile some of the poorest people and those
who remained in the city, along with the rest of the craftsmen
and those who had gone over to the king of Babylon. 16But
Nebuzaradan left behind the rest of the poorest people of the
land to work the vineyards and fields.**

We do not know who added this postscript to the prophecy of Jeremiah, and it is useless to speculate. We can be sure it was added at the Lord's command, and that it is his Word. According to the closing verses of the chapter it was written about twenty years after Jerusalem fell. This account chronicles in great detail the fall of Jerusalem. Its purpose was to show that the Lord keeps his word. It was also intended to raise the hopes of those Jews who were living in exile.

The first verses recount the actual fall of Jerusalem and the cruel punishment the Babylonians meted out to Zedekiah and the officials of his government when they tried to escape. The message of this postscript is simple. All this happened because Judah rebelled against the Lord. All this happened just as the Lord had said it would (Jeremiah 38:18).

**17The Babylonians broke up the bronze pillars, the movable
stands and the bronze Sea that were at the temple of the LORD
and they carried all the bronze to Babylon. 18They also took
away the pots, shovels, wick trimmers, sprinkling bowls, dishes
and all the bronze articles used in the temple service. 19The
commander of the imperial guard took away the basins,**

censers, sprinkling bowls, pots, lampstands, dishes and bowls used for drink offerings—all that were made of pure gold or silver.

[20]The bronze from the two pillars, the Sea and the twelve bronze bulls under it, and the movable stands, which King Solomon had made for the temple of the LORD, was more than could be weighed. [21]Each of the pillars was eighteen cubits high and twelve cubits in circumference; each was four fingers thick, and hollow. [22]The bronze capital on top of the one pillar was five cubits high and was decorated with a network and pomegranates of bronze all around. The other pillar, with its pomegranates, was similar. [23]There were ninety-six pomegranates on the sides; the total number of pomegranates above the surrounding network was a hundred.

[24]The commander of the guard took as prisoners Seraiah the chief priest, Zephaniah the priest next in rank and the three doorkeepers. [25]Of those still in the city, he took the officer in charge of the fighting men, and seven royal advisers. He also took the secretary who was chief officer in charge of conscripting the people of the land and sixty of his men who were found in the city. [26]Nebuzaradan the commander took them all and brought them to the king of Babylon at Riblah. [27]There at Riblah, in the land of Hamath, the king had them executed.

So Judah went into captivity, away from her land. [28]This is the number of the people Nebuchadnezzar carried into exile:

in the seventh year, 3,023 Jews;
[29] in Nebuchadnezzar's eighteenth year,
832 people from Jerusalem;
[30] in his twenty-third year,
745 Jews taken into exile by Nebuzaradan
the commander of the imperial guard.
There were 4,600 people in all.

With these verses the author adds new information about the fall of Jerusalem. Early in the reign of Zedekiah some of the priests and the false prophets had said that the plunder Nebuchadnezzar had taken from the temple (598/597 B.C.) would be returned. In sharp contrast, Jeremiah had told the Jews by the Word of the Lord that not only would nothing be returned but that all the remaining furnishings of the temple would also be taken to Babylon (Jeremiah 27:19-22). The writer describes in detail how all of the remaining vessels and articles in the temple were broken down and carried away to Babylon. The Lord kept his word. The prophet had spoken the truth.

Jeremiah had also told King Zedekiah that if he did not surrender to the Babylonians both he and his officials would be captured (Jeremiah 34:21). In chapter 39 Jeremiah recorded the capture and the subsequent punishment of Zedekiah and the execution of "all the nobles of Judah" (Jeremiah 39:6). The writer of this postscript lists the names of those officials. Again, the Lord had kept his word.

The writer gives an account of various deportations of Jews which Nebuchadnezzar ordered throughout his reign. The relatively small number of those carried into exile may reflect the staggering losses the nation had suffered because of its disobedience. Of course, not all of Jerusalem's inhabitants were carried into exile. Some fled to other places. Some of the poorest were left behind. But these numbers, for the most part, represented the brightest and best, the future hope of God's chosen nation. That any of them survived is a testimony to the grace of God. By that same grace this small remnant would not die out in exile but would grow back into a large nation again.

Jehoiachin Released

31In the thirty-seventh year of the exile of Jehoiachin king of Judah, in the year Evil-Merodach became king of Babylon, he

released Jehoiachin king of Judah and freed him from prison on the twenty-fifth day of the twelfth month. 32He spoke kindly to him and gave him a seat of honor higher than those of the other kings who were with him in Babylon. 33So Jehoiachin put aside his prison clothes and for the rest of his life ate regularly at the king's table. 34Day by day the king of Babylon gave Jehoiachin a regular allowance as long as he lived, till the day of his death.

The Lord had promised his people through Jeremiah that their exile would last seventy years (Jeremiah 25:12). In the year 562 B.C., after a reign of over forty years, Nebuchadnezzar, the great builder and conqueror, died. His son Evil-Merodach succeeded him to the throne.

This change of rulers marked a significant milestone in Judah's exile. Jehoiachin's years of exile represented about half of the seventy, the number of years God had told his people they would live in exile. Upon succeeding his father, Evil-Merodach showed kindness to Jehoiachin the exiled king. He had succeeded his father in 598/597 B.C., but he reigned for only three months before Nebuchadnezzar carried him away to Babylon. Jehoiachin had languished in prison for thirty-seven years when Evil-Merodach freed him and gave him a place of honor at the royal table with other nobles and dignitaries. For the rest of his life Jehoiachin would live in comfort and dignity. Jehoiachin's new status was a sign of hope. The Lord keeps his word. He would deliver Judah from exile after the seventy years, just as he had promised. The final books of the Old Testament tell us that he did.

LAMENTATIONS

INTRODUCTION

The Structure

The Hebrew title for this book of the Bible is taken from the first word, "How." When, during the Intertestamental Period, the Jews translated this book into Greek they gave it the title, "The Tears of Jeremiah." When the Greek was translated into Latin, it was named "The Lamentations of Jeremiah," the title we use today. Lamentations consists of five individual poems. The first four (chapters 1—4) use a poetic device known as "acrostic." In an acrostic each new line of poetry begins with a successive letter of the alphabet. In chapters 1,2, and 4 each verse begins with a new letter of the Hebrew alphabet. Since the Hebrew alphabet has twenty-two letters, each of these chapters has twenty-two verses. In chapter 3 the author triples the acrostic. Every three verses begin with a new letter of the alphabet, so chapter 3 has sixty-six verses.

The Author

We do not know positively who wrote the book of Lamentations. We do know that the author lived at the time Jerusalem fell to the Babylonians, for he was an eyewitness to its fall. The author also was a capable poet. Tradition assigns the authorship to Jeremiah, and he is a very good choice. He certainly was a capable poet and did write in the style of poetry common to Lamentations (2 Chronicles 35:25). Many of the pictures and images found throughout Jeremiah's prophecy also appear in Lamentations. In chapter 3 the author mentions his own life's troubles and applies them to the nation. They match well with some of the troubles we know Jeremiah himself experienced. Throughout the commentary that follows we shall assume that Jeremiah wrote Lamentations.

The Purpose

In the face of Jerusalem's destruction, the prophet encouraged the believers to keep on clinging to the Lord. The nation was without excuse. It had plenty of time to repent, but it chose the path of sin. Now its sins had brought the present terror. On its own the nation could not deliver itself. Its only hope lay in a return to the Lord, and the Lord did not fail. Even in this disaster, believers could see his gracious hand. "Because of the LORD's great love we are not consumed, for his compassions never fail. They are new every morning; great is your faithfulness" (Lamentations 3:22,23). Even under suffering, the believer can confidently wait for the salvation he knows will come.

The Outline

LAMENTATIONS: A DIRGE OVER FALLEN JERUSALEM

I. There is no disaster like it (1)

II. The extent of the disaster is numbing (2)

III. The past mercies of the Lord give hope and courage to the survivors (3)

IV. There was never a bleaker time (4)

V. A prayer goes up to the Lord for compassion (5)

THE FALL OF JERUSALEM: THERE IS NO DISASTER LIKE IT

LAMENTATIONS 1

1 How deserted lies the city,
once so full of people!
How like a widow is she,
who once was great among the nations!
She who was queen among the provinces
has now become a slave.

2 Bitterly she weeps at night,
tears are upon her cheeks.
Among all her lovers
there is none to comfort her.
All her friends have betrayed her;
they have become her enemies.

3 After affliction and harsh labor,
Judah has gone into exile.
She dwells among the nations;
she finds no resting place.
All who pursue her have overtaken her
in the midst of her distress.

4 The roads to Zion mourn,
for no one comes to her appointed feasts.
All her gateways are desolate,
her priests groan,
her maidens grieve,
and she is in bitter anguish.

5 Her foes have become her masters;
her enemies are at ease.
The LORD has brought her grief
because of her many sins.

Her children have gone into exile,
captive before the foe.

6 **All the splendor has departed**
from the Daughter of Zion.
Her princes are like deer
that find no pasture;
in weakness they have fled
before the pursuer.

7 **In the days of her affliction and wandering**
Jerusalem remembers all the treasures
that were hers in days of old.
When her people fell into enemy hands,
there was no one to help her.
Her enemies looked at her
and laughed at her destruction.

As he sat outside the city, perhaps on a hill overlooking it, nothing struck the prophet more than its emptiness. Memories flooded over him like they would a person who returns to the quiet, but deserted, ruins of his childhood—perhaps an old farm house slowly going to ruin. For a moment he does not see the weeds pushing through the rotted porch, the broken windows, or the sagging roof. No, he hears the voices of children playing. He smells freshly baked bread put out to cool. He joins in the big family picnic and the baseball game that followed. But soon the quiet returns and he leaves, for what he saw and smelled is all in the past.

So the prophet reflected on the silence of the great city. For forty years he had moved among its bustle. For forty years he had preached in its streets and in the temple courtyard, but no one had listened. Now Jerusalem's streets were silent and its temple gone.

The writer captures the city's deep pain and disappointment with the words repeated throughout this chapter, "there is none to comfort her" (verse 2). The friends and allies the Jewish nation had so carefully cultivated had abandoned her. Not one of them had tried to help her. Many of them, in fact, became her enemies. They attacked Jews who were being led off as prisoners of war; they laid claim to property that had to be left behind when the exiles were led off to Babylon. The false gods upon which the citizens of Jerusalem had lavished so much of their wealth and attention had proved powerless. The Lord had warned his people not to trust in the strength of great men or in military alliances. He had invited, even begged them to lean only upon him, but to no avail. Jerusalem had rejected the one Comforter who could have helped her. There was no other.

The citizens of Jerusalem saw their leaders lose heart. The people had looked to them for spiritual guidance but were disappointed, for they too had failed. Now her leaders had been led away in chains. No more would they feast at tables filled with delicacies. Now they would gladly give their former wealth for a little good bread.

The priests were in particular distress, for the temple lay in ruins, its services stopped. They had failed to do their duty, to serve as mediators between sinners and the holy God. They had not rebuked or silenced the false prophets. They had allowed, even encouraged, pagan and idolatrous practices within the very confines of the temple. They had closed their eyes to sin. They had failed in their duty. Now they no longer had any duties in the temple. The Lord had taken their calling from them. They could offer comfort neither to their people nor to themselves.

As priest, prince, and people contemplated their misery, they remembered "all the treasures that were hers in days of old" (verse 7). Certainly among those treasures was the abundance of goods and possessions with which the Lord had blessed them. How seldom they had given thanks and how little they had returned in offerings to the Lord!

Their greatest loss, however, was something they had considered worthless. They had despised the Lord's love, a love freely and abundantly offered them through their temple worship and the preaching of the prophets. That love, that grace, was theirs for the taking every day. But God's abundant love seemed so commonplace, they imagined they could never lose it. By sheer neglect they had drifted into unbelief, which led them to overestimate their own abilities to take care of themselves. It led them to turn their backs on the Lord and finally drove them to their ruin. From this ruin there was no escape except by the power of the very love they had despised. Fortunately that love is beyond tracing out. The Lord remained faithful. He will not turn away from the penitent.

8 Jerusalem has sinned greatly
and so has become unclean.
All who honored her despise her,
for they have seen her nakedness;
she herself groans
and turns away.

9 Her filthiness clung to her skirts;
she did not consider her future.
Her fall was astounding;
there was none to comfort her.
"Look, O LORD, on my affliction,
for the enemy has triumphed."

10 The enemy laid hands
on all her treasures;
she saw pagan nations
enter her sanctuary—
those you had forbidden
to enter your assembly.

11 **All her people groan**
as they search for bread;
they barter their treasures for food
to keep themselves alive.
"Look, O LORD, and consider,
for I am despised."

Without the white robes of the Lord's righteousness, Jerusalem could see herself for what she really was, filthy and unclean. By herself she could not shake off the filthiness of her sin. Confronted by her sin at every turn, she sank into despair. She had enjoyed the sinning while it lasted, but "she did not consider her future." Sin had blinded her.

That's the very nature of sin. It blinds people to the results it will bring them in the end. Sin focuses only on the pleasure we enjoy right now but deceives about the long-term future by denying any judgment or hell. It leads the sinner to go about his sinning as if he had nothing to worry about. "God is far away, he does not care. After death there is nothing, don't worry, do what you please," it whispers. So it deceives and leads to destruction. Jerusalem learned the power of sin's deception and was miserable. She groaned over what it had led her to do.

Jerusalem's false confidence in the temple as a magic charm that would protect her and her failure to trust the Lord had thrown the doors of the temple open to the soldiers of the enemy. The pagans poured through those doors but not to worship (Psalm 74:4-8; 79:1-4). They desecrated the temple and made it useless for worship. They shattered the means the Lord had established for his people to approach him.

No greater loss was imaginable. God's ancient people would not soon recover the precious privilege of fellowship with their God in the temple. They also knew, however, that the Lord does not dwell in a temple made with hands. Despite their great sin they could still know his love and fellowship. The continuation of that Savior-love would renew them and lead them to yearn for the time when they could worship him in a new temple. They could also look forward to that day when the Lord would take up his dwelling among them, not in a temple building, but in the person of Jesus Christ. They could look forward to Christ's coming.

They had sacrificed the temple and its worship on the altar of their own greed and covetousness. They had made wealth their number one goal in life. They had violated God's sabbath and the law of brotherly love in order to pile up more wealth. But in doing so, they had lost their true wealth, the Wealth Giver, the Lord.

The treasures they had heaped up for their own pleasure and enjoyment now went for survival. They had to barter away what little they had left just to stay alive. They had learned too late that "life [is] more important than food, and the body more important than clothes" (Matthew 6:25). They had learned too late that the abundance of a person's life does not consist in the things that he possesses (Luke 12:15). They had put the wrong things first and had lost not only their things but also their Lord.

12 "Is it nothing to you, all you who pass by?
Look around and see.
Is any suffering like my suffering
that was inflicted on me,
that the LORD brought on me
in the day of his fierce anger?

13 "From on high he sent fire,
sent it down into my bones.
He spread a net for my feet
and turned me back.

He made me desolate,
faint all the day long.

14 **"My sins have been bound into a yoke;**
by his hands they were woven together.
They have come upon my neck
and the Lord has sapped my strength.
He has handed me over
to those I cannot withstand.

15 **"The Lord has rejected**
all the warriors in my midst;
he has summoned an army against me
to crush my young men.
In his winepress the Lord has trampled
the Virgin Daughter of Judah.

The remnants of Jerusalem's population pleaded with the passers-by to feel something. How could anyone walk by without stopping to notice the destruction and the pain? Their plea brought little response. Judah's once privileged position meant nothing to strangers. The survivors could expect little sympathy from those who had heard their arrogant boast in the Lord. After all, they had gotten what they had deserved.

The people of Judah confessed indeed that they had gotten what they deserved. Their pain was so great it had gone into their bones, to the very seat of the emotions. The heavy weight of their sins had crushed them. The Lord had fastened their sins around their neck like a heavy yoke. The rebellion and sin that once seemed so insignificant had woven themselves tightly around Judah, leaving no escape. The Lord was not nearly so distant and unconcerned as they had imagined. His law and curse weighed heavily upon them. They were without excuse and knew they had no one but themselves to blame.

16 "This is why I weep
and my eyes overflow with tears.
No one is near to comfort me,
no one to restore my spirit.
My children are destitute
because the enemy has prevailed."

17 Zion stretches out her hands,
but there is no one to comfort her.
The LORD has decreed for Jacob
that his neighbors become his foes;
Jerusalem has become
an unclean thing among them.

18 "The LORD is righteous,
yet I rebelled against his command.
Listen, all you peoples;
look upon my suffering.
My young men and maidens
have gone into exile.

19 "I called to my allies
but they betrayed me.
My priests and my elders
perished in the city
while they searched for food
to keep themselves alive.

20 "See, O LORD, how distressed I am!
I am in torment within,
and in my heart I am disturbed,
for I have been most rebellious.
Outside, the sword bereaves;
inside, there is only death.

21 "People have heard my groaning,
but there is no one to comfort me.
All my enemies have heard of my distress;
they rejoice at what you have done.

May you bring the day you have announced
so they may become like me.

22 **"Let all their wickedness come before you;**
deal with them
as you have dealt with me
because of all my sins.
My groans are many
and my heart is faint."

Again Judah confessed her sin—this time calling it what it was: rebellion, open and willful defiance against the Lord. She had no excuse. She pleaded with no excuse. This sin had brought unbelievable trouble to her. She had lost her future, her young men and maidens. Her leaders were dying of starvation, and she was in constant torment. She had paid a fearful price for her affair with sin. She confessed this to God in the hope that the Lord would recognize the genuineness of her sorrow and have pity.

She warned her enemies not to rejoice over her fall. She reminded them, as they had so quickly reminded her, that the Lord her God had done this to her. She warned them to listen and learn from her mistakes. She begged them to find no joy in the fall of a sinner, because the Lord finds no pleasure in such a fall. Her pitiful example cried out to them that the Lord keeps his promise of punishment. He does not make empty threats. Like her, they had the opportunity to turn away from God, so they have opportunity to repent. If they would not, their end would be as hers.

Because her enemies rejoiced over her ruin, however, and because they were not ready to repent, Judah prayed against them. She asked the Lord to treat them the same way he had treated her. She begged him to act righteously in accord with his holiness. She asked him to keep his promises to "bring the day you have announced." The Lord had announced his judgments against the nations in chapters 46—51 of Jeremiah. Unless they repented, he would swiftly judge them. The judgment he had rendered against Judah testified to that.

THE EXTENT OF THE DISASTER IS NUMBING

LAMENTATIONS 2

2 How the Lord has covered the Daughter of Zion
with the cloud of his anger!
He has hurled down the splendor of Israel
from heaven to earth;
he has not remembered his footstool
in the day of his anger.

2 Without pity the Lord has swallowed up
all the dwellings of Jacob;
in his wrath he has torn down
the strongholds of the Daughter of Judah.
He has brought her kingdom and its princes
down to the ground in dishonor.

3 In fierce anger he has cut off
every horn of Israel.
He has withdrawn his right hand
at the approach of the enemy.
He has burned in Jacob like a flaming fire
that consumes everything around it.

4 Like an enemy he has strung his bow;
his right hand is ready.
Like a foe he has slain
all who were pleasing to the eye;
he has poured out his wrath like fire
on the tent of the Daughter of Zion.

5 The Lord is like an enemy;
he has swallowed up Israel.
He has swallowed up all her palaces
and destroyed her strongholds.
He has multiplied mourning and lamentation
for the Daughter of Judah.

Judah had forgotten its real greatness. It had begun to boast in itself, in its ability, and in its own resources. But it was no more than the Lord's footstool. Apart from the grace of God it was nothing. In no way could it boast before the Lord. Because Judah forgot this grace and rejected the Lord, the Lord showed her what she would be if he removed his protection from her.

After Jerusalem was destroyed, the people of the city began to realize how they had taken the Lord for granted. He had stood between them and their enemies just as in the days of Moses in the desert he had stood between Israel and its enemies in a pillar of fire. He had protected them just as he had promised. But they had taken the Lord for granted and finally rejected him in unbelief. So the Lord removed his protection to show them that as the Giver of the gift he could also take it back.

Instead of being their protector, God now became their enemy. With great ferocity he had attacked them. Having removed every bit of their strength, every "horn," he easily swallowed them up. In a moment he brought down what generations had built. In his anger he cleared away with fire the abominations they had constructed for other gods.

Their unbelief had taken them out of the circle of his grace. They had to learn the hard way that it is a fearful thing to fall into the hands of the living God. Even though he had to carry out his judgment, the Lord found no joy in it. In bringing judgment down on his own people it was as if he were moving against himself, for he is love. He is the Savior, not the Crusher. But their unbelief and stubbornness of heart had compelled him to do what he did.

6 He has laid waste his dwelling like a garden;
he has destroyed his place of meeting.

The LORD has made Zion forget
her appointed feasts and her Sabbaths;
in his fierce anger he has spurned
both king and priest.

7 The Lord has rejected his altar
and abandoned his sanctuary.
He has handed over to the enemy
the walls of her palaces;
they have raised a shout in the house of the LORD
as on the day of an appointed feast.

8 The LORD determined to tear down
the wall around the Daughter of Zion.
He stretched out a measuring line
and did not withhold his hand from destroying.
He made ramparts and walls lament;
together they wasted away.

9 Her gates have sunk into the ground;
their bars he has broken and destroyed.
Her king and her princes are exiled
among the nations,
the law is no more,
and her prophets no longer find
visions from the LORD.

10 The elders of the Daughter of Zion
sit on the ground in silence;
they have sprinkled dust on their heads
and put on sackcloth.
The young women of Jerusalem
have bowed their heads to the ground.

Jerusalem and its inhabitants had fallen as low as they could go. The only noises to be heard in the temple were the celebrations of the enemy or the sounds of the scavenger. Just as he said (Jeremiah 7), the Lord had destroyed their boast in the temple. The sabbaths they had so long neglected and despised, they no longer had a chance to celebrate. Now, with their city in ruins, they were forced to take a rest, to observe the days off commanded by the law (Jeremiah 17).

They had rejected God's wisdom and his Word. They had refused to listen to his voice as he spoke through his prophets. The priests had failed to instruct the people from the law, for they treated God's Word as if it were an unimportant thing. So the Lord silenced the priests. "The law is no more," because those called to teach were unable to practice its provisions. The false prophets who were so quick to speak visions out of their own hearts now hid their faces in shame. The true prophets of the Lord were silent. The people listened in vain for some word from the Lord. He had cut them off, as they deserved. His Word, once so abundant and easily available, now was hard to find. They had cut themselves off from the only means the Lord had given them to come to him, and they could only mourn.

11 My eyes fail from weeping,
I am in torment within,
my heart is poured out on the ground
because my people are destroyed,
because children and infants faint
in the streets of the city.

12 They say to their mothers,
"Where is bread and wine?"
as they faint like wounded men
in the streets of the city,
as their lives ebb away
in their mothers' arms.

13 What can I say for you?
With what can I compare you,
O Daughter of Jerusalem?

To what can I liken you,
that I may comfort you,
O Virgin Daughter of Zion?
Your wound is as deep as the sea.
Who can heal you?

14 **The visions of your prophets**
were false and worthless;
they did not expose your sin
to ward off your captivity.
The oracles they gave you
were false and misleading.

15 **All who pass your way**
clap their hands at you;
they scoff and shake their heads
at the Daughter of Jerusalem:
"Is this the city that was called
the perfection of beauty,
the joy of the whole earth?"

16 **All your enemies open their mouths**
wide against you;
they scoff and gnash their teeth
and say, "We have swallowed her up.
This is the day we have waited for;
we have lived to see it."

The pain of the person who spoke these words was almost beyond description. It tears at one's heart. Even though they had deserved every bit of what had happened to them, the sympathetic prophet could not but feel for them. Infants and children were dying in their mothers' arms. They begged for food but no one offered them any. If only the parents had thought of their children before! If only they had instructed their children to worship the Lord alone! If only they themselves had followed the way of the Lord, none of this would be happening. Their sin had caught up to them.

In his attempt to comfort them, Jeremiah searched for something to say, some word that might ease their pain, but he could find none. He had no comparison to describe their wound. It went deeper than the depths of the sea. No ordinary physician could heal it, and they certainly could not heal themselves. With the question, "Who can heal you?" Jeremiah pointed to the answer. There is one who can do the impossible, who can heal wounds and take away sin, one who drowns sins in the very depths of the sea. The Lord himself could heal their wound. The Lord himself wanted to heal their wound. He was waiting for them to come to their senses and turn to him.

17 The LORD has done what he planned;
he has fulfilled his word,
which he decreed long ago.
He has overthrown you without pity,
he has let the enemy gloat over you,
he has exalted the horn of your foes.

18 The hearts of the people
cry out to the Lord.
O wall of the Daughter of Zion,
let your tears flow like a river
day and night;
give yourself no relief,
your eyes no rest.

19 Arise, cry out in the night,
as the watches of the night begin;
pour out your heart like water
in the presence of the Lord.
Lift up your hands to him
for the lives of your children,

who faint from hunger
at the head of every street.

20 **"Look, O LORD, and consider:**
Whom have you ever treated like this?
Should women eat their offspring,
the children they have cared for?
Should priest and prophet be killed
in the sanctuary of the Lord?

21 **"Young and old lie together**
in the dust of the streets;
my young men and maidens
have fallen by the sword.
You have slain them in the day of your anger;
you have slaughtered them without pity.

22 **"As you summon to a feast day,**
so you summoned against me terrors on every side.
In the day of the LORD's anger
no one escaped or survived;
those I cared for and reared,
my enemy has destroyed."

The destruction of Jerusalem surprised no one. The Lord had done exactly as he said he would do. His action serves as a warning to all future generations, to all future readers. God means what he says. He carries out every threat he makes. The people of Judah did not believe. They stubbornly resisted the message of law and gospel God had given them. But their unbelief did not prevent the Lord's punishment.

In that grim and unrelenting purpose of the Lord, however, lies a kernel of hope. If he determined to punish, despite all his love and great patience, how much more will he be ready to help and to show mercy. Jeremiah urged his people to turn to the Lord with all their might. Day and night, from every street and shack they should pray without ceasing. Counting on the Lord's free grace, they should pray for the children, not for themselves. The Lord had promised that from their descendants would come the One in whom all the nations of the earth would be blessed. Their prayer would find its power in that promise, the promise he himself had given to them, and he is a God who keeps his every word.

Enough is enough. God had promised to leave them a remnant. His worst threats had now come true. He had warned that, during the eighteen-month siege of Jerusalem, mothers would use their own children for food, and that grim prophecy had come true. Few had escaped God's wrath. The flock which Jeremiah had shepherded was scattered. They knew the fearsome power of the Lord when it had turned against them. They had learned their lesson. The time for healing was surely at hand.

THE PAST MERCIES OF THE LORD GIVE HOPE AND COURAGE TO THE SURVIVORS

LAMENTATIONS 3

3 I am the man who has seen affliction
by the rod of his wrath.
2 He has driven me away and made me walk
in darkness rather than light;
3 indeed, he has turned his hand against me
again and again, all day long.

4 He has made my skin and my flesh grow old
and has broken my bones.
5 He has besieged me and surrounded me
with bitterness and hardship.
6 He has made me dwell in darkness
like those long dead.

7 He has walled me in so I cannot escape;
he has weighed me down with chains.
Even when I call out or cry for help,
he shuts out my prayer.
9 He has barred my way with blocks of stone;
he has made my paths crooked.

10 Like a bear lying in wait,
like a lion in hiding,
11 he dragged me from the path and mangled me
and left me without help.
12 He drew his bow
and made me the target for his arrows.

13 He pierced my heart
with arrows from his quiver.
14 I became the laughingstock of all my people;
they mock me in song all day long.

15 He has filled me with bitter herbs
and sated me with gall.

16 He has broken my teeth with gravel;
he has trampled me in the dust.
17 I have been deprived of peace;
I have forgotten what prosperity is.
18 So I say, "My splendor is gone
and all that I had hoped from the LORD."
19 I remember my affliction and my wandering,
the bitterness and the gall.
20 I well remember them,
and my soul is downcast within me.
21 Yet this I call to mind
and therefore I have hope:

This chapter and its message are the very center of Lamentations. The writer emphasizes its importance by tripling the poetic device of the acrostic. Instead of a single verse, he begins every three verses with a new letter of the Hebrew alphabet.

Jeremiah uses his own experience during his long prophetic ministry as a way to express what he and his fellow believers felt when they saw Jerusalem fall and in the days and months that followed. Time after time during his preaching Jeremiah had been overwhelmed and crushed (Jeremiah 15;21). At every turn he had failed to bring the people to repentance. None of his preaching had had the effect he wanted. At times Jeremiah even felt that the Lord himself stood in his way. He felt as though the Lord had used and abused him. His preaching had made him an outcast, the butt of jokes on every street corner. Despair and depression were his constant companions.

Yet Jeremiah could not escape his calling from God. The Lord's Word could not be silenced within him; he had to preach. Again and again he stood powerless and exposed before the stony silence of the crowds. Their unbelief afflicted his body and spirit. Deep sadness filled every fiber of his being. Nevertheless, that experience did not crush him. Instead, it proved the enormity of the Lord's love for the inhabitants of Jerusalem. It proved again and again the long-suffering of the Lord and his faithfulness to every promise he had made to Jeremiah. Jeremiah survived all. He remained faithful to his calling and to his Lord. He even experienced some small successes. All this now came to his mind and gave him hope, a hope he shared with his hearers who were going through the very things he had already felt.

22 Because of the LORD's great love we are not consumed,
for his compassions never fail.
23 They are new every morning;
great is your faithfulness.
24 I say to myself, "The LORD is my portion;
therefore I will wait for him."
25 The LORD is good to those whose hope is in him,
to the one who seeks him;
26 it is good to wait quietly
for the salvation of the LORD.

The words that the apostle Paul would later speak about himself and his fellow apostles apply well to the condition of Jeremiah and the handful of believers who remained after the fall of Jerusalem. "We are hard pressed on every side, but not crushed; perplexed, but not in despair; persecuted, but not abandoned; struck down, but not destroyed" (2 Corinthians 4:8,9).

It seemed to Jeremiah and his fellow Jews that they could fall no lower. They had no visible resources, either from within or from without. The whole world had declared them a loss. They were thrown back upon their one last resource, in truth their first and only resource, the Lord. At the very center of his lament Jeremiah broke out of the gloom by turning his attention to the character of the Lord, whose Word he had come to know and whose person he had learned to trust.

Because of the Lord's great love, God's people would survive. God's loyal love which first made them his people would keep them and protect them. By an oath and a promise the Lord had separated them from all other nations. Purely by grace he had called them to belong to him. Because of his promise to Abraham, Isaac, and Jacob, he had rescued them from Egypt. Because of that same promise, he had kept them through forty years of wandering in the wilderness. Because of that same promise, he had loved them down to the very end, always trying to reach them with the Word that would change their hearts and lead them to appreciate how much he cared for them.

His love had shown itself in his actions again and again. He could not help himself. His love fired his compassion so that out of his deep feeling for them he was stirred to come to their rescue time after time. Their history was a record of his love and action on their behalf. Every morning, every week, every year of their national and personal existence, they had received new evidence of God's mercy. Nevertheless, they brought themselves to this desperate condition. They had failed. They had broken faith on their part. Even so, they could still rely on their God. He does not break faith. He keeps his word. They could still confess joyfully: "Great is your faithfulness!"

Deprived of all, they still had an inheritance. It is an inheritance richer than any man could supply. The Lord himself was their portion. As the psalmist says, "The boundary lines have fallen for me in pleasant places" (Psalm 16:6). As members of the Lord's family and his heirs through faith, his people simply and quietly waited for the riches that would surely come to them. They already had the greatest possession: they belonged to the Lord. Sitting in the ashes of their ruined city, they could wait with confidence and hope, knowing he would not disappoint them.

Jeremiah was certain of what the future held, and he began the next verses with the word "good." He himself had experienced the goodness of God. To those who hope in him, he is good. To those who seek him, he gives good things, for he has promised, "Seek and you will find." Knowing that he is good and knowing that good will surely come, it is good for us to wait quietly for the salvation of the Lord. His goodness will not fail.

27 It is good for a man to bear the yoke
while he is young.

28 Let him sit alone in silence,
for the LORD has laid it on him.
29 Let him bury his face in the dust—
there may yet be hope.
30 Let him offer his cheek to one who would strike him,
and let him be filled with disgrace.

Jeremiah urged his readers to show godly endurance and patience. They would find the strength to bear up under the yoke if they remembered that the Lord had sent it. They could endure the insults and the put-downs, the shame and the disgrace. For they could be sure that the Lord had sent these chastisements and that these were designed to strip away all pretense and self-righteousness. The nightmare of grief they had gone through could teach them to throw themselves wholly upon the Lord and to wait for the good to come.

31 For men are not cast off
by the Lord forever.
32 Though he brings grief, he will show compassion,
so great is his unfailing love.
33 For he does not willingly bring affliction
or grief to the children of men.

34 To crush underfoot
all prisoners in the land,
35 to deny a man his rights
before the Most High,
36 to deprive a man of justice—
would not the Lord see such things?

37 Who can speak and have it happen
if the Lord has not decreed it?
38 Is it not from the mouth of the Most High
that both calamities and good things come?
39 Why should any living man complain
when punished for his sins?

Again the prophet directed his hearers to God's covenant love. So great and certain is that love, a love that offered hope for an end to their suffering. This is the hope that upholds every believer. The Lord does not fail those whom he has embraced and to whom he has given his name. He will surely help those whom he has taken into his family and into the circle of his protection and security.

Believers can be sure of this protection and security because God does not "willingly bring affliction or grief to the children of men." (or more literally, "not from the heart"). The Lord had acted in Jerusalem's case, as it were, against his nature. He had wanted to love because he is love. But the sin and impenitence of his people forced him to act out his love in a different way. To bring them around, to turn them back to him, he was forced to use tough love. His people could be sure, however, that he would not forget them or stop loving them. He would not overlook the injustice done to them, nor would he fail to act justly toward them. He would forgive them and restore them.

To be sure, the Lord had taken action against them, but they had no cause for complaint. He makes the rain fall upon the just and the unjust. From his hand both good and bad come, as part of his design to lead people to himself. No one can claim anything from God, certainly none of the people who had lived in Jerusalem. Everyone sins. Our sins bring us only what we deserve. God owes no one anything. All live by grace alone, a grace that has been rich toward us in ways far beyond our imagination. That grace came to us in Christ, through whom God gave us his eternal riches and wealth, a place in his family, and the promise of a place at his side. Because in Christ we have everything, we may confess with Job, "The LORD gave and the LORD has taken away; may the name of the LORD be praised" (Job 1:21).

40 Let us examine our ways and test them,
and let us return to the LORD.
41 Let us lift up our hearts and our hands
to God in heaven, and say:
42 "We have sinned and rebelled
and you have not forgiven.

43 "You have covered yourself with anger and pursued us;
you have slain without pity.
44 You have covered yourself with a cloud
so that no prayer can get through.
45 You have made us scum and refuse
among the nations.

Jeremiah reminded his hearers, "This is no time to complain. We have better things to do than complain. Let us honestly examine ourselves and put our lives to the test." Believers need not fear such examination. True, we will find much that is distressing and downright ugly in our lives. But we know that the Lord has covered it all with the fresh clean cover of Christ's righteousness. "Let us return to the Lord boldly," Jeremiah urges.

"Let us confess our sins because we have sinned." Little is harder in life than admitting to the hurt we have caused another person or God. How hard it is to break through the barriers we have erected between ourselves and those against whom we have sinned. This would be impossible if it were not for the love we know in Christ. We could not open the way back to God, but Christ did. In our place and on our behalf, he opened the way to the Father. In his name we may approach our God and Father and each other. In Christ we are brought together.

46 "All our enemies have opened their mouths
wide against us.
47 We have suffered terror and pitfalls,
ruin and destruction."
48 Streams of tears flow from my eyes
because my people are destroyed.

49 My eyes will flow unceasingly,
without relief,
50 until the LORD looks down
from heaven and sees.
51 What I see brings grief to my soul
because of all the women of my city.

Though he, together with his fellow believers, knew the Lord would bring good to them, their situation was desperate. Their enemies had triumphed completely over them. Jeremiah's grief brought him to tears and to the Lord. He vowed to keep on praying until the Lord would look down and answer. Jeremiah prayed with confidence, knowing that the Lord hears and answers the prayers of his people. The Lord loves his people; he is ready to act on their behalf. "And will not God bring about justice for his chosen ones, who cry out to him day and night? Will he keep putting them off? I tell you, he will see that they get justice, and quickly" (Luke 18:7,8).

52 Those who were my enemies without cause
hunted me like a bird.
53 They tried to end my life in a pit
and threw stones at me;
54 the waters closed over my head,
and I thought I was about to be cut off.

55 I called on your name, O LORD,
from the depths of the pit.
56 You heard my plea: "Do not close your ears
to my cry for relief."
57 You came near when I called you,
and you said, "Do not fear."

Jeremiah again returned to his personal experience, which he presented as a model for the whole nation. Just as the Jewish nation was at the point of death, so Jeremiah was at the point of death (Jeremiah 38). His enemies had thrown him into a cistern with no intention of ever bothering to check on him again. They hoped that in his pit-prison he would die. He was a man without hope. As far as he could see, life was over. No escape seemed possible.

But hoping against hope, believing that nothing with God is impossible, Jeremiah prayed to the Lord. Taking his cue from his fellow prophet Jonah, from within the "belly" of his cistern, he cried to the Lord. Jeremiah knew that the

Lord would hear and give him a ready answer, and he was not disappointed.

The Lord drew near to Jeremiah in his distress. The Lord took charge of Jeremiah's life, proving once again that the Lord controls all things, using whatever might come, for the good of those who love him. To his disheartened prophet he spoke words designed to remove his doubt: "Do not fear." These words ring out over all the storms and troubles of life as did the words of Jesus over the raging water of Galilee, "Take courage! It is I. Don't be afraid" (Mark 6:50). Jeremiah comforted his fellow sufferers and believers with the same comfort. As the Lord had rescued and delivered him from his impossible situation so the Lord would rescue and deliver his people.

58 O Lord, you took up my case;
you redeemed my life.
59 You have seen, O LORD, the wrong done to me.
Uphold my cause!
60 You have seen the depth of their vengeance,
all their plots against me.

61 O LORD, you have heard their insults,
all their plots against me—
62 what my enemies whisper and mutter
against me all day long.
63 Look at them! Sitting or standing,
they mock me in their songs.

64 Pay them back what they deserve, O LORD,
for what their hands have done.
65 Put a veil over their hearts,
and may your curse be on them!
66 Pursue them in anger and destroy them
from under the heavens of the LORD.

Jeremiah continued to use his example to encourage his fellow believers in their distress. The Lord was not deaf to Jeremiah's prayer. He just took up Jeremiah's case. He saved Jeremiah's life and protected him through the dangerous times that followed the fall of Jerusalem. Jeremiah's enemies had treated him unfairly. They had made him their enemy because they opposed the Lord and his Word. Their real problem was with the Lord. Because of that, rather than destroying Jeremiah, they destroyed themselves instead. Because of their opposition to the Lord, Jeremiah had called down the judgment of God upon them, and God fulfilled that judgment. He kept his dire threats against them. Everything happened to them just as Jeremiah had said it would.

Jeremiah's example gave the beleaguered believers hope. God had used an enemy nation as his tool to punish unbelievers and to discipline his children. God carried out this action in the hope that both the Jews and those who served as his instruments in their punishment would learn. The Babylonians, of course, did not recognize this. They did not understand that they were only tools in the Lord's hands. They never learned that the unrighteous, whoever they may be, will not escape the Lord's wrath. The prophet therefore called upon the Lord to show his righteous anger against those who had so willingly destroyed and ravaged his people.

THERE WAS NEVER A BLEAKER TIME

LAMENTATIONS 4

4 How the gold has lost its luster,
the fine gold become dull!
The sacred gems are scattered
at the head of every street.

2 How the precious sons of Zion,
once worth their weight in gold,
are now considered as pots of clay,
the work of a potter's hands!

3 Even jackals offer their breasts
to nurse their young,
but my people have become heartless
like ostriches in the desert.

4 Because of thirst the infant's tongue
sticks to the roof of its mouth;
the children beg for bread,
but no one gives it to them.

5 Those who once ate delicacies
are destitute in the streets.
Those nurtured in purple
now lie on ash heaps.

6 The punishment of my people
is greater than that of Sodom,
which was overthrown in a moment
without a hand turned to help her.

7 Their princes were brighter than snow
and whiter than milk,
their bodies more ruddy than rubies,
their appearance like sapphires.

8 But now they are blacker than soot;
they are not recognized in the streets.
Their skin has shriveled on their bones;
it has become as dry as a stick.

9 Those killed by the sword are better off
than those who die of famine;
racked with hunger, they waste away
for lack of food from the field.

10 With their own hands compassionate women
have cooked their own children,
who became their food
when my people were destroyed.

When the time was right, the Lord would return to his people and have mercy on them. But for the time being, the reality of God's heavy hand resting upon them overshadowed everything else. Their circumstances were hard and cruel. The devastation all around them and the prolonged starvation had driven the survivors to acts of inhuman cruelty. Gold that once fueled their lust and charmed their eyes had lost all its appeal. Gold and silver mean nothing if there is no food to buy. Costly jewels could be found lying in the streets. No one bothered to pick them up because they were useless.

The words of the prophet Ezekiel come to mind. He, too, described the intense pain of the Lord's judgment and its effect upon those who experience it. "They will throw their silver into the streets, and their gold will be an unclean thing. Their silver and gold will not be able to save them in the day of the LORD's wrath" (Ezekiel 7:19). We can only imagine what the survivors felt when we read that gold and silver meant nothing to them. That report reminds us once again that gold and silver cannot bring anyone peace and security. In the Lord alone do we find safety.

If gold and silver mean nothing, how much less will people mean! Even those in ancient Jerusalem who once counted for something were regarded as no more important than cheap pieces of pottery. Status meant nothing. The princes and leaders who once clothed themselves in the finest and ate the best lay in the streets in rags. No one took notice of them; no one even recognized them. And if these prominent citizens counted for nothing, what about the common people who were without name and position? God's punishment for sin is heavy indeed to bear.

The conditions under which Jerusalem's survivors had to live led some of them to unspeakable acts of inhumanity. Acting against the deepest feelings of their hearts, mothers actually used their own children for food. One could expect to find little compassion among any of the people if even the most compassionate among them had fallen this low. Jeremiah compared them to the ostrich who buried its eggs in the desert and then appeared to abandon them. This action on the part of the ostrich became synonymous with cruelty. Under such conditions, "those killed by the sword are better off."

11 The LORD has given full vent to his wrath;
he has poured out his fierce anger.
He kindled a fire in Zion
that consumed her foundations.

12 The kings of the earth did not believe,
nor did any of the world's people,
that enemies and foes could enter
the gates of Jerusalem.

13 But it happened because of the sins of her prophets
and the iniquities of her priests,
who shed within her
the blood of the righteous.

[14] Now they grope through the streets
like men who are blind.
They are so defiled with blood
that no one dares to touch their garments.

[15] "Go away! You are unclean!" men cry to them.
"Away! Away! Don't touch us!"
When they flee and wander about,
people among the nations say,
"They can stay here no longer."

[16] The LORD himself has scattered them;
he no longer watches over them.
The priests are shown no honor,
the elders no favor.

The impossible had happened to Jerusalem. From a military, economic, and diplomatic standpoint such a fall had seemed impossible. What happened? Jeremiah repeated the answer so no one could possibly miss it. "It happened because of the sins of her prophets and . . . her priests." They failed to do their duty. God had commanded them to carry out the law. They were to speak the Lord's Word and not their own; they were to act on behalf of those who were powerless; they were to see that justice was done. Instead they themselves trampled on God's revealed truth and on those whom it was designed to protect.

The Lord had given priests and prophets in Israel a great responsibility. We have it from the lips of our Lord: "From the one who has been entrusted with much, much more will be asked" (Luke 12:48). Because of their special privilege and calling, they now had to bear an extra measure of responsibility and an extra measure of punishment. They had thrown away the knowledge they had, so now they had to stumble through the streets, groping like blind men. They had no answers. People treated them as lepers. No one wanted to touch them or be near them. No one wanted them around. The Lord who had once protected and watched out for these public servants of his had abandoned them. They had forgotten whom they were to serve, and now they were paying the price of their neglect.

Those ancient prophets and priests can serve as warning examples for all whom the Lord has blessed and called to any kind of service to himself. God's blessing and his call place the same responsibility upon those blessed and called as it laid upon the prophets and priests of Jeremiah's time. Such blessings and responsibilities remind us that we are not to serve ourselves for our own purposes. It is only by God's grace that we serve; he outlines the service, and he gives the gifts from which he expects the returns.

17 Moreover, our eyes failed,
looking in vain for help;
from our towers we watched
for a nation that could not save us.

18 Men stalked us at every step,
so we could not walk in our streets.
Our end was near, our days were numbered,
for our end had come.

19 Our pursuers were swifter
than eagles in the sky;
they chased us over the mountains
and lay in wait for us in the desert.

20 The LORD's anointed, our very life breath,
was caught in their traps.
We thought that under his shadow
we would live among the nations.

21 Rejoice and be glad, O Daughter of Edom,
you who live in the land of Uz.

But to you also the cup will be passed;
you will be drunk and stripped naked.

22 O Daughter of Zion, your punishment will end;
he will not prolong your exile.
But, O Daughter of Edom, he will punish your sin
and expose your wickedness.

The priests and the prophets were not alone in rebelling against God's good will. The entire nation had put its confidence in the wrong place, so that when disaster came there was no escape. Instead of looking to the Lord, they looked everywhere else, including to their king, "the Lord's anointed."

They repeated the sin for which God had rebuked them when they first begged him to give them a king. At that time they had requested a king for the following reason: "Then we will be like all the other nations, with a king to lead us and to go out before us and fight our battles" (1 Samuel 8:20). They looked to their king as the one who would save them.

The Lord warned them when he said to Samuel, "It is not you they have rejected, but they have rejected me as their king" (1 Samuel 8:7). In their attempts to guarantee their national security, they forgot who stood behind the king and was their real protector. Their lack of faith in the Lord and their trust in human ingenuity and ability led them to ruin. "God [alone] is our refuge and strength" (Psalm 46:1).

None were happier about the mistakes the Jews had made than their cousins to the south, the Edomites. They were exuberant over the fall of Jerusalem and the humiliation of the Jews (Psalm 137:7). They helped the enemy bring Jerusalem down. Jeremiah warned the Edomites that, though God had set a limit to the exile and punishment of his people (Jeremiah 25:12), he set no such limit to the cup of punishment he would give the Edomites to drink (Jeremiah 49:7-22). God's promise to end the exile and to punish those who had failed to learn from it would bring some small comfort to the believers who survived the fall of the city.

A PRAYER GOES UP TO THE LORD FOR COMPASSION

LAMENTATIONS 5

5 Remember, O LORD, what has happened to us;
look, and see our disgrace.
2 Our inheritance has been turned over to aliens,
our homes to foreigners.
3 We have become orphans and fatherless,
our mothers like widows.
4 We must buy the water we drink;
our wood can be had only at a price.
5 Those who pursue us are at our heels;
we are weary and find no rest.
6 We submitted to Egypt and Assyria
to get enough bread.

Jeremiah closes his lamentation with a final appeal to the Lord's compassion and love. He speaks on behalf of the survivors who represent a new generation and a new beginning. They begged the Lord to see the full extent of their condition. They had become strangers in the land he had given them for an inheritance. They no longer had any rights. They owned nothing. They had become dispossessed like widows and orphans. With few resources, the burden of living had become intolerable. They were forced to buy all their necessities at high cost, even the water they drank.

They felt under pressure all the time. Attacks from the outside were constant. As the invading armies retreated, bands of raiders and robbers moved in. Lawlessness became the norm. The food they had hoped to secure from their former allies never materialized. Now they had to spend most of their time just trying to find enough to eat. They had little leisure for anything else.

> **7 Our fathers sinned and are no more,**
> **and we bear their punishment.**
> **8 Slaves rule over us,**
> **and there is none to free us from their hands.**
> **9 We get our bread at the risk of our lives**
> **because of the sword in the desert.**
> **10 Our skin is hot as an oven,**
> **feverish from hunger.**
> **11 Women have been ravished in Zion,**
> **and virgins in the towns of Judah.**
> **12 Princes have been hung up by their hands;**
> **elders are shown no respect.**
> **13 Young men toil at the millstones;**
> **boys stagger under loads of wood.**
> **14 The elders are gone from the city gate;**
> **the young men have stopped their music.**
> **15 Joy is gone from our hearts;**
> **our dancing has turned to mourning.**
> **16 The crown has fallen from our head.**
> **Woe to us, for we have sinned!**

The Lord had visited the sins of the fathers upon their descendants who, against better knowledge, had repeated those sins. They keenly felt the consequences of their sin and had to live with those consequences. Because in hardness they had reenacted the sins of the previous generation, this generation had to serve as slaves. They too had lost the blessing of good government and had to live with the curse of disorder and defeat.

Their condition was in sharp contrast to that which they had once enjoyed when they ruled the land. Now they risked their lives to find food. They were fortunate to find enough to ward off starvation. Their women could not walk safely in the streets, and even their homes provided no security. Their leaders were utterly despised. Young men were forced to serve as slaves, turning millstones to grind grain or carrying loads of wood from the countryside. Life in Jerusalem no longer offered any enjoyment or pleasure. Who could have imagined such a turn of events? They had once been prosperous, but they had chosen to ignore the Word and will of the Lord. Now they wished for the time and opportunity to hear that Word.

17 Because of this our hearts are faint,
because of these things our eyes grow dim
18 for Mount Zion, which lies desolate,
with jackals prowling over it.

19 You, O LORD, reign forever;
your throne endures from generation to generation.
20 Why do you always forget us?
Why do you forsake us so long?
21 Restore us to yourself, O LORD, that we may return;
renew our days as of old
22 unless you have utterly rejected us
and are angry with us beyond measure.

The new generation confesses that it, too, had sinned. It is not only for the sin of their fathers that this all had happened to them. The sight of the ruined temple desolated their spirit, for it symbolized the emptiness of the nation. They no longer had reason for any expression of joy. They had no hope as they looked to the future, a future they once thought they had made secure. They could no longer deceive themselves with the devices people so often use to hide from the truth. The truth of their situation simply overwhelmed all denials. Their lives were lives of despair though not total despair.

Though they in no way deserved God's mercy, they knew that a merciful Lord controls the future as he had the past. This Lord of might and mercy rules in heaven, and his will is done on earth. In him they found hope in their despair. This hope was not an illusion, as their former hopes had been. It rested in the nature of a God whose character and will had been revealed to them throughout their national history. He was and is the God who saves purely by grace.

They turned to the Lord, not as the last resort, but as the first. All renewal begins with him. They prayed that he might change them and restore them, so that they might once again serve him and enjoy his fellowship. They knew from experience what their sin had done to them. They acknowledged that the Lord had no reason to do them any good. He had every right to forsake them forever, but he could not, for he had loved them with an everlasting love. He is the God of Abraham, Isaac, and Jacob, the God of promise, a God who keeps his word. He is the God who has confirmed that word and spoken to all people the great "AMEN" in Jesus Christ his Son. "For no matter how many promises God has made, they are 'Yes' in Christ" (2 Corinthians 1:20).

Lamentations is not a pleasant book to read. It weighs one down. It brings home to the reader the inescapable results of sin and unbelief. But even more it points to the Lord, the God of love and grace. It assures us that in him we are never without hope.